Microsoft® Excel 2002
Illustrated Introductory

Elizabeth Eisner Reding
Lynn Wermers

COURSE TECHNOLOGY
THOMSON LEARNING

Australia • Canada • Mexico • Singapore • Spain • United Kingdom • United States

COURSE TECHNOLOGY

THOMSON LEARNING

Microsoft Excel 2002 - Illustrated Introductory

Elizabeth Eisner Reding, Lynn Wermers

Managing Editor:
Nicole Jones Pinard

Product Manager:
Emily Heberlein

Associate Product Manager:
Emeline Elliott

Production Editor:
Karen Jacot

Developmental Editor:
Barbara Clemens

Editorial Assistant:
Christina Kling Garrett

QA Manuscript Reviewers:
John Freitas, Ashlee Welz, Alex White, Harris Bierhoff, Serge Palladino, Holly Schabowski, Jeff Schwartz

Text Designer:
Joseph Lee, Black Fish Design

Composition House:
GEX Publishing Services

COPYRIGHT © 2002 Course Technology, a division of Thomson Learning™. Thomson Learning™ is a trademark used herein under license.

Printed in the United States of America

3 4 5 6 7 8 9 BM 05 04 03 02

For more information, contact Course Technology, 25 Thomson Place, Boston, Massachusetts, 02210.

Or you can visit us on the World Wide Web at www.course.com

ALL RIGHTS RESERVED. No part of this work covered by the copyright hereon may be reproduced or used in any form or by any means - graphic, electronic, or mechanical, including photocopying, recording, taping, Web distribution, or information storage and retrieval systems - without the written permission of the publisher.

For permission to use material from this text or product, contact us by
Tel (800) 730-2214
Fax (800) 730-2215
www.thomsonrights.com

Trademarks
Some of the product names and company names used in this book have been used for identification purposes only and may be trademarks or registered trademarks of their respective manufacturers and sellers.

Microsoft and the Office logo are either registered tradmarks or trademarks of Microsoft Corporation in the Unites States and/or other countries. Course Technology is an independent entity from Microsoft Corporation, and not affiliated with Microsoft in any manner.

This text may be used in assisting students to prepare for a Microsoft Office User Specialist Exam. Neither Microsoft Corporation, its designated review company, nor Course Technology warrants that use of this text will ensure passing the relevant exam.

Use of the Microsoft Office User Specialist Approved Courseware Logo on this product signifies that it has been independently reviewed and approved in complying with the following standards: "Includes acceptable coverage of all content related to the Microsoft Office Exam entitled Microsoft Excel 2002 Core, and sufficient performance-based exercises that relate closely to all required content, based on sampling of text."

"When used in conjunction with *Microsoft Excel 2002 – Illustrated Second Course,* includes acceptable coverage of all content related to the Microsoft Office Exams entitled Microsoft Excel 2002 Core and Microsoft Excel 2002 Expert, and sufficient performance-based exercises that relate closely to all required content, based on sampling of text."

ISBN 0-619-04504-3

The Illustrated Series Vision

Teaching and writing about computer applications can be extremely rewarding and challenging. How do we engage students and keep their interest? How do we teach them skills that they can easily apply on the job? As we set out to write this book, our goals were to develop a textbook that:

- works for a beginning student
- provides varied, flexible and meaningful exercises and projects to reinforce the skills
- serves as a reference tool
- makes your job as an educator easier, by providing resources above and beyond the textbook to help you teach your course

Our popular, streamlined format is based on advice from instructional designers and customers. This flexible design presents each lesson on a two-page spread, with step-by-step instructions on the left, and screen illustrations on the right. This signature style, coupled with high-caliber content, provides a comprehensive yet manageable introduction to Microsoft Excel 2002—it is a teaching package for the instructor and a learning experience for the student.

ACKNOWLEDGMENTS

Thanks to the reviewers who provided invaluable feedback and ideas to us: Judy Irvine and Glenn Rogers (Western Nevada Community College).

Elizabeth Eisner Reding

Creating a book of this magnitude is a team effort: I would like to thank my husband, Michael, for putting up with my ridiculous mood swings, Emily Heberlein, the project manager, and my development editors, Barbara Clemens and Kitty Pinard, for their insightful suggestions and corrections. I would also like to thank the production and editorial staff for all their hard work that made this project a reality.

Lynn Wermers

Thanks to my editor, Barbara Clemens, for her helpful suggestions and encouragement.

Preface

Welcome to *Microsoft Excel 2002 —Illustrated Introductory*. Each lesson in the book contains elements pictured to the right in the sample two-page spread.

▶ How is the book organized?
The book is organized into eight units on Excel, covering creating and editing worksheets, formatting worksheets, and working with charts, formulas and functions. Managing workbooks, automating tasks, and using lists are also covered.

▶ What kinds of assignments are included in the book? At what level of difficulty?
The lesson assignments use MediaLoft, a fictional chain of bookstore cafés, as the case study. The assignments on the blue pages at the end of each unit increase in difficulty. Project files and case studies, with many international examples, provide a great variety of interesting and relevant business applications for skills. Assignments include:

- **Concepts Reviews** include multiple choice, matching, and screen identification questions.

- **Skills Reviews** provide additional hands-on, step-by-step reinforcement.

- **Independent Challenges** are case projects requiring critical thinking and application of the skills learned in the unit. The Independent Challenges increase in difficulty, with the first Independent Challenge in each unit being the easiest (most step-by-step with detailed instructions). Independent Challenges 2 and 3 become increasingly open-ended, requiring more independent thinking and problem solving.

- **E-Quest Independent Challenges** are case projects with a Web focus. E-Quests require the use of the World Wide Web to conduct research to complete the project.

- **Visual Workshops** show a completed file and require that the file be created without any step-by-step guidance, involving problem solving and an independent application of the unit skills.

Each 2-page spread focuses on a single skill.

Concise text that introduces the basic principles in the lesson and integrates the brief case study (indicated by the paintbrush icon).

Changing Attributes and Alignment

Excel 2002 — Unit C

Attributes are styling formats such as bold, italics, and underlining that you can apply to affect the way text and numbers look in a worksheet. You can also change the **alignment** of labels and values in cells to be left, right, or center. You can apply attributes and alignment options from the Formatting toolbar or from the Alignment tab of the Format Cells dialog box. See Table C-2 for a list and description of the available attribute and alignment toolbar buttons. 🖌 Now that you have applied new fonts and font sizes to his worksheet labels, Jim wants you to further enhance the worksheet's appearance by adding bold and underline formatting and centering some of the labels.

Steps

1. Press **[Ctrl][Home]** to move to cell A1, then click the **Bold button** on the Formatting toolbar
   The title appears in bold.

2. Select the range **A3:J3**, then click the **Underline button** on the Formatting toolbar
   Excel underlines the text in the column headings in the selected range.

3. Click cell **A3**, click the **Italics button** on the Formatting toolbar, then click
   The word "Type" appears in boldface italic type. Notice that the Bold, Italics, and Underline buttons are selected.

   QuickTip: Overuse of any attribute can be distracting and make a workbook less readable. Be consistent, adding emphasis the same way throughout.

4. Click
   Excel removes italics from cell A3 but the bold and underline formatting attributes remain.

   QuickTip: Use formatting shortcuts on any selected range: [Ctrl][B] to bold, [Ctrl][I] to italicize, and [Ctrl][U] to underline.

5. Select the range **B3:J3**, then click
   Bold formatting is added to the rest of the labels in the column headings. The title would look better if it were centered over the data columns.

6. Select the range **A1:J1**, then click the **Merge and Center button** on the Formatting toolbar
   The Merge and Center button creates one cell out of the 10 cells across the row, then centers the text in that newly created large cell. The title "MediaLoft NYC Advertising Expenses" is centered across the 10 columns you selected. You can change the alignment within individual cells using toolbar buttons; you can split merged cells into their original components by selecting the merged cells, then clicking.

   QuickTip: To clear all formatting, click Edit on the menu bar, point to Clear, then click Formats.

7. Select the range **A3:J3**, then click the **Center button** on the Formatting toolbar
   Compare your screen to Figure C-7. Although they may be difficult to read, notice that all the headings are centered within their cells.

8. Click the **Save button** on the Standard toolbar

CLUES TO USE: Rotating and indenting cell entries
In addition to applying fonts and formatting attributes, you can rotate or indent cell data within a cell to further change its appearance. You can rotate text within a cell by altering its alignment. To change alignment, select the cells you want to modify, click Format on the menu bar, click Cells, then click the Alignment tab. Click a position in the Orientation box, or type a number in the degrees text box to change from the default horizontal alignment, then click OK. You can indent cell contents using the Increase Indent button on the Formatting toolbar, which moves cell contents to the right one space, or the Decrease Indent button, which moves cell contents to the left one space.

▶ EXCEL C-6 FORMATTING A WORKSHEET

Hints as well as troubleshooting advice, right where you need it — next to the step itself.

▶ IV

Quickly accessible summaries of key terms, toolbar buttons, or keyboard alternatives connected with the lesson material. Students can refer easily to this information when working on their own projects at a later time.

Every lesson features large, full-color representations of what the screen should look like as students complete the numbered steps.

FIGURE C-7: Worksheet with formatting attributes applied

- Center button
- Title centered across columns
- Formatting buttons outlined
- Column headings centered, bolded, and underlined

TABLE C-2: Attribute and Alignment buttons on the Formatting toolbar

button	description	button	description
B	Bolds text		Aligns text on the left side of the cell
I	Italicizes text		Centers text horizontally within the cell
U	Underlines text		Aligns text on the right side of the cell
	Adds lines or borders		Centers text across columns, and combines two or more selected adjacent cells into one cell

Clues to Use

Using AutoFormat

Excel has 17 predefined worksheet formats to make formatting easier and to give you the option of consistently styling your worksheets. AutoFormats are designed for worksheets with labels in the left column and top rows, and totals in the bottom row or right column. To use AutoFormat, select the data to be formatted—or place your mouse pointer anywhere within the range to be selected (Excel can automatically detect a range of cells)—click Format on the menu bar, click AutoFormat, select a format from the sample boxes, as shown in Figure C-8, then click OK.

FIGURE C-8: AutoFormat dialog box

Samples of available formats

FORMATTING A WORKSHEET EXCEL C-7

Clues to Use boxes provide concise information that either expands on the major lesson skill or describes an independent task that in some way relates to the major lesson skill.

The pages are numbered according to unit. C indicates the unit, 7 indicates the page.

▶ Is this book MOUS Certified?

Microsoft Excel 2002 – Illustrated Introductory covers the Core objectives for Excel and has received certification approval as courseware for the MOUS program. See the inside front cover for more information on other Illustrated titles meeting MOUS certification.

The first page of each unit includes MOUS symbols to indicate which skills covered in the unit are MOUS skills. A grid in the back of the book lists all the exam objectives and cross-references them with the lessons and exercises.

▶ What online content solutions are available to accompany this book?

Visit www.course.com for more information on our online content for Illustrated titles. Options include:

MyCourse.com

Need a quick, simple tool to help you manage your course? Try MyCourse.com, the easiest to use, most flexible syllabus and content management tool available. MyCourse.com offers you brand new content, including Topic Reviews, Extra Case Projects, and Quizzes, to accompany this book.

WebCT

Course Technology and WebCT have partnered to provide you with the highest quality online resources and Web-based tools for your class. Course Technology offers content for this book to help you create your WebCT class, such as a suggested Syllabus, Lecture Notes, Practice Test questions, and more.

Blackboard

Course Technology and Blackboard have also partnered to provide you with the highest quality online resources and Web-based tools for your class. Course Technology offers content for this book to help you create your Blackboard class, such as a suggested Syllabus, Lecture Notes, Practice Test questions, and more.

V

Instructor Resources

The Instructor's Resource Kit (IRK) CD is Course Technology's way of putting the resources and information needed to teach and learn effectively into your hands. All the components are available on the IRK, (pictured below), and many of the resources can be downloaded from www.course.com.

ASSESSING YOUR STUDENTS

Solution Files
Solution Files are Project Files completed with comprehensive sample answers. Use these files to evaluate your students' work. Or distribute them electronically or in hard copy so students can verify their own work.

ExamView
ExamView is a powerful testing software package that allows you to create and administer printed, computer (LAN-based), and Internet exams. ExamView includes hundreds of questions that correspond to the topics covered in this text, enabling students to generate detailed study guides that include page references for further review. The computer-based and Internet testing components allow students to take exams at their computers, and also save you time by grading each exam automatically.

PRESENTING YOUR CLASS

Figure Files
Figure Files contain all the figures from the book in .jpg format. Use the figure files to create transparency masters or in a PowerPoint presentation.

STUDENT TOOLS

Project Files and Project Files List
To complete most of the units in this book, your students will need **Project Files**. Put them on a file server for students to copy. The Project Files are available on the Instructor's Resource Kit CD-ROM, the Review Pack, and can also be downloaded from www.course.com.

Instruct students to use the **Project Files List** at the end of the book. This list gives instructions on copying and organizing files.

PLANNING YOUR CLASS

Instructor's Manual
Available as an electronic file, the Instructor's Manual is quality-assurance tested and includes unit overviews, detailed lecture topics for each unit with teaching tips, comprehensive sample solutions to all lessons and end-of-unit material, and extra Independent Challenges. The Instructor's Manual is available on the Instructor's Resource Kit CD-ROM, or you can download it from www.course.com.

Sample Syllabus
Prepare and customize your course easily using this sample course outline (available on the Instructor's Resource Kit CD-ROM).

SAM, Skills Assessment Manager for Microsoft Office XP
SAM is the most powerful Office XP assessment and reporting tool that will help you gain a true understanding of your students' proficiency in Microsoft Word, Excel, Access, and PowerPoint 2002. (Available separately from the IRK CD.)

TOM, Training Online Manager for Microsoft Office XP
TOM is Course Technology's MOUS-approved training tool for Microsoft Office XP. Available via the World Wide Web and CD-ROM, TOM allows students to actively learn Office XP concepts and skills by delivering realistic practice through both guided and self-directed simulated instruction.

Brief Contents

The Illustrated Series Vision   III
Preface   IV
Instructor Resources   VI
Read This Before You Begin   XVI

Excel 2002	
Getting Started with Excel 2002	EXCEL A-1
Building and Editing Worksheets	EXCEL B-1
Formatting a Worksheet	EXCEL C-1
Working with Charts	EXCEL D-1
Working with Formulas and Functions	EXCEL E-1
Automating Worksheet Tasks	EXCEL F-1
Managing Workbooks and Preparing Them for the Web	EXCEL G-1
Using Lists	EXCEL H-1

Project Files   1
MOUS Certification Objectives   5
Glossary   9
Index   13

Contents

Illustrated Series Vision ... III
Preface ... IV
Instructor Resources ... VI
Read this Before you Begin ... XVI

EXCEL 2002

Getting Started with Excel 2002 — EXCEL A-1

Defining Spreadsheet Software ... EXCEL A-2

Starting Excel 2002 ... EXCEL A-4

Viewing the Excel Window ... EXCEL A-6

   Working with toolbars and menus in Excel 2002 ... EXCEL A-7

Opening and Saving a Workbook ... EXCEL A-8

   Creating a new workbook ... EXCEL A-8

Opening a workbook using a template ... EXCEL A-9

Entering Labels and Values ... EXCEL A-10

   Navigating a worksheet ... EXCEL A-11

Naming and Moving a Sheet ... EXCEL A-12

   Copying worksheets ... EXCEL A-13

Previewing and Printing a Worksheet ... EXCEL A-14

   Using Zoom in Print Preview ... EXCEL A-15

Getting Help ... EXCEL A-16

Changing the Office Assistant ... EXCEL A-16

Closing a Workbook and Exiting Excel ... EXCEL A-18

Concepts Review ... EXCEL A-20

Skills Review ... EXCEL A-21

Independent Challenges ... EXCEL A-22

Visual Workshop ... EXCEL A-24

Contents

Building and Editing Worksheets — EXCEL B-1

Planning and Designing a Worksheet .... EXCEL B-2
Editing Cell Entries .... EXCEL B-4
   Recovering a lost workbook file .... EXCEL B-5
Entering Formulas .... EXCEL B-6
Creating Complex Formulas .... EXCEL B-8
   Editing formulas .... EXCEL B-8
   Order of precedence in Excel formulas .... EXCEL B-9
Introducing Excel Functions .... EXCEL B-10
   Using the MIN and MAX functions .... EXCEL B-11
Copying and Moving Cell Entries .... EXCEL B-12
   Using the Office Clipboard .... EXCEL B-13
Understanding Relative and Absolute Cell References .... EXCEL B-14
   Using a mixed reference .... EXCEL B-15
Copying Formulas with Relative Cell References .... EXCEL B-16
   Filling cells with sequential text or values .... EXCEL B-17
Copying Formulas with Absolute Cell References .... EXCEL B-18
   Inserting and deleting selected cells .... EXCEL B-19
Concepts Review .... EXCEL B-20
Skills Review .... EXCEL B-21
Independent Challenges .... EXCEL B-22
Visual Workshop .... EXCEL B-24

Formatting a Worksheet — EXCEL C-1

Formatting Values .... EXCEL C-2
   Using the Format Painter .... EXCEL C-3
Using Fonts and Font Sizes .... EXCEL C-4
   Inserting Clip Art .... EXCEL C-5

Changing Attributes and Alignment .... **EXCEL C-6**
    Rotating and indenting cell entries .... **EXCEL C-6**
    Using AutoFormat .... **EXCEL C-7**
Adjusting Column Widths .... **EXCEL C-8**
    Specifying row height .... **EXCEL C-9**
Inserting and Deleting Rows and Columns .... **EXCEL C-10**
    Adding and editing comments .... **EXCEL C-11**
Applying Colors, Patterns, and Borders .... **EXCEL C-12**
Using Conditional Formatting .... **EXCEL C-14**
    Deleting conditional formatting .... **EXCEL C-15**
Checking Spelling .... **EXCEL C-16**
    Using e-mail to send a workbook .... **EXCEL C-16**
Concepts Review .... **EXCEL C-18**
Skills Review .... **EXCEL C-19**
Independent Challenges .... **EXCEL C-21**
Visual Workshop .... **EXCEL C-24**

Working with Charts   EXCEL D-1

Planning and Designing a Chart .... **EXCEL D-2**
Creating a Chart .... **EXCEL D-4**
Moving and Resizing a Chart .... **EXCEL D-6**
    Identifying chart objects .... **EXCEL D-7**
Editing a Chart .... **EXCEL D-8**
    Rotating a 3-D chart .... **EXCEL D-9**
Formatting a Chart .... **EXCEL D-10**
Enhancing a Chart .... **EXCEL D-12**
    Changing text alignment in charts .... **EXCEL D-13**
Annotating and Drawing on a Chart .... **EXCEL D-14**
    Exploding a pie slice .... **EXCEL D-15**

Contents

Previewing and Printing a Chart ....**EXCEL D-16**

    Using the Page Setup dialog box for a chart ....**EXCEL D-17**

Concepts Review ....**EXCEL D-18**

Skills Review ....**EXCEL D-19**

Independent Challenges ....**EXCEL D-21**

Visual Workshop ....**EXCEL D-24**

Working with Formulas and Functions   **EXCEL E-1**

    Creating a Formula with Several Operators ....**EXCEL E-2**

    Using Paste Special to paste formulas and values and to perform calculations ....**EXCEL E-3**

Using Names in a Formula ....**EXCEL E-4**

    Producing a list of names ....**EXCEL E-5**

Generating Multiple Totals with AutoSum ....**EXCEL E-6**

    Quick calculations with AutoCalculate ....**EXCEL E-6**

Using Dates in Calculations ....**EXCEL E-8**

    Custom number and date formats ....**EXCEL E-9**

Building a Conditional Formula with the IF Function ....**EXCEL E-10**

    Correcting circular references ....**EXCEL E-11**

Using Statistical Functions ....**EXCEL E-12**

Calculating Payments with the PMT Function ....**EXCEL E-14**

    Calculating future value with the FV function ....**EXCEL E-15**

Displaying and Printing Formula Contents ....**EXCEL E-16**

    Setting margins and alignment when printing part of a worksheet ....**EXCEL E-18**

Concepts Review ....**EXCEL E-18**

Skills Review...**EXCEL E-19**

Independent Challenges ....**EXCEL E-21**

Visual Workshop ....**EXCEL E-24**

Managing Workbooks and Preparing Them for the Web — EXCEL F-1

Freezing Columns and Rows ....EXCEL F-2
   Splitting the worksheet into multiple panes ....EXCEL F-3
Inserting and Deleting Worksheets ....EXCEL F-4
   Previewing and printing multiple worksheets ....EXCEL F-4
   Specifying headers and footers ....EXCEL F-5
Consolidating Data with 3-D References ....EXCEL F-6
   Linking data between workbooks ....EXCEL F-7
Hiding and Protecting Worksheet Areas ....EXCEL F-8
   Changing workbook properties ....EXCEL F-9
Saving Custom Views of a Worksheet ....EXCEL F-10
Creating a workspace ....EXCEL F-11
Controlling Page Breaks and Page Numbering ....EXCEL F-12
Using Page Break Preview ....EXCEL F-13
Creating a Hyperlink Between Excel Files ....EXCEL F-14
   Using hyperlinks to navigate large worksheets ....EXCEL F-14
   Finding and replacing data and formats ....EXCEL F-15
Saving an Excel File as a Web Page ....EXCEL F-16
   Holding Web discussions ....EXCEL F-17
Concepts Review ....EXCEL F-18
Skills Review ....EXCEL F-19
Independent Challenges ....EXCEL F-21
Visual Workshop ....EXCEL F-24

Contents

Automating Worksheet Tasks — EXCEL G-1

Planning a Macro ....EXCEL G-2
   Macros and viruses ....EXCEL G-3
Recording a Macro ....EXCEL G-4
Running a Macro ....EXCEL G-6
Editing a Macro ....EXCEL G-8
   Adding comments to Visual Basic code ....EXCEL G-9
Using Shortcut Keys with Macros ....EXCEL G-10
Using the Personal Macro Workbook ....EXCEL G-12
   Working with the Personal Macro Workbook ....EXCEL G-13
Adding a Macro as a Menu Item ....EXCEL G-14
   Adding a custom menu ....EXCEL G-14
Creating a Toolbar for Macros ....EXCEL G-16
Concepts Review ....EXCEL G-18
Skills Review ....EXCEL G-19
Independent Challenges ....EXCEL G-21
Visual Workshop ....EXCEL G-24

Using Lists — EXCEL H-1

Planning a List ....EXCEL H-2
   Using lists versus databases ....EXCEL H-3
Creating a List ....EXCEL H-4
   Filtering lists using AutoFilter ....EXCEL H-5
Adding Records with the Data Form ....EXCEL H-6

XIV

Finding Records ....**EXCEL H-8**
   Using wildcards to fine-tune your search ....**EXCEL H-8**
Deleting Records ....**EXCEL H-10**
   Deleting records using the worksheet ....**EXCEL H-11**
   Sorting a List on One Field ....**EXCEL H-12**
Sorting a List on Multiple Fields ....**EXCEL H-14**
   Specifying a custom sort order ....**EXCEL H-15**
Printing a List ....**EXCEL H-16**
   Setting a print area ....**EXCEL H-17**
Concepts Review..**EXCEL H-18**
Skills Review ....**EXCEL H-19**
Independent Challenges ....**EXCEL H-21**
Visual Workshop ....**EXCEL H-24**

Project Files   1
MOUS Certification Objectives   5
Glossary   9
Index   13

Read This Before You Begin

Software Information and Required Installation

This book was written and tested using Microsoft Office XP - Professional Edition, with a typical installation on Microsoft Windows 2000, with Internet Explorer 5.0 or higher. There are several instances where, in order to cover a software feature clearly, an additional feature not part of the typical installation is referenced. To insure that all the steps and exercises can be completed as written, make sure the following features are available before beginning this unit: Excel Unit A (page A-8): Using Excel Templates (Clues to Use).

What are Project Files?

To complete many of the units in this book, you need to use Project Files. You use a Project File, which contains a partially completed document used in an exercise, so you don't have to type in all the information you need in the document. Your instructor will either provide you with a copy of the Project Files or ask you to make your own copy. Detailed instructions on how to organize your files, as well as a complete listing of all the files you'll need and will create, can be found in the back of the book (look for the yellow pages) in the Project Files List.

Why is my screen different from the book?

1. Your Desktop components and some dialog box options might be different if you are using an operating system other than Windows 2000

2. Depending on your computer hardware capabilities and the Windows Display settings on your computer, you may notice the following differences:
   - Your screen may look larger or smaller because of your screen resolution (the height and width of your screen)
   - The colors of the title bar in your screen may be a solid blue, and the cells in Excel may appear different from the purple and gray because of your color settings

3. Depending on your Office settings, your toolbars may display on a single row and your menus may display with a shortened list of frequently used commands. Office menus and toolbars can modify themselves to your working style by displaying only the most frequently used buttons and menu commands.

Toolbars on one row

To view buttons not currently displayed, click a Toolbar Options button at the end of either the Standard or Formatting toolbar. To view the full list of menu commands, click the double arrow at the bottom of the menu.

In order to have your toolbars display on two rows, showing all buttons, and to have the full menus display, you must turn off the personalized menus and toolbars feature. Click Tools on the menu bar, Click Customize, select the show Standard and Formatting toolbars on two rows and Always show full menus check boxes on the Options tab, then click Close. This book assumes you are displaying toolbars on two rows and full menus.

Toolbars on two rows

Excel 2002

Unit A

Getting Started with Excel 2002

Objectives

- ▶ Define spreadsheet software
- ▶ Start Excel 2002
- ▶ View the Excel window
- MOUS ▶ Open and save a workbook
- MOUS ▶ Enter labels and values
- MOUS ▶ Name and move a sheet
- MOUS ▶ Preview and print a worksheet
- ▶ Get Help
- ▶ Close a workbook and exit Excel

In this unit, you will learn how to start Microsoft Excel 2002 and identify elements in the Excel window. You will also learn how to open and save existing files, enter data in a worksheet, manipulate worksheets, and use the extensive Help system. Jim Fernandez is the office manager at MediaLoft, a nationwide chain of bookstore cafés selling books, CDs, DVDs, and videos. MediaLoft cafés sell coffee and pastries. Jim wants you to help him use Excel to analyze a worksheet summarizing budget information for the MediaLoft Café in the New York City store.

Defining Spreadsheet Software

Excel 2002 — Unit A

Microsoft Excel is an electronic spreadsheet program that runs on Windows computers. You use an **electronic spreadsheet** to produce professional-looking documents that perform numeric calculations rapidly and accurately. These calculations are updated automatically so that accurate information is always available. See Table A-1 for common ways spreadsheets are used in business. The electronic spreadsheet that you produce when using Excel is also referred to as a **worksheet**. Individual worksheets are stored within a **workbook**, which is a file with the .xls file extension. Each new workbook contains three worksheets. Jim uses Excel extensively to track MediaLoft finances. Figure A-1 shows a budget worksheet that Jim created using pencil and paper, while Figure A-2 shows the same worksheet Jim created using Excel.

Details

The advantages of using Excel include:

▶ **Enter data quickly and accurately**

With Excel, you can enter information faster and more accurately than with pencil and paper. For example, in the MediaLoft NYC Café budget, certain expenses, such as rent, cleaning supplies, and products supplied on a yearly contract (coffee, creamers, sweeteners), remain constant for the year. You can copy the expenses that don't change from quarter to quarter, and then use Excel to calculate Total Expenses and Net Income for each quarter by supplying the data and formulas.

▶ **Recalculate data easily**

Fixing typing errors or updating data using Excel is easy, and the results of a changed entry are recalculated automatically. For example, if you receive updated expense figures for Quarter 4, you enter the new numbers and Excel recalculates the worksheet.

▶ **Perform a what-if analysis**

The Excel ability to change data and let you quickly view the recalculated results makes it a powerful decision-making tool. For instance, if the salary budget per quarter is increased to $14,500, you can enter the new figure into the worksheet and immediately see the impact on the overall budget. Any time you use a worksheet to ask the question "what if?" you are performing a **what-if analysis**.

▶ **Change the appearance of information**

Excel provides powerful features for making information visually appealing and easy to understand. For example, you can use boldface type and colored or shaded text headings or numbers to emphasize important worksheet data and trends.

▶ **Create charts**

Excel makes it easy to create charts based on worksheet information. Charts are updated automatically as data changes. The worksheet in Figure A-2 includes a 3-D pie chart that shows the distribution of the budget expenses for the MediaLoft NYC Café.

▶ **Share information with other users**

Because everyone at MediaLoft is now using Microsoft Office, it's easy for them to share worksheet data. For example, you can complete the MediaLoft budget that your manager started creating in Excel. Simply access the files you need or want to share through the network or from a disk, or through the use of online collaboration tools (such as intranets and the Internet), and then make any changes or additions.

▶ **Create new worksheets from existing ones quickly**

It's easy to take an existing Excel worksheet and quickly modify it to create a new one. When you are ready to create next year's budget, you can open the file for this year's budget, save it with a new filename, and use the existing data as a starting point. An Excel file can also be created using a special format called a **template**, which lets you open a new file based on an existing workbook's design and/or content. Office comes with many prepared templates you can use.

▶ EXCEL A-2   GETTING STARTED WITH EXCEL 2002

FIGURE A-1: Traditional paper worksheet

```
                    MediaLoft NYC Café Budget

                  Qtr 1    Qtr 2    Qtr 3    Qtr 4    Total

Net Sales        56,000   84,000   72,000   79,000   291,000
Expenses
  Salary         14,500   14,500   14,500   14,500    58,000
  Rent            4,000    4,000    4,000    4,000    16,000
  Advertising     3,750    8,000    3,750    3,750    19,250
  Cleansers       1,500    1,500    1,500    1,500     6,000
  Pastries        2,500    2,500    2,500    2,500    10,000
  Milk/Cream      1,000    1,000    1,000    1,000     4,000
  Coffee/Tea      4,700    4,750    4,750    4,750    18,950
  Sweeteners        300      300      300      300     1,200
Total Expenses   32,250   36,550   32,300   32,300   133,400

Net Income       23,750   47,450   39,700   46,700   157,600
```

FIGURE A-2: Excel worksheet

Office Assistant provides help when needed

TABLE A-1: Common business uses for electronic spreadsheets

spreadsheets are used to	by
Maintain values	Calculating numbers
Represent values graphically	Creating charts based on worksheet figures
Create consecutively numbered pages using multiple workbook sheets	Printing reports containing workbook sheets
Organize data	Sorting data in ascending or descending order
Analyze data	Creating data summaries and short-lists using PivotTables or AutoFilters
Create what-if data scenarios	Using variable values to investigate and sample different outcomes

GETTING STARTED WITH EXCEL 2002 EXCEL A-3

Excel 2002
Starting Excel 2002

To start any Windows program, you use the Start button on the taskbar. A slightly different procedure might be required for computers on a network and those that use Windows-enhancing utilities. If you need assistance, ask your instructor or technical support person. Jim is ready to begin work on the budget for the MediaLoft Café in New York City. He begins by starting Excel.

Steps

1. **Point to the Start button on the taskbar**
   The Start button is on the left side of the taskbar. You use it to start programs on your computer.

2. **Click Start**
   Microsoft Excel is located in the Programs folder, which is at the top of the Start menu, as shown in Figure A-3.

3. **Point to Programs**
   The Programs menu opens. All the programs on your computer, including Microsoft Excel, are listed on this menu. See Figure A-4. Your program menu might look different, depending on the programs installed on your computer.

   Trouble?
   If you don't see the Microsoft Excel icon, see your instructor or technical support person.

4. **Click the Microsoft Excel program icon on the Programs menu**
   Excel opens and a blank worksheet appears. In the next lesson, you will learn about the elements of the Excel worksheet window.

5. **If necessary, click the Maximize button on the title bar**

FIGURE A-3: Start menu

Click here to open Start menu

Microsoft Excel located in this folder

FIGURE A-4: Programs list

Microsoft Excel program icon

Your Programs menu might differ

GETTING STARTED WITH EXCEL 2002   EXCEL A-5

Viewing the Excel Window

Excel 2002 — Unit A

When you start Excel, the **worksheet window** appears on your screen. The worksheet window includes the tools that enable you to create and work with worksheets. Jim needs to familiarize himself with the Excel worksheet window and its elements before he starts working with the budget worksheet. Compare the descriptions below to the elements shown in Figure A-5.

Details

▶ The **worksheet window** contains a grid of columns and rows. Columns are labeled alphabetically (A, B, C, etc.) and rows are labeled numerically (1, 2, 3, etc.). The worksheet window displays only a small fraction of the whole worksheet, which has a total of 256 columns and 65,536 rows. The intersection of a column and a row is called a **cell**. Cells can contain text, numbers, formulas, or a combination of all three. Every cell has its own unique location or **cell address**, which is identified by the coordinates of the intersecting column and row. For example, the cell address of the cell in the upper-left corner of a worksheet is A1. The **new workbook pane** appears to the right of the worksheet window and lets you quickly open new or existing workbooks. The **Task pane list arrow** lets you display other panes.

▶ The **cell pointer** is a dark rectangle that outlines the cell you are working in. This cell is called the **active cell**. In Figure A-5, the cell pointer is located at A1, so A1 is the active cell. The column and row headings for the active cell are purple; inactive column and row headings are gray. To activate a different cell, just click any other cell or press the arrow keys on your keyboard to move the cell pointer elsewhere.

> **Trouble?**
> If your screen does not display cells in purple and gray as shown in the figure, ask your technical support person to check your Windows color settings.

▶ The **title bar** displays the program name (Microsoft Excel) and the filename of the open worksheet (in this case the default filename, Book1). As shown in Figure A-5, the title bar also contains a control menu box, a Close button, and resizing buttons, which are common to all Windows programs.

▶ The **menu bar** contains menus from which you choose Excel commands. As with all Windows programs, you can choose a menu command by clicking it with the mouse pointer or by pressing [Alt] plus the underlined letter in the menu command name. When you click a menu, only a short list of commonly used commands may appear at first; you can wait or click the double arrows at the bottom of the menu to see expanded menus with more commands.

▶ The **name box** displays the active cell address. In Figure A-5, "A1" appears in the name box, indicating that A1 is the active cell.

▶ The **formula bar** allows you to enter or edit data in the worksheet.

▶ The **toolbars** contain buttons for frequently used Excel commands. The **Standard toolbar** is located just below the menu bar and contains buttons that perform actions within the worksheet. The **Formatting toolbar**—beneath the Standard toolbar—contains buttons that change the worksheet's appearance. Each button contains an image representing its function. For instance, the Print button contains an image of a printer. To choose any button, click it with the left mouse button.

▶ **Sheet tabs** below the worksheet grid let you keep your work in a collection called a **workbook**. Each workbook contains three worksheets by default and can contain a maximum of 255 sheets. Sheet tabs allow you to name your worksheets with meaningful names. **Sheet tab scrolling buttons** help you display hidden worksheets.

▶ The **status bar** is located at the bottom of the Excel window. The left side of the status bar provides a brief description of the active command or task in progress. The right side of the status bar shows the status of important keys such as [Caps Lock] and [Num Lock].

FIGURE A-5: Excel worksheet window elements

Labels on figure:
- Control menu box
- Menu bar
- Standard toolbar
- Formatting toolbar
- Name box
- Cell pointer highlights active cell
- Title bar
- Formula bar
- Sheet tab scrolling buttons
- Sheet tabs
- Status bar
- Close button
- Resizing buttons
- Task pane
- Task pane list arrow
- Pane lets you create new workbooks
- Worksheet window
- Office Assistant may appear in a different location, or not at all

CLUES TO USE

Working with toolbars and menus in Excel 2002

Although you can configure Excel so that your toolbars and menus modify themselves to conform to your working style, the lessons in this book assume you have turned off personalized menus and toolbars and are working with all menu commands and toolbar buttons displayed. When you use personalized toolbars, the Standard and Formatting toolbars appear on the same row and display only the most frequently used buttons, as shown in Figure A-6. To use a button that is not visible on a toolbar, you click the Toolbar Options button at the end of the toolbar, then click the button on the Toolbar Options list. As you work, Excel adds the buttons you use to the visible toolbars and drops the buttons you don't often use to the Toolbar Options list. Similarly, Excel menus adjust to your work habits, so that the commands you use most often appear on shortened menus. You can see all the menu commands by clicking the double arrows at the bottom of a menu. It is often easier to work with full toolbars and menus displayed. To turn off personalized toolbars and menus, click Tools on the menu bar, click Customize, on the Options tab select the Show Standard and Formatting toolbars on two rows and Always show full menus check boxes, and then click Close. The Standard and Formatting toolbars appear on separate rows and display all the buttons, and the menus display the complete list of menu commands. (You can quickly display the toolbars on two rows by clicking a Toolbar Options button and then clicking Show Buttons on Two Rows.)

FIGURE A-6: Toolbars in one row

Toolbar options buttons

GETTING STARTED WITH EXCEL 2002 EXCEL A-7

Excel 2002 Unit A

Opening and Saving a Workbook

Sometimes it's more efficient to create a new worksheet by modifying one that already exists. This saves you from having to retype information from previous work. Throughout this book, you will create new workbooks by opening a file from the location where your Project Files are stored, using the Save As command to create a copy of the file with a new name, and then modifying the new file by following the lesson steps. Use the Save command to store changes made to an existing file. It is a good idea to save your work every 10 or 15 minutes and before printing. Saving the files with new names keeps your original Project Files intact, in case you have to start the unit over again or you wish to repeat an exercise. ✐ Jim wants you to complete the New York City MediaLoft Café budget that a member of the accounting staff has been working on.

Steps

1. Click **More Workbooks** in the New Workbook task pane
The Open dialog box opens. See Figure A-7. If no workbooks have been opened on your computer, the command will read "Workbooks."

> **QuickTip**
> You can also click the Open button on the Standard toolbar.

2. Click the **Look in list arrow**, then click the drive and folder where your Project Files are located
The Look in list arrow lets you navigate to folders and disk drives on your computer. A list of your Project Files appears in the Open dialog box.

> **QuickTip**
> If you don't see the three-letter extension .xls on the filenames in the Open dialog box, don't worry. Windows can be set up to display or not to display the file extensions.

3. Click the file **EX A-1**, then click **Open**
The workbook file EX A-1 opens. The new workbook pane no longer appears.

4. Click **File** on the menu bar, then click **Save As**
The Save As dialog box opens, displaying the drive where your Project Files are stored.

> **QuickTip**
> You can create a new folder from within the Save As dialog box by clicking on the dialog box toolbar, typing a name in the Name text box, then clicking OK. To open a file from a folder you create, double-click folders or use the Look in list arrow in the Open dialog box to open the folder, click the filename, then click Open.

5. In the File name text box, select the current filename (if necessary), type **MediaLoft Cafe Budget**, as shown in Figure A-8, then click **Save**
Both the Save As dialog box and the file EX A-1 close, and a duplicate file named MediaLoft Cafe Budget opens, as shown in Figure A-9. The Office Assistant may or may not appear on your screen.

CLUES TO USE

Creating a new workbook

You can create your own worksheets from scratch by opening a new workbook. To create a new workbook, click the New button on the Standard toolbar. You can also use the New Workbook pane (located on the right side of the screen) to open a new file. Click the Blank Workbook button in the New Workbook pane, and a new workbook will open. Each new workbook automatically contains 3 sheets, although you can insert as many as you need.

EXCEL A-8 GETTING STARTED WITH EXCEL 2002

FIGURE A-7: Open dialog box

- Your folder contents might differ
- Your files and folders appear here
- Selected filename will appear here
- Look in list arrow
- My Documents folder opens by default

FIGURE A-8: Save As dialog box

- Your list of files might differ
- Current drive or folder (yours may differ)
- Type new filename here

FIGURE A-9: MediaLoft Café Budget workbook

- Purple column and row headers define active cell

Opening a workbook using a template

You can create a workbook by entering data and formats into a blank workbook, or you can use predesigned workbooks called templates that are included with Excel. Templates let you automatically create workbooks such as balance sheets, expense statements, loan amortizations, sales invoices, or timecards. Templates save you time because they contain labels, values, formulas, and formatting. To open a new document based on a template, click General Templates from the New Workbook task pane, save it under a new name, then add your own information. You may need to have the Office CD available to install the templates.

GETTING STARTED WITH EXCEL 2002 EXCEL A-9

Excel 2002 Unit A

Entering Labels and Values

Labels help you identify the data in worksheet rows and columns, making your worksheet more readable and understandable. Try to enter all labels in your worksheet before entering the data. Labels can contain text and numerical information not used in calculations, such as dates, times, or addresses. Labels are left-aligned by default. **Values**, which include numbers, formulas, and functions, are used in calculations. Excel recognizes an entry as a value when it is a number or begins with special symbols: +, -, =, @, #, or $. Because Excel treats labels and values differently, you can have a label such as '2003 Sales' without affecting values used in a totals column. All values are right-aligned by default. When a cell contains both text and numbers it is not a valid formula; Excel recognizes the entry as a label. Jim wants you to enter labels identifying the rest of the expense categories, and the values for Qtr 3 and Qtr 4 into the MediaLoft Café Budget worksheet.

Steps

1. **Click cell A8 to make it the active cell**
   Notice that the cell address A8 appears in the name box. As you work, the mouse pointer takes on a variety of appearances, depending on where it is and what Excel is doing. Table A-2 lists and identifies some mouse pointers. The labels in cells A8:A15 identify the expenses.

2. **Type Salary, as shown in Figure A-10, then click the Enter button on the formula bar**
   As you type, the word "Enter" appears in the status bar. Clicking the Enter button indicates that you are finished typing or changing your entry, and the word "Ready" appears in the status bar. Because the cell is still selected, its contents still appear in the formula bar. You can also confirm a cell entry by pressing [Enter], [Tab], or one of the keyboard arrow keys. These three methods also select an adjacent cell. To confirm an entry and leave the same cell selected, you can press [Ctrl][Enter]. If a label does not fit in a cell, Excel displays the remaining characters in the next cell to the right, as long as it is empty. Otherwise, the label is **truncated**, or cut off.

   > **Trouble?**
   > If you notice a mistake in a cell entry after entering it, double-click the cell, use [Backspace] or [Delete], make your corrections, then press [Enter]. You can also click Edit on the menu bar, point to Clear, then click Contents to remove a cell's contents.

3. **Click cell A9, type Rent, press [Enter] to confirm the entry and move the cell pointer to cell A10, type Advertising in cell A10, then press [Enter]**
   The remaining expense values have to be added to the worksheet.

4. **Click cell D8, press and hold down the left mouse button, drag to cell E8 then down to cell E15, then release the mouse button**
   You have selected a **range**, which is two or more adjacent cells. The active cell is still cell D8, and the cells in the range are shaded in purple.

   > **QuickTip**
   > To enter a number that will not be used as part of a calculation, such as a telephone number, type an apostrophe (') before the number.

5. **Type 14500, press [Enter], type 4000 in cell D9, press [Enter], type 3750 in cell D10, press [Enter], type 1500 in cell D11, press [Enter], type 2500 in cell D12, press [Enter], type 1000 in cell D13, press [Enter], type 4750 in cell D14, press [Enter], type 300 in cell D15, then press [Enter]**
   You will often enter data in multiple columns and rows; selecting a range makes working with data entry easier because pressing [Enter] makes the next cell in the range active. You have entered all the values in the Qtr 3 column, as shown in Figure A-11. The cell pointer is now in cell E8.

6. **Using Figure A-11 as a guide, type the remaining values for cells E8 through E15**
   Before confirming a cell entry, you can click the Cancel button on the formula bar or press [Esc] to cancel or delete the entry. Notice that the AutoCalculate area in the status bar displays "Sum=64550," which is the sum of the figures in the selected range. This sum changes if you change any of the numbers in the selected range.

7. **Click cell D8, type 14550, press [Enter], then select cells D8:E15**
   Notice that the AutoCalculate area in the status bar now says "Sum=64600".

8. **Press [Ctrl][Home] to return to cell A1**

9. **Click the Save button on the Standard toolbar**
   You can also press [Ctrl][S] to save a worksheet.

EXCEL A-10   GETTING STARTED WITH EXCEL 2002

FIGURE A-10: Worksheet with first label entered

FIGURE A-11: Worksheet with new labels and values

TABLE A-2: Commonly used pointers

name	pointer	use to
Normal	✥	Select a cell or range; indicates Ready mode
Copy	▸⁺	Create a duplicate of the selected cell(s)
Fill handle	➕	Create an alphanumeric series in a range
I-beam	I	Edit contents of formula bar
Move	✥	Change the location of the selected cell(s)

Clues to Use

Navigating a worksheet

With over a million cells available to you, it is important to know how to move around, or navigate, a worksheet. You can use the arrow keys on the keyboard ([↑] [↓] [←] or [→]) to move a cell or two at a time, or use [Page Up] or [Page Down] to move a screenful at a time. To move a screen to the left press [Alt][Page Up]; to move a screen to the right press [Alt][Page Down]. You can also use the mouse pointer to click the desired cell. If the desired cell is not visible in the worksheet window, use the scroll bars or the Go To command on the Edit menu to move the location into view. To return to the first active cell in a worksheet, click cell A1, or press [Ctrl][Home].

GETTING STARTED WITH EXCEL 2002   EXCEL A-11

Excel 2002

Naming and Moving a Sheet

Each workbook initially contains three worksheets, named Sheet1, Sheet2, and Sheet3. When you open a workbook, the first worksheet is the active sheet. To move from sheet to sheet, you can click any sheet tab at the bottom of the worksheet window. The sheet tab scrolling buttons, located to the left of the sheet tabs, allow you to display hidden sheet tabs. To make it easier to identify the sheets in a workbook, you can rename each sheet, add color to the tabs, and then organize them in a logical way. The sheet name appears on the sheet tab. For instance, to better track performance goals, you could name each workbook sheet for an individual salesperson; then you could move the sheets so they appeared in alphabetical order. Jim wants to be able to easily identify the actual expenses and the projected expenses. He wants you to name two sheets in his workbook, add color to distinguish them, then change their order.

Steps

1. **Click the Sheet2 tab**
   Sheet2 becomes active; this is the worksheet that contains the actual quarterly expenses. Its tab moves to the front, and Sheet1 moves to the background.

2. **Click the Sheet1 tab**
   Sheet1, which contains the projected expenses, becomes active again. Once you have confirmed which sheet is which, you can assign them each a name that you can easily remember.

   QuickTip: You can also rename a sheet by right-clicking the tab, clicking Rename, typing the new name, then pressing [Enter].

3. **Double-click the Sheet2 tab**
   Sheet 2 becomes the active sheet with the default sheet name ("Sheet2") selected.

4. **Type Actual, then press [Enter]**
   The new name automatically replaces the default name in the tab. Worksheet names can have up to 31 characters, including spaces and punctuation.

5. **Right-click the Actual tab, then click Tab Color**
   The Format Tab Color dialog box appears, as shown in Figure A-12.

   QuickTip: To delete a worksheet, select the worksheet you want to delete, click Edit on the menu bar, then click Delete sheet. To insert a worksheet, click Insert on the menu bar, then click Worksheet.

6. **Click the color red (first column, third row), click OK, double-click the Sheet1 tab, type Projected, then press [Enter]**
   Notice that when you renamed Sheet1, the color of the entire Actual tab changed to red. Jim decides to rearrange the order of the sheets, so that Actual comes before Projected.

7. **Click the Actual sheet tab and hold down the mouse button, then drag it to the left of the Projected sheet tab**
   As you drag, the pointer changes to, the sheet relocation pointer, and a small, black triangle shows its position. See Figure A-13. The first sheet in the workbook is now the Actual sheet. When you have more worksheets than can appear at once, click the leftmost tab scrolling button to display the first sheet tab; click the rightmost navigation button to display the last sheet tab. The left and right buttons move one sheet in their respective directions.

8. **Click the Projected sheet tab, enter your name in cell A20, then press [Ctrl][Home]**
   Your name identifies your worksheet as yours, which is helpful if you are sharing a printer.

9. **Click the Save button on the Standard toolbar**

FIGURE A-12: Format Tab Color dialog box

Available colors

Click to remove existing color from a tab

FIGURE A-13: Moving Actual sheet before Projected sheet

Sheet 1 renamed

Sheet 2 renamed

Sheet relocation pointer

Indicates tab color

Clues to Use

Copying worksheets

There are times when you may want to copy a worksheet. To copy it, press [Ctrl] as you drag the sheet tab and release the mouse button before you release [Ctrl]. You can also move and copy worksheets between workbooks. You must have the workbook that you are copying to, as well as the workbook that you are copying from, open. Select the sheet to copy or move, click Edit on the menu bar, then click Move or Copy sheet. Complete the information in the Move or Copy dialog box. Be sure to click the Create a Copy check box if you are copying rather than moving the worksheet. Carefully check your calculation results whenever you move or copy a worksheet.

GETTING STARTED WITH EXCEL 2002   EXCEL A-13

Excel 2002

Previewing and Printing a Worksheet

After you complete a worksheet, you may want to print it to have a paper copy for reference or to give to others. You can also print a worksheet that is not complete to review your work when you are not at a computer. Before you print a worksheet, you should save any changes. That way, if anything happens to the file as it is being sent to the printer, you will have your latest work saved. Then you should preview it to make sure it will fit on a page the way you want. When you **preview** a worksheet, you see a copy of the worksheet exactly as it will appear on paper. See Table A-3 for a summary of printing tips. Jim is finished entering the labels and values into the MediaLoft Café budget. He has already saved his changes, so he asks you to preview and print a copy of the worksheet he can review on the way home.

Steps

1. **Make sure the printer is on and contains paper**
   If a file is sent to print and the printer is off, an error message appears.

2. **Click the Print Preview button on the Standard toolbar**
   A miniature version of the worksheet appears on the screen, as shown in Figure A-14. If your worksheet requires more than one page, you could click the Next button or the Previous button to move between pages. Because your worksheet is only one page, the Next and Previous buttons are dimmed.

   > **QuickTip**
   > To print the worksheet using existing settings without previewing it, click 🖨 on the Standard toolbar.

3. **Click Print**
   The Print dialog box opens, as shown in Figure A-15.

4. **Make sure that the Active Sheet(s) option button is selected in the Print what section and that 1 appears in the Number of copies text box in the Copies section**
   Adjusting the value in the Number of copies text box enables you to print multiple copies. You could also print a selected range by clicking the Selection option button.

   > **QuickTip**
   > After previewing or printing a worksheet, dotted lines appear on the screen indicating individual page breaks in the printout. Page break positions vary with each printer.

5. **Click OK**
   A Printing dialog box appears briefly while the file is sent to the printer. Note that the dialog box contains a Cancel button. You can use it to cancel the print job provided you can catch it before the file is sent to the printer.

TABLE A-3: Worksheet printing tips

before you print	recommendation
Save your work	Make sure your work is saved
Check the printer	Make sure that the printer is turned on and is online, that it has paper, and that there are no error messages or warning signals
Preview the worksheet	Check the formatted image for page breaks, page setup (vertical or horizontal), and overall appearance of the worksheet
Check the printer selection	Look in the Print dialog box to verify that the correct printer is selected
Check the Print what options	Verify that you are printing either the active sheet, the entire workbook, or just a selected range

▶ EXCEL A-14 GETTING STARTED WITH EXCEL 2002

FIGURE A-14: Print Preview screen

- Move to another page
- Enlarge the screen image
- Print the worksheet
- Change print options
- Return to worksheet
- Zoom pointer

FIGURE A-15: Print dialog box

- Your printer may differ
- Prints the current worksheet
- Indicates the number of copies to be printed

Using Zoom in Print Preview

When you are in the Print Preview window, you can enlarge the image by clicking the Zoom button. You can also position the Zoom pointer over a specific part of the worksheet page, then click it to view that section of the page. Figure A-16 shows a magnified section of a document. While the image is zoomed in, use the scroll bars to view different sections of the page.

FIGURE A-16: Enlarging the preview using Zoom

GETTING STARTED WITH EXCEL 2002

Excel 2002 Unit A

Getting Help

Excel features an extensive **Help system** that gives you immediate access to definitions, steps, explanations, and useful tips. The animated Office Assistant provides help in two ways. You can type a **keyword**, a representative word on which Excel can search your area of interest, or you can access a question and answer format to research your Help topic. The Office Assistant provides **Office Assistant Tips** (indicated by a light bulb) on the current action you are performing. You can click the light bulb to display a dialog box containing relevant choices that you can refer to as you work. In addition, you can press [F1] at any time to get immediate help. Alternately, the **Ask a Question list arrow** on the menu bar is always available for asking questions. You can click the text box and type a question at any time to display related help topics. Questions from your current Excel session are stored, and you can access them at any time by clicking the Ask a Question list arrow, then clicking the question of interest. Jim wants to find out more about ranges so he can work more efficiently with them. He asks you to find more information by using the animated Office Assistant.

Steps

QuickTip
If the Office Assistant is displayed, click it to access Help. If it is not displayed, clicking opens the Office Assistant. A previous user may have turned off the Office Assistant. To turn it on, click Help on the menu bar, click Show the Office Assistant, then click the Office Assistant to open the dialog balloon.

1. **Click the Microsoft Excel Help button on the Standard toolbar**
   An Office Assistant dialog balloon opens, asking what you want to do. You can get information by typing a keyword or question in the white box, known as the **query box**. If the text within the query box is highlighted, your text will automatically replace it. The Office Assistant provides help based on the text in the query box.

2. **Type Define a range**
   See Figure A-18.

3. **Click Search**
   The Office Assistant searches for relevant topics from the Help files in Excel and then displays a list of topics for you to choose from.

QuickTip
Clicking the Print button in the Help window prints the information.

4. **Click See More, then click Name cells on more than one worksheet**
   A Help window containing information about ranges opens, as shown in Figure A-19.

5. **Read the text, then click the Close button on the Help window title bar**
   The Help window closes.

6. **Click the Microsoft Excel button on the taskbar to display it, if necessary.**
   The Office Assistant is no longer visible on the worksheet. Hiding the Office Assistant does not turn it off; it only hides it temporarily.

Clues to Use

Changing the Office Assistant

The default Office Assistant character is Clippit, but there are others from which you can choose. To change the appearance of the Office Assistant, right-click the Office Assistant, then click Options. Click the Gallery tab shown in Figure A-17, click the Back and Next buttons until you find an Assistant you want to use, then click OK. (You may need to insert your Microsoft Office CD to perform this task.) Each Office Assistant character makes its own unique sounds. Animate any assistant by right-clicking it, then clicking Animate!

FIGURE A-17: Office Assistant dialog box

EXCEL A-16   GETTING STARTED WITH EXCEL 2002

FIGURE A-18: Office Assistant

- Ask a Question list arrow
- Office Assistant on your screen may offer a list of options to choose from
- Query box
- Click to close the dialog balloon

FIGURE A-19: Help window

- Your topic list may differ
- Click to print a topic
- Your Help window may be wider or narrower

GETTING STARTED WITH EXCEL 2002

Closing a Workbook and Exiting Excel

Excel 2002 — Unit A

When you have finished working, you need to save the workbook file and close it. When you have completed all your work in Excel you need to exit the program. You can exit Excel by clicking Exit on the File menu. ✒ Jim has completed his work on the MediaLoft Café budget. He wants you to close the workbook and then exit Excel.

Steps

1. **Click File on the menu bar**
   The File menu opens. See Figure A-20.

2. **Click Close**
   Excel closes the workbook, asking if you want to save your changes; if you have made any changes be sure to save them. You could also click the workbook Close button instead of using the File menu.

3. **Click File on the menu bar, then click Exit**
   You could also click the program Close button to exit the program. Excel closes and you return to the desktop.

> **QuickTip**
> To exit Excel and close several files at once, click Exit on the File menu. Excel will prompt you to save changes to each open workbook before exiting.

FIGURE A-20: Closing a workbook using the File menu

- Program control menu box
- Workbook control menu box
- Close command
- Your list may differ
- Exit command

GETTING STARTED WITH EXCEL 2002   EXCEL A-19

Excel 2002 Practice

▶ Concepts Review

Label the elements of the Excel worksheet window shown in Figure A-21.

FIGURE A-21

Match each term with the statement that describes it.

7. Cell pointer
8. Formula bar
9. Worksheet window
10. Name box
11. Cell
12. Workbook

a. Area that contains a grid of columns and rows
b. The intersection of a column and row
c. Allows you to enter or edit worksheet data
d. Collection of worksheets
e. Rectangle indicating the active cell
f. Displays the active cell address

Select the best answer from the list of choices.

13. An electronic spreadsheet can perform all of the following tasks, except:
    a. Display information visually.
    b. Calculate data accurately.
    c. Plan worksheet objectives.
    d. Recalculate updated information.
14. Each of the following is true about labels, except:
    a. They are left-aligned by default.
    b. They are not used in calculations.
    c. They are right-aligned by default.
    d. They can include numerical information.

▶ EXCEL A-20　GETTING STARTED WITH EXCEL 2002

Practice

15. Each of the following is true about values, except:
    a. They can include labels.
    b. They are right-aligned by default.
    c. They are used in calculations.
    d. They can include formulas.
16. What symbol is typed before a number to make the number a label?
    a. "
    b. !
    c. '
    d. ;
17. You can get Excel Help in any of the following ways, except:
    a. Clicking Help on the menu bar, then clicking Microsoft Excel Help.
    b. Pressing [F1].
    c. Clicking 🗊.
    d. Minimizing the program window.
18. The following key(s) can be used to confirm cell entries, except:
    a. [Enter].
    b. [Tab].
    c. [Esc].
    d. [Ctrl][Enter].
19. Which button is used to preview a worksheet?
    a. 🗋
    b. 🔍
    c. 💾
    d. 🖨
20. Which feature is used to enlarge a Print Preview view?
    a. Magnify
    b. Enlarge
    c. Amplify
    d. Zoom
21. Each of the following is true about the Office Assistant, except:
    a. It provides tips based on your work habits.
    b. It provides help using a question-and-answer format.
    c. You can change the appearance of the Office Assistant.
    d. It can complete certain tasks for you.

▶ Skills Review

1. **Start Excel 2002.**
   a. Point to **Programs** in the Start menu.
   b. Click the **Microsoft Excel** program icon.
   c. In what area of the Start menu are all the programs on your computer located?
   d. What appears when Excel opens?
2. **Open and save a workbook.**
   a. Open the workbook EX A-2 from the drive and folder where your Project Files are located.
   b. Save the workbook as **MediaLoft Toronto Cafe** using the Save As command on the File menu; use the New Folder button to save it in a new folder called **Toronto** in the drive and folder where your Project Files are located.
   c. Close the file.
   d. Open it again from the new folder you created.
   e. Open a workbook based on the Balance Sheet template: Display the task pane, select General Templates, display the Spreadsheet Solutions tab, then double-click Balance Sheet.
   f. Save the workbook as **MediaLoft Balance Sheet** in the drive and folder where your Project Files are stored, then close the workbook.

TABLE-4: MediaLoft Toronto Café

	On-Hand	Cost Each	Sale Price
Water	32	9.57	
Coffee	52	13.71	
Bread	36	15.22	
Muffins	25	16.99	
Sweets	43	11.72	
Sodas	52	9.61	

GETTING STARTED WITH EXCEL 2002

Excel 2002 | Practice

3. **Enter labels and values.**
   a. Enter the necessary labels shown in Table A-4.
   b. Enter the values shown in Table A-4.
   c. Clear the contents of cell A9 using the Edit menu, then type **Tea** in cell A9.
   d. Save the workbook using the Save button.
4. **Name and move a sheet.**
   a. Name the Sheet1 tab **Inventory**, then name the Sheet2 tab **Sales**.
   b. Move the Inventory sheet so it comes after the Sales sheet.
   c. Change the tab color of the Inventory sheet to yellow (third column, fifth row).
   d. Change the tab color of the Sales sheet to aqua (fifth column, fourth row).
   e. Save the workbook.
5. **Preview and print a worksheet.**
   a. Make the Inventory sheet active.
   b. View it in Print Preview.
   c. Use the Zoom button to get a better look at your worksheet.
   d. Add your name to cell A11, then print one copy of the worksheet.
6. **Get Help.**
   a. Display the Office Assistant if it is not already displayed.
   b. Ask the Office Assistant for information about creating a formula.
   c. Print the information offered by the Office Assistant, using the Print button in the Help window.
   d. Close the Help window.
7. **Close a workbook and exit Excel.**
   a. Close the file using the Close command.
   b. If asked if you want to save the worksheet, click **No**.
   c. Exit Excel.

▶ Independent Challenge 1

The Excel Help feature provides definitions, explanations, procedures, and other helpful information. It also provides examples and demonstrations to show you how Excel features work. Topics include elements such as the active cell, status bar, buttons, and dialog boxes, as well as detailed information about Excel commands and options.

a. Start Excel and open a new workbook using the New Workbook task pane.
b. Click the **Office Assistant**; display it if necessary using the Show Office Assistant command on the Help menu.
c. Type a question that will give you information about opening and saving a workbook. (*Hint*: You may have to ask the Office Assistant more than one question.)
d. Print the information, close the Help window, then exit Excel.

▶ Independent Challenge 2

Spreadsheet software has many uses that can affect the way people work. The beginning of this unit discusses some examples of people using Excel. Use your own personal or business experiences to come up with five examples of how Excel could be used in a business setting.

a. Start Excel.
b. Write down five business tasks that you could complete more efficiently by using an Excel worksheet.
c. Sketch a sample of each worksheet. See Table A-5, a sample payroll worksheet, as a guide.
d. Open a new workbook and save it as **Sample Payroll** in the drive and folder where your Project Files are stored.

Practice

e. Give your worksheet a title in cell A1, then type your name in cell B1.
f. Enter the labels shown in Table A-5. Enter Hours Worked in column C and Hourly Wage in Column E.
g. Enter sample data for Hours Worked and Hourly Wage in the worksheet.
h. Save your work, then preview and print the worksheet.
i. Close the worksheet and exit Excel.

TABLE A-5: Sample payroll

Employee Name	Hours Worked	Hourly Wage
Dale Havorford		
Chris Wong		
Sharon Armenta		
Belinda Swanson		
Total		

▶ Independent Challenge 3

You are the office manager for Christine's Car Parts, a small auto parts supplier. Although the company is just three years old, it is expanding rapidly, and you are continually looking for ways to make your job easier. Last year you began using Excel to manage and maintain data on inventory and sales, which has greatly helped you to track information accurately and efficiently. The owner of the company has just approved your request to hire an assistant, who will be starting work in a week. You want to create a short training document that acquaints your new assistant with basic Excel skills.

a. Start Excel.
b. Create a new workbook and save it as **Training Workbook** in the drive and folder where your Project Files are located.
c. Enter a title for the worksheet in cell A1.
d. Make up and enter the values and labels for a sample spreadsheet. Make sure you have labels in column A.
e. Enter your name in cell D1.
f. Change the name of Sheet1 to Sample Data, then change the tab color of the Sample Data to another color.
g. Preview the worksheet, then print it.
h. Open a workbook based on a template from the Spreadsheet Solutions tab in the Templates dialog box. (You may need to insert your Office CD in order to do this.)
i. Save the workbook as **Template Sample**, then close the files and exit Excel.

ⓔ Independent Challenge 4

You can use the World Wide Web to help make informed purchasing decisions. Your supervisor has just given you approval for buying a new computer. While cost is not a limiting factor, you do need to provide a list of hardware and software requirements. You can use data found on the World Wide Web and use Excel to create a worksheet that details your purchase decision.

a. Connect to the Internet, then go to the CNET site at computers.com.
b. Use any of the links to locate information about the type of computer you want to purchase.
c. Locate data for the type of system you want using at least two vendors from within this site. When you find systems that meet your needs, print out the information. Be sure to identify each system's key features, such as the processor chip, hard drive capacity, RAM, and monitor size.
d. When you are finished gathering data, disconnect from the Internet.
e. Start Excel, open a new workbook and save it in the drive and folder where your Project Files are stored as **New Computer Data**.
f. Enter the manufacturers' names in columns and computer features (RAM, etc.) in rows. List the systems you found through your research, including the features you want (e.g., CD-ROM drive, etc.) and the cost for each system.
g. List the tax and shipping costs the manufacturer charges.
h. Indicate on the worksheet your final purchase decision by including descriptive text in a prominent cell. Enter your name in one of the cells.
i. Save, preview, and then print your worksheet.
j. Close the file and exit Excel.

GETTING STARTED WITH EXCEL 2002   EXCEL A-23

Excel 2002 | Practice

▶ Visual Workshop

Create a worksheet similar to Figure A-22 using the skills you learned in this unit. Save the workbook as **Carrie's Camera and Darkroom** to the drive and folder where your Project Files are stored. Type your name in cell A11, then preview and print the worksheet.

FIGURE A-22

	A	B	C	D	E
1	Carrie's Camera and Darkroom				
2					
3	Quarterly Sales				
4					
5		Quarter 1	Quarter 2	Quarter 3	Quarter 4
6	Camera	47213	52669	53074	57221
7	Supplies	20201	20761	23421	22049
8	Film	1069	1264	1202	1250
9	Gadgets	983	1066	1146	1608
10					
11					

Excel 2002

Unit B

Building
and Editing Worksheets

Objectives

- Plan and design a worksheet
- Edit cell entries
- Enter formulas
- Create complex formulas
- Introduce Excel functions
- Copy and move cell entries
- Understand relative and absolute cell references
- Copy formulas with relative cell references
- Copy formulas with absolute cell references

Using your understanding of Excel basics, you can now plan and build your own worksheets. When you build a worksheet, you enter labels, values, and formulas into worksheet cells. Once you create a worksheet, you can save it in a workbook file and then print it. The MediaLoft marketing department has asked Jim Fernandez for an estimate of the average number of author appearances this summer. Marketing hopes that the number of appearances will increase 20% over last year's figures. Jim asks you to create a worksheet that summarizes appearances for last year and forecasts the summer appearances for this year.

Planning and Designing a Worksheet

Excel 2002 — Unit B

Before you start entering data into a worksheet, you need to know the purpose and approximate layout of the worksheet. To increase store traffic and sales, MediaLoft encourages authors to come to stores and sign their books. Jim wants to forecast MediaLoft's 2003 summer author appearances. The goal, already identified by the Marketing department, is to increase the year 2002 signings by 20%. Using the planning guidelines below, work with Jim as he plans this worksheet.

Details

In planning and designing a worksheet it is important to:

▶ **Determine the purpose of the worksheet and give it a meaningful title**
Jim needs to forecast summer appearances for 2003. Jim titles the worksheet "Summer 2003 MediaLoft Author Events Forecast."

▶ **Determine your worksheet's desired results, or "output"**
Jim needs to begin scheduling author events and will use these forecasts to determine staffing and budget needs if the number of author events increases by 20%. He also wants to calculate the average number of author events because the Marketing department uses this information for corporate promotions.

▶ **Collect all the information, or "input," that will produce the results you want**
Jim gathers together the number of author events that occurred at four stores during the 2002 summer season, which runs from June through August.

▶ **Determine the calculations, or formulas, necessary to achieve the desired results**
First, Jim needs to total the number of events at each of the selected stores during each month of the summer of 2002. Then he needs to add these totals together to determine the grand total of summer appearances. Because he needs to determine the goal for the 2003 season, the 2002 monthly totals and grand total are multiplied by 1.2 to calculate the projected 20% increase for the 2003 summer season. He'll use the Average function to determine the average number of author appearances for the Marketing department.

▶ **Sketch on paper how you want the worksheet to look; identify where to place the labels and values**
Jim decides to put the store locations in rows and the months in columns. He enters the data in his sketch and notes the location of the monthly totals and the grand total. Below the totals, he writes out the formula for determining a 20% increase in 2002 appearances. He also includes a label for the average number of events calculations. Jim's sketch of his worksheet is shown in Figure B-1.

▶ **Create the worksheet**
Jim enters the labels first, to establish the structure of the worksheet. He then enters the values—the data summarizing the events—into his worksheet. Finally, he enters the formulas necessary to calculate totals, averages, and forecasts. These values and formulas will be used to calculate the necessary output. The worksheet Jim creates is shown in Figure B-2.

▶ EXCEL B-2   BUILDING AND EDITING WORKSHEETS

FIGURE B-1: Worksheet sketch showing labels, values, and calculations

Summer 2003 MediaLoft Author Events Forecast

	June	July	August	Total	Average
Boston	22	15	19		
New York	28	18	22		
Seattle	20	17	12		
Houston	15	26	21		
Total	June Total	July Total	August Total	Grand Total	
20% rise	Total X 1.2				

FIGURE B-2: Jim's forecasting worksheet

- Labels
- Values to be used in calculations
- Formulas will calculate results
- Workbook title

BUILDING AND EDITING WORKSHEETS

Excel 2002 Unit B

Editing Cell Entries

You can change the contents of a cell at any time. To edit the contents of a cell, you first select the cell you want to edit. Then you have two options: you can click the formula bar or press [F2]. This puts Excel into Edit mode. Alternately, you can double-click any cell and start editing. To make sure you are in Edit mode, look at the **mode indicator** on the far-left side of the status bar. After planning and creating his worksheet, Jim notices that he entered the wrong value for the August Seattle events, and that Houston should replace San Diego. He asks you to edit these entries to correct them.

Steps

> **QuickTip**
> In the Open dialog box, you can double-click the filename to open the workbook in one step.

1. **Start Excel, open the workbook EX B-1 from the drive and folder where your Project Files are stored, then save it as Author Events Forecast**

2. **Click cell D5**
   This cell contains August events for the Seattle store, which you want to change to reflect the correct numbers.

3. **Click to the right of 12 in the formula bar**
   Excel goes into Edit mode, and the mode indicator on the status bar displays "Edit." A blinking vertical line called the **insertion point** appears in the formula bar, and if you move the mouse pointer to the formula bar, the pointer changes to I, which is used for editing. See Figure B-3.

4. **Press [Backspace], type 8, then click the Enter button on the formula bar**
   The value in cell D5 is changed from 12 to 18, and cell D5 remains selected.

5. **Click cell A6, then press [F2]**
   Excel returns to Edit mode, and the insertion point appears in the cell.

> **QuickTip**
> The Undo button allows you to reverse up to 16 previous actions, one at a time.

6. **Press [Backspace] nine times, type Houston, then press [Enter]**
   The label changes to Houston, and cell A7 becomes the active cell. If you make a mistake, you can click the Cancel button on the formula bar *before* confirming the cell entry. If you notice the mistake *after* you have confirmed the cell entry, click the Undo button on the Standard toolbar.

7. **Double-click cell C6**
   Double-clicking a cell also puts Excel into Edit mode with the insertion point in the cell.

8. **Press [Delete] twice, then type 19**
   The number of book signings for July in Houston has been corrected. See Figure B-4.

9. **Click to confirm the entry, then click the Save button on the Standard toolbar**

▶ EXCEL B-4 **BUILDING AND EDITING WORKSHEETS**

FIGURE B-3: Worksheet in Edit mode

Insertion point in formula bar

Pointer used for editing

Edit mode indicator

FIGURE B-4: Edited worksheet

Name box

Insertion point in cell

Clues to Use

Recovering a lost workbook file

Sometimes while you are using Excel, you may experience a power failure or your computer may "freeze," making it impossible to continue working. If this type of interruption occurs, Excel has a built-in recovery feature that allows you to open and save files that were open at the time of the interruption. When you restart Excel after an interruption, the Document Recovery task pane opens on the left side of your screen displaying both original and recovered versions of the files that were open. If you're not sure which file to open (original or recovered), it's usually better to open the recovered file because it will have retained the latest information. You can, however, open and review all the versions of the file that were recovered and save the best one. Each file listed in the Document Recovery task pane has a list arrow with options that allow you to open the file, save the file, delete the file, or show repairs made to the file.

BUILDING AND EDITING WORKSHEETS   EXCEL B-5

Entering Formulas

Excel 2002 Unit B

You use **formulas** to perform numeric calculations such as adding, multiplying, and averaging. Formulas in an Excel worksheet usually start with the equal sign (=), called the **formula prefix**, followed by cell addresses and range names. Arithmetic formulas use one or more **arithmetic operators** to perform calculations; see Table B-1. Using a cell address or range name in a formula is called **cell referencing**. If you change a value in a cell, any formula containing that cell reference will be automatically recalculated using the new value. Jim needs to total the values for the monthly author events for June, July, and August. He asks you to create formulas to perform these calculations.

Steps

1. **Click cell B8**
   This is the cell where you want to enter the calculation that totals the number of June events.

2. **Type = (the equal sign)**
   Placing an equal sign at the beginning of an entry tells Excel that a formula is about to be entered, rather than a label or a value. "Enter" appears on the status bar. The total number of June events is equal to the sum of the values in cells B3, B4, B5, and B6.

   Trouble?
   If you type an incorrect character, press [Backspace].

3. **Type b3+b4+b5+b6**
   Compare your worksheet to Figure B-5. Each cell address in the equation is shown in a matching color in the worksheet. For example, the cell address B3 is written in blue in the equation and is outlined in blue in the worksheet. This makes it easy to identify each cell in a formula.

   Trouble?
   If the formula instead of the result appears in the cell after you click ✓, make sure you began the formula with = (the equal sign).

4. **Click the Enter button ✓ on the formula bar**
   The result, 85, appears in cell B8. Cell B8 remains selected, and the formula appears in the formula bar. Excel is not case-sensitive: it doesn't matter if you type uppercase or lowercase characters when you enter cell addresses. Typing cell addresses is only one way of creating a formula. A more accurate method involves **pointing** at cells using the mouse, then using the keyboard to supply arithmetic operators.

5. **Click cell C8, type =, click cell C3, type +, click cell C4, type +, click cell C5, type +, click cell C6, then click the Enter button ✓ on the formula bar**
   When you clicked cell C3, a moving border surrounded the cell. This **moving border** indicates the cell used in the calculation. Moving borders can appear around a single cell or a range of cells. The total number of author appearances for July, 69, appears in cell C8. The pointing method of creating a formula is more accurate than typing, because it is easy to type a cell address incorrectly. Cell D8 also needs a total.

6. **Click cell D8, type =, click cell D3, type +, click cell D4, type +, click cell D5, type +, click cell D6, then click the Enter button ✓ on the formula bar**
   The total number of appearances for August, 80, appears in cell D8. Compare your worksheet to Figure B-6.

7. **Click the Save button 💾 on the Standard toolbar**

FIGURE B-5: Worksheet showing cells in a formula

Formula displayed in cell

Formula displayed in formula bar

FIGURE B-6: Completed formulas

TABLE B-1: Excel arithmetic operators

operator	purpose	example
+	Addition	=A5+A7
–	Subtraction or negation	=A5–10
*	Multiplication	=A5*A7
/	Division	=A5/A7
%	Percent	=35%
^ (caret)	Exponent	=6^2 (same as 6^2)

BUILDING AND EDITING WORKSHEETS EXCEL B-7

Creating Complex Formulas

Excel 2002 — Unit B

The formula you entered is a simple formula containing one arithmetic operator, the plus sign. You can create a **complex formula**—an equation that uses more than one type of arithmetic operator. For example, you may need to create a formula that uses addition and multiplication. You can use arithmetic operators to separate tasks within a complex equation. In formulas containing more than one arithmetic operator, Excel uses the order of precedence rules to determine which operation to perform first. Jim wants you to total the values for the monthly author events for June, July, and August, and forecast what the 20% increase in appearances will be. You create a complex formula to perform these calculations.

Steps

1. **Click cell B10, type =, click cell B8, then type *.2**
   This part of the formula calculates 20% of the cell contents by multiplying the June total by .2 (or 20%). Because this part of the formula uses multiplication, it will be calculated first according to the rules of precedence.

2. **Type +, then click cell B8**
   The second part of the formula adds the 20% increase to the original value of the cell. The mode indicator says Point, indicating you can add more cell references. Compare your worksheet to Figure B-7.

   > **QuickTip**
   > Press [Esc] to turn off a moving border.

3. **Click ✓ on the formula bar**
   The result, 102, appears in cell B10.

4. **Click cell C10, type =, click cell C8, type *.2, type +, click cell C8, then click ✓**
   The result, 82.8, appears in cell C10.

5. **Click cell D10, type =, click cell D8, type *.2, type +, click cell D8, then click ✓**
   The result, 96, appears in cell D10. Compare your completed worksheet to Figure B-8.

6. **Click the Save button 💾 on the Standard toolbar**

CLUES TO USE

Editing formulas

You can edit formulas the same way you edit cell entries: you can click the cell containing the formula then edit it in the formula bar; you can also double-click a cell or press [F2] to enter Edit mode, and then edit the formula in the cell. After you are in Edit mode, use the arrow keys to move the insertion point left or right in the formula. Use [Backspace] or [Delete] to delete characters to the left or right of the insertion point, then type or point to new cell references or operators.

► EXCEL B-8   BUILDING AND EDITING WORKSHEETS

FIGURE B-7: Elements of a complex formula

FIGURE B-8: Multiple complex formulas

Formula calculates a 20% increase over the value in cell D8 and displays the result in cell D10

Clues to Use

Order of precedence in Excel formulas

A formula can include several mathematical operations. When you work with formulas that have more than one operator, the order of precedence is very important. If a formula contains two or more operators, such as 4+.55/4000*25, the computer performs the calculations in a particular sequence based on these rules: Operations inside parentheses are calculated before any other operations. Exponents are calculated next, then any multiplication and division—from left to right. Finally, addition and subtraction are calculated from left to right. In the example 4+.55/4000*25, Excel performs the arithmetic operations by first dividing 4000 into .55, then multiplying the result by 25, then adding 4. You can change the order of calculations by using parentheses. For example, in the formula (4+.55)/4000*25, Excel would first add 4 and .55, then divide that amount by 4000, then finally multiply by 25.

BUILDING AND EDITING WORKSHEETS

Introducing Excel Functions

Functions are predefined worksheet formulas that enable you to perform complex calculations easily. Like formulas, functions always begin with the formula prefix = (the equal sign). You can type functions, or you can use the Insert Function button to select the function you need from a list. The **AutoSum** button on the Standard toolbar enters the most frequently used function, SUM. A function can be used by itself within a cell, or as part of a formula. For example, to calculate monthly sales tax, you could create a formula that adds a range of cells (using the SUM function) and then multiplies the total by a decimal. Jim asks you to use the SUM function to calculate the grand totals in his worksheet and the AVERAGE function to calculate the average number of author events per store.

Steps

1. **Click cell E3**
   This is where you want the total of all Boston author events for June, July, and August.

2. **Click the AutoSum button Σ on the Standard toolbar, then click the Enter button ✓ on the formula bar**
   The formula =SUM(B3:D3) appears in the formula bar and the result, 56, appears in cell E3. By default, AutoSum adds the values in the cells above the cell pointer. If there are one or fewer values there, AutoSum adds the values to its left—in this case, the values in cells B3, C3, and D3. The information inside the parentheses is the **argument**, or the information Excel uses to calculate the function result. In this case, the argument is the range B3:D3.

3. **Click cell E4, click Σ, then click ✓**
   The total for the New York events appears in cell E4.

4. **Click cell E5, then click Σ**
   AutoSum sets up a function to add the two values in the cells above the active cell, but this time the default argument is not correct.

   > **QuickTip**
   > The ScreenTip 1R x 3C tells you the size of the range is 1 row and 3 columns.

5. **Click cell B5 and hold down the mouse button, drag to cell D5 to select the range B5:D5, then click ✓**
   As you drag, the argument in the SUM function changes to reflect the selected range, and a yellow Argument ToolTip shows the function syntax. You can click any part of the ToolTip to display Help on the function.

6. **Click cell E6, type =SUM(, click cell B6 and drag to cell D6, click ✓, click cell E8, type =SUM(, click cell B8 and drag to cell D8, click ✓, click cell E10, type =SUM(, click cell B10 and drag to cell D10, then click ✓**
   Compare your screen to Figure B-9. Excel adds the closing parenthesis.

   > **Trouble?**
   > If the Office Assistant opens, click No, don't provide help now.

7. **Click cell F3, then click the Insert Function button ƒx on the formula bar**
   The Insert Function dialog box and Wizard opens. Here you can select a function from a list. See Table B-2 for frequently used functions. The function you need to calculate averages—named AVERAGE—appears in the Most Recently Used function category.

   > **QuickTip**
   > Modify a function's range by clicking the Collapse dialog box button, defining the range with your mouse, then clicking the Expand dialog box button to return to the Function Arguments dialog box.

8. **Click AVERAGE in the Select a function list box, click OK; the Function Arguments dialog box opens; type B3:D3 in the Number 1 text box, as shown in Figure B-10, then click OK**

9. **Click cell F4, click ƒx, verify that AVERAGE is selected, click OK, type B4:D4, click OK, click cell F5, click ƒx, click AVERAGE, click OK, type B5:D5, click OK, click cell F6, click ƒx, click AVERAGE, click OK, type B6:D6, then click OK**
   The result for Boston (cell F3) is 18.66667; the result for New York (cell F4) is 22.66667; the result for Seattle (cell F5) is 18.33333; and the result for Houston (cell F6) is 18.33333, giving you the averages for all four stores.

10. **Enter your name in cell A25, click the Save button on the Standard toolbar, then click the Print button on the Standard toolbar**

EXCEL B-10 BUILDING AND EDITING WORKSHEETS

FIGURE B-9: Worksheet with SUM functions entered

(Screenshot of Excel worksheet showing Summer 2003 MediaLoft Author Events Forecast with SUM formula =SUM(B10:D10) in cell E10 displaying result 280.8)

Callouts:
- AutoSum button
- SUM function entered in cell
- Insert Function button
- Result of SUM function shown in formula bar

FIGURE B-10: Using Insert Function to create a formula

(Screenshot showing Function Arguments dialog box for AVERAGE function with Number1 set to B3:D3, result = 18.66666667)

Callouts:
- Click Collapse Dialog Box button to define an argument using your mouse
- Argument appears here

TABLE B-2: Frequently used functions

function	description
SUM (*argument*)	Calculates the sum of the arguments
AVERAGE (*argument*)	Calculates the average of the arguments
MAX (*argument*)	Displays the largest value among the arguments
MIN (*argument*)	Displays the smallest value among the arguments
COUNT (*argument*)	Calculates the number of values in the arguments

(Handwritten note: =countA(A3:A6) for name lines)

Clues to Use

Using the MIN and MAX functions

Other commonly used functions include MIN and MAX. You use the MIN function to calculate the minimum, or smallest, value in a selected range; the MAX function calculates the maximum, or largest, value in a selected range. The MAX function is included in the Most Recently Used function category in the Insert Function dialog box, while both the MIN and MAX function can be found in the Statistical category. These functions are particularly useful in larger worksheets.

BUILDING AND EDITING WORKSHEETS EXCEL B-11

Excel 2002 Unit B

Copying and Moving Cell Entries

Using the Cut, Copy, and Paste buttons or the Excel drag-and-drop feature, you can copy or move information from one cell or range in your worksheet to another. When you cut or move information, the original data does not remain in the original location. You can also cut, copy, and paste labels and values from one worksheet to another. Jim needs to include the 2003 forecast for spring and fall author events. He's already entered the spring data and will finish entering the labels and data for the fall. He asks you to copy information from the spring report to the fall report.

Steps

1. **Click the Spring-Fall sheet tab of the Author Events Forecast workbook**
   The store names in cells A6:A7 are incorrect.

2. **Click the Summer sheet tab, select the range A5:A6, then click the Copy button on the Standard toolbar**
   The selected range (A5:A6) is copied to the Office Clipboard, a temporary storage area that holds the selected information you copy or cut. A moving border surrounds the selected range until you press [Esc] or copy additional information to the Clipboard. The information you copied remains in the selected range.

   > **Trouble?**
   > If the Clipboard task pane does not open, click Edit on the menu bar, then click Office Clipboard.

3. **Click the Spring-Fall sheet tab, select the range A6:A7, click the Paste button on the Standard toolbar, select the range A4:A9, then click**
   The Clipboard task pane opens when you copy a selection to the already-occupied Clipboard. You can use the Clipboard task pane to copy, cut, store, and paste up to 24 items. Each item in the pane displays its contents.

   > **QuickTip**
   > After you paste an item, the Paste Options button appears. If you move the pointer over it, the Paste Options list arrow appears, letting you choose whether to paste the contents or only the formatting.

4. **Click cell A13, click [Boston New York Seattle Houston Total] in the Clipboard Task Pane to paste the contents in cell A13, then click the Close button in the Task Pane title bar to close it**
   The item is copied into the range A13:A18. When pasting an item from the Clipboard into the worksheet, you only need to specify the top-left cell of the range where you want to paste the selection. The Total label in column E is missing from the fall forecast.

5. **Click cell E3, position the pointer on any edge of the cell until the pointer changes to ⇖, then press and hold down [Ctrl]**
   The pointer changes to the copy pointer.

6. **While still pressing [Ctrl], press and hold the left mouse button, drag the cell contents to cell E12, release the mouse button, then release [Ctrl]**
   This drag-and-drop technique is useful for copying cell contents. As you dragged, an outline of the cell moved with the pointer, as shown in Figure B-11, and a ScreenTip appeared tracking the current position of the item as you moved it. When you released the mouse button, the Total label appeared in cell E12. You can also use drag and drop to move data to a new cell.

   > **Trouble?**
   > When you use drag and drop to move data into occupied cells, Excel asks if you want to replace the existing cells. Click OK to replace the contents with those of the cell you are moving.

7. **Click cell C1, position the pointer on the edge of the cell until it changes to ⇖, then drag the cell contents to A1**
   You don't use [Ctrl] when moving information with drag and drop. You can easily enter the fall events data into the range B13:D16.

8. **Using the information shown in Figure B-12, enter the author events data for the fall into the range B13:D16**

9. **Click the Save button on the Standard toolbar**

EXCEL B-12 BUILDING AND EDITING WORKSHEETS

FIGURE B-11: Using drag-and-drop to copy information

- Copy button
- Paste button
- Copied cell
- Outline of copied cell
- Drag-and-drop pointer with ScreenTip

FIGURE B-12: Worksheet with fall author event data entered

Sum of selected range appears in status bar

Clues to Use

Using the Office Clipboard

The Office Clipboard, shown in the task pane in Figure B-13, lets you copy and paste multiple items such as text, images, tables, or Excel ranges within or between Microsoft Office applications. The Office Clipboard can hold up to 24 items copied or cut from any Office program. The Clipboard task pane displays the items stored on the Office Clipboard. You choose whether to delete the first item from the Clipboard when you copy the 25th item. The collected items remain in the Office Clipboard and are available to you until you close all open Office programs. You can specify when and where to show the Office Clipboard task pane by clicking the options list arrow at the bottom of the Clipboard pane.

FIGURE B-13: Office Clipboard task pane

Clipboard entry from another Office program

BUILDING AND EDITING WORKSHEETS   EXCEL B-13

Understanding Relative and Absolute Cell References

Excel 2002 — Unit B

As you work in Excel, you will often want to reuse formulas in different parts of the worksheet. This will save you time because you won't have to retype them. For example, you may want to perform a what-if analysis showing one set of sales figures using a lower forecast in one part of the worksheet and another set using a higher forecast in another area. But when you copy formulas, it is important make sure that they refer to the correct cells. To do this, you need to understand relative and absolute cell references. ✒ Jim often reuses formulas in different parts of his worksheets to examine different possible outcomes, so he wants you to understand relative and absolute cell references.

Details

▶ Use relative references when cell relationships remain unchanged.

When you create a formula that references other cells, Excel normally does not "record" the exact cell references, but instead the relationship to the cell containing the formula. For example, in Figure B-14, cell E5 contains the formula: =SUM(B5:D5). When Excel retrieves values to calculate the formula in cell E5, it actually looks for "the cell three columns to the left of the formula, which in this case is cell B5", "the cell two columns to the left of the formula" and so on. This way, if you copy the cell to a new location such as cell E6, the results will reflect the new formula location, and will automatically retrieve the values in cells B6, C6, and D6. This is called **relative cell referencing**, because Excel is recording the input cells *in relation to* the formula cell.

In most cases, you will use relative cell references, which is the Excel default. In Figure B-14, the formulas in E5:E9 and in B9:E9 contain relative cell references. They total the "three cells to the left of" or the "four cells above" the formulas.

▶ Use absolute cell references when one relationship changes.

There are times when you want Excel to retrieve formula information from a specific cell, and you don't want that cell to change when you copy the formula to a new location. For example, you might have a price in a specific cell that you want to use in all formulas, regardless of their location. If you used relative cell referencing, the formula results would be incorrect, because Excel would use a different cell every time you copied the formula. Therefore you need to use an **absolute cell reference**, a reference that does not change when you copy the formula.

You create an absolute cell reference by placing a $ (dollar sign) before both the column letter and the row number for the cell's address, using the [F4] function key on the keyboard. Figure B-15 displays the formulas used in Figure B-14. The formulas in cells B15 to D18 use absolute cell references to refer to a potential sales increase of 50%, shown in cell B12.

▶ EXCEL B-14 BUILDING AND EDITING WORKSHEETS

FIGURE B-14: Location of relative references

Formula contains relative references
Cells contain relative references
Cells contain relative references

FIGURE B-15: Absolute and relative reference formulas

Cell referenced in absolute formulas
Relative reference
Absolute reference

Clues to Use

Using a mixed reference

Sometimes when you copy a formula, you'll want to change the row reference but keep the column reference the same. This type of cell referencing combines elements of both absolute and relative referencing and is called a mixed reference. When copied, the mixed reference C$14 changes the column relative to its new location but prevents the row from changing. In the mixed reference $C14, the column would not change but the row would be updated relative to its location. Like the absolute reference, a mixed reference can be created using the [F4] function key. With each press of the [F4] key, you cycle through all the possible combinations of relative, absolute, and mixed references ($C$14, C$14, $C14, C14).

BUILDING AND EDITING WORKSHEETS   EXCEL B-15

Copying Formulas with Relative Cell References

Excel 2002 Unit B

Copying and moving formulas allows you to reuse formulas you've already created. Copying formulas, rather than retyping them, is faster and helps to prevent typing errors. You can use the Copy and Paste commands or the Fill Right method to copy formulas. Jim wants you to copy the formulas that total the appearances by region and by month from the spring to the fall.

Steps

1. **Click cell E4, then click the Copy button on the Standard toolbar**
   The formula for calculating the total number of spring Boston author events is copied to the Clipboard. Notice that the formula =SUM(B4:D4) appears in the formula bar.

2. **Click cell E13, then click the Paste button on the Standard toolbar**
   The formula from cell E4 is copied into cell E13, where the new result of 59 appears. Notice in the formula bar that the cell references have changed, so that the range B13:D13 appears in the formula. This formula contains **relative cell references**, which tell Excel to copy the formula to a new cell, but to substitute new cell references so that the relationship of the cells to the formula in its new location remains unchanged. In this case, Excel adjusted the formula so that cells D13, C13, and B13—the three cell references immediately to the left of E13—replaced cells D4, C4, and B4, the three cell references to the left of E4. Notice that the bottom-right corner of the active cell contains a small square, called the **fill handle**. You can use the fill handle to copy labels, formulas, and values. This option is called **AutoFill**.

   > **QuickTip**
   > To specify components of the copied cell or range prior to pasting, click Edit on the menu bar, then click Paste Special. You can selectively copy formulas, values, comments, validation, and formatting attributes, and specify calculations, as well as transpose cells or paste the contents as a link.

3. **Position the pointer over the fill handle until it changes to +, press and hold the left mouse button, then drag the fill handle to select the range E13:E16**
   See Figure B-16.

4. **Release the mouse button**
   A formula similar to the one in cell E13 now appears in the range E14:E16. Again, because the formula uses relative cell references, cells E14 through E16 correctly display the totals for the fall author events. After you release the mouse button, the **AutoFill Options button** appears. If you move the pointer over it and click its list arrow, you can specify what you want to fill and whether or not you want to include formatting.

5. **Click cell B9, click Edit on the menu bar, then click Copy**

6. **Click cell B18, click Edit on the menu bar, then click Paste**
   See Figure B-17. The formula for calculating the September events appears in the formula bar. You also need totals to appear in cells C18, D18, and E18. You could use the fill handle again, but another option is to use a menu command.

   > **Trouble?**
   > If the Clipboard task pane opens, click the Close button. If the Office Assistant appears, right-click it, then click Hide.

7. **Select the range B18:E18**

8. **Click Edit on the menu bar, point to Fill, then click Right**
   The rest of the totals are filled in correctly. Compare your worksheet to Figure B-18.

9. **Click the Save button on the Standard toolbar**

► EXCEL B-16   BUILDING AND EDITING WORKSHEETS

FIGURE B-16: Using the fill handle

12	Fall	September	October	November	Total	
13	Boston	22	17	20	59	← Formula in cell E13 will be copied to E14:E16
14	New York	27	16	24		
15	Seattle	19	19	18		← Fill handle
16	Houston	15	25	18		
17						
18	Total				+	← Mouse pointer

FIGURE B-17: Copied formula

[Screenshot of Microsoft Excel - Author Events Forecast.xls showing the Spring-Fall worksheet with cell B18 selected containing =SUM(B13:B16) with result 83]

- Copied formula result
- Paste Options button
- Copied formula cell references

FIGURE B-18: Completed worksheet with all formulas copied

12	Fall	September	October	November	Total
13	Boston	22	17	20	59
14	New York	27	16	24	67
15	Seattle	19	19	18	56
16	Houston	15	25	18	58
17					
18	Total	83	77	80	240

Clues To Use

Filling cells with sequential text or values

Often, you'll need to fill cells with sequential text: months of the year, days of the week, years, or text plus a number (Quarter 1, Quarter 2, . . .). You can easily fill cells using sequences by dragging the fill handle. As you drag the fill handle, Excel automatically extends the existing sequence. (The contents of the last filled cell appear in the ScreenTip.) Use the Fill Series command on the Edit menu to examine all of the available fill series options.

BUILDING AND EDITING WORKSHEETS EXCEL B-17

Copying Formulas with Absolute Cell References

Excel 2002 — Unit B

When copying formulas, you might want a cell reference to always refer to a particular cell address. In such an instance, you would use an absolute cell reference. An **absolute cell reference** always refers to a specific cell address when the formula is copied. You create an absolute reference by placing a dollar sign ($) before the row letter and column number of the address (for example $A$1). The staff in the Marketing department hopes the number of author events will increase by 20% over last year's figures. Jim wants you to add a column that calculates a possible increase in the number of spring events in 2003. He asks you to do a what-if analysis and recalculate the spreadsheet several times, changing the percentage by which the number of appearances might increase each time.

Steps

1. **Click cell G1, type Change, then press [→]**
   You can store the increase factor that will be used in the what-if analysis in cell H1.

2. **Type 1.1, then press [Enter]**
   The value in cell H1 represents a 10% increase in author events.

3. **Click cell G3, type What if?, then press [Enter]**

4. **Click cell G4, type =, click E4, type *, click H1, then click the Enter button on the formula bar**
   The result, 56.1, appears in cell G4. This value represents the total spring events for Boston if there is a 10% increase. Jim wants to perform a what-if analysis for all the stores.

5. **Drag the fill handle to extend the selection from G4 to G7**
   The resulting values in the range G5:G7 are all zeros. When you copy the formula it adjusts so that the formula in cell G5 is =E5*H2. Because there is no value in cell H2, the result is 0, an error. You need to use an absolute reference in the formula to keep the formula from adjusting itself. That way, it will always reference cell H1. You can change the relative cell reference to an absolute cell reference by using [F4].

6. **Click cell G4, press [F2] to change to Edit mode, then press [F4]**
   When you press [F2], the **range finder** outlines the equation's arguments in blue and green. When you press [F4], dollar signs appear, changing the H1 cell reference to an absolute reference. See Figure B-19.

7. **Click on the formula bar, then drag the fill handle to extend the selection to range G5:G7**
   The formula correctly contains an absolute cell reference, and the value of G4 remains unchanged at 56.1. The correct values for a 10% increase appear in cells G4:G7. You complete the what-if analysis by changing the value in cell H1 to indicate a 25% increase in events.

8. **Click cell H1, type 1.25, then click**
   The values in the range G4:G7 change to reflect the 25% increase. Compare your completed worksheets to Figure B-20. Because events only occur in whole numbers, the numbers' appearance can be changed later.

9. **Enter your name in cell A25, click the Save button on the Standard toolbar, click the Print button on the Standard toolbar, close the workbook, then exit Excel**

> **QuickTip**
> Before you copy or move a formula, check to see if you need to use an absolute cell reference.

EXCEL B-18 BUILDING AND EDITING WORKSHEETS

FIGURE B-19: Absolute cell reference in cell G4

	A	B	C	D	E	F	G	H
1	Spring and Fall Events						Change	1.1
2								
3	Spring	March	April	May	Total		What if?	
4	Boston	20	13	18	51		=E4*$H$1	
5	New York	26	17	19	62		0	
6	Seattle	18	15	13	46		0	
7	Houston	13	22	16	51		0	
8								
9	Total	77	67	66	210			

- Absolute cell references in formula
- Incorrect values due to relative references in copied formulas

FIGURE B-20: Completed worksheets

Summer 2003 MediaLoft Author Events Forecast

	June	July	August	Total	Average
Boston	22	15	19	56	18.66667
New York	28	18	22	68	22.66667
Seattle	20	17	18	55	18.33333
Houston	15	19	21	55	18.33333
Total	85	69	80	234	
20% rise	102	82.8	96	280.8	

Spring and Fall Events   Change   1.25

Spring	March	April	May	Total	What if?
Boston	20	13	18	51	63.75
New York	26	17	19	62	77.5
Seattle	18	15	13	46	57.5
Houston	13	22	16	51	63.75
Total	77	67	66	210	

Fall	September	October	November	Total
Boston	22	17	20	59
New York	27	16	24	67
Seattle	19	19	18	56
Houston	15	25	18	58
Total	83	77	80	240

Clues to Use

Inserting and deleting selected cells

As you add formulas to your workbook, you may need to insert or delete cells, not entire rows or columns. When you do this, Excel automatically adjusts cell references to reflect their new locations. To insert cells, click Insert on the menu bar, then click Cells. The Insert dialog box opens, asking if you want to insert a cell and move the selected cell down or to the right of the new one. To delete one or more selected cells, click Edit on the menu bar, click Delete, and, in the Delete dialog box, indicate which way you want to move the adjacent cells. When using this option, be careful not to disturb row or column alignment that may be necessary to make sense of the worksheet.

BUILDING AND EDITING WORKSHEETS   EXCEL B-19

Excel 2002

Practice

▶ Concepts Review

Label each element of the Excel worksheet window shown in Figure B-21.

FIGURE B-21

Match the term or button with the statement that describes it.

8. Fill handle
9. Function
10. [icon]
11. [icon]
12. Formula

a. A predefined formula that provides a shortcut for commonly used calculations
b. A cell entry that performs a calculation in an Excel worksheet
c. Used to copy labels, formulas, and values
d. Adds the selected range to the Office Clipboard.
e. Used to paste cells

Select the best answer from the list of choices.

13. What type of cell reference changes when it is copied?
    a. Absolute
    b. Circular
    c. Looping
    d. Relative

14. What character is used to make a reference absolute?
    a. &
    b. ^
    c. $
    d. @

▶ EXCEL B-20 **BUILDING AND EDITING WORKSHEETS**

15. Which button is used to enter data in a cell?
    a. ↶
    b. ✗
    c. 📋
    d. ✓

▶ Skills Review

1. **Edit cell entries and work with ranges.**
    a. Start Excel, open the workbook EX B-2 from the drive and folder where your Project Files are stored then save it as **Office Furnishings**.
    b. Change the quantity of Tables to **27**.
    c. Change the price of Desks to **285**.
    d. Change the quantity of Easels to **18**.
    e. Enter your name in cell A40, then save the workbook.
2. **Enter formulas.**
    a. In cell B6, use the pointing method to enter the formula **B2+B3+B4+B5**.
    b. In cell D2, use the pointing method to enter the formula **B2*C2**.
    c. Save your work.
3. **Create complex formulas.**
    a. In cell B8, enter the formula **(B2+B3+B4+B5)/4**.
    b. In cell C8, enter the formula **(C2+C3+C4+C5)/4**.
    c. Save your work.
4. **Introduce Excel functions.**
    a. Enter the label **Min Price** in cell A9.
    b. In cell C9, enter the function **MIN(C2:C5)**.
    c. Enter the label **Max Price** in cell A10.
    d. Create a formula in cell C10 that determines the maximum price.
    e. Save your work.
5. **Copy and move cell entries.**
    a. Select the range **A1:C6**, then copy the range to cell A12.
    b. Select the range **D1:E1**, then use drag and drop to copy the range to cell D12.
    c. Move the contents of cell G1 to cell E9, then save your work.
6. **Copy formulas with relative cell references.**
    a. Copy the formula in D2 into cells D3:D5.
    b. Copy the formula in D2 into cells D13:D16.
    c. Save the worksheet.
7. **Copy formulas with absolute cell references.**
    a. In cell E10, enter the value **1.375**.
    b. In cell E2, create a formula containing an absolute reference that multiplies D2 and E10.
    c. Use the fill handle to copy the formula in E2 into cells **E3:E5**.
    d. Use the copy and paste buttons to copy the formula in E2 into cells **E13:E16**.
    e. Delete cells A13:E13, shifting the cells up, then edit the formula in cell B16 so the missing reference is removed.
    f. Change the amount in cell E10 to **2.873**.
    g. Select cells A1:E1 and insert cells, shifting cells down.
    h. Enter **Inventory Estimate** in cell A1.
    i. Save, preview, print, and close the workbook, then exit Excel.

Excel 2002 | Practice

▶ Independent Challenge 1

You are the box office manager for the Young Brazilians Jazz Band, a popular new group. Your responsibilities include tracking seasonal ticket sales for the band's concerts and anticipating ticket sales for the next season. The group sells four types of tickets: reserved, general, senior, and student tickets.

The 2003–2004 season includes five scheduled concerts: Spring, Summer, Fall, Winter, and Thaw. You will plan and build a worksheet that tracks the sales of each of the four ticket types for all five concerts.

FIGURE B-22

	A	B	C	D	E	F	G	H
1			2003-2004 Season					
2			Young Brazilians Jazz Band					Increase
3								1.05
4		Reserved	General	Senior	Student			
5	Concerts	Seating	Admission	Citizens	Tickets	Totals		What if?
6	Spring	285	50	30	20	385		404.25
7	Summer	135	25	35	20	215		225.75
8	Fall	130	50	25	20	225		236.25
9	Winter	160	100	30	20	310		325.5
10	Thaw	250	60	35	20	365		383.25
11	Total	960	285	155	100	1500		1575

a. Think about the results you want to see, the information you need to build into these worksheets, and what types of calculations must be performed.

b. Sketch sample worksheets on a piece of paper to indicate how the information should be laid out. What information should go in the columns? In the rows?

c. Start Excel, open a new workbook, then save it as **Young Brazilians** in the drive and folder where your Project Files are stored.

d. Plan and build a worksheet that tracks the sales of each of the four ticket types for all five concerts. Build the worksheets by entering a title, row labels, column headings, and formulas.

e. Enter your own sales data. No concert sold more than 400 tickets, and the Reserved category was the most popular.

f. Calculate the total ticket sales for each concert, the total sales for each of the four ticket types, and the total sales for all tickets.

g. Name the worksheet **Sales Data** and color the tab Red.

h. Copy the Sales Data worksheet to a blank worksheet, name the copied worksheet **5% Increase**, and color the tab aqua.

i. Modify the 5% increase sheet so that a 5% increase in sales of all ticket types is shown in a separate column. See Figure B-22 for a sample worksheet.

j. Enter your name in a worksheet cell.

k. Save your work, preview and print the worksheets, then close the workbook and exit Excel.

▶ Independent Challenge 2

The Beautiful You Salon is a small but growing beauty salon that has hired you to organize its accounting records using Excel. The owners want you to track its expenses using Excel. Before you were hired, one of the bookkeepers entered last year's expenses in a workbook, but the analysis was never completed.

a. Start Excel, open the workbook EX B-3 then save it as **Beautiful You Finances** in the drive and folder where your Project Files are stored. The worksheet includes labels for functions such as the Average, Maximum, and Minimum amounts of each of the expenses in the worksheet.

b. Think about what information would be important for the bookkeeping staff to know.

c. Create your sketch using the existing worksheet as a foundation.

d. Create formulas in the Total column and row using the AutoSum function.

e. Create formulas in the Average, Maximum, and Minimum columns and rows using the appropriate functions, dragging to select the range.

f. Rename Sheet1 **Expenses** and add a color to the tab.

g. Enter your name in a worksheet cell.

h. Save your work, preview and print the worksheet, then close the workbook and exit Excel.

▶ EXCEL B-22 **BUILDING AND EDITING WORKSHEETS**

Practice

▶ Independent Challenge 3

You have been promoted to computer lab manager at Learn-It-All, a local computer training center. It is your responsibility to make sure there are enough computers for students during scheduled classes. Currently, you have five classrooms: four with IBM PCs and one with Macintoshes. Classes are scheduled Monday, Wednesday, and Friday in two-hour increments from 9 a.m. to 5 p.m. (the lab closes at 7 p.m.), and each room can currently accommodate 30 computers.

You plan and build a worksheet that tracks the number of students who can currently use the available computers per room. You create your enrollment data. Using an additional worksheet, you show the impact of an enrollment increase of 25%.

a. Think about how to construct these worksheets to create the desired output.
b. Sketch sample paper worksheets to indicate how the information should be laid out.
c. Start Excel, open a new workbook, then save it as **Learn-it-All** in the drive and folder where your Project Files are stored.
d. Create a worksheet by entering a title, row labels, column headings, data, and formulas. Name the sheet to easily identify its contents.
e. Create a second sheet by copying the information from the initial sheet.
f. Name the second sheet to easily identify its contents.
g. Add color to each sheet tab.
h. Enter your name in a cell in each sheet.
i. Save your work, preview and print each worksheet, then close the workbook and exit Excel.

e Independent Challenge 4

Your company is opening a branch office in Great Britain and your boss is a fanatic about keeping the thermostats at a constant temperature during each season of the year. Because she grew up in the U.S., she is only familiar with Fahrenheit temperatures and doesn't know how to convert them to Celsius. She has asked you to find out the Celsius equivalents for the thermostatic settings she wants to use. She prefers the temperature to be 65 degrees F in the winter, 62 degrees F in the spring, 75 degrees in the summer, and 70 degrees F in the fall. You can use the Web and Excel to determine the new settings.

a. Start Excel, open a new workbook, then save it as **Temperature Conversions** in the drive and folder where your Project Files are stored.
b. Go to the Alta Vista search engine at www.altavista.com and enter search text such as "temperature conversions". You can also use Yahoo!, Excite, Infoseek, or another search engine of your choice. Locate a site that tells you how to convert Fahrenheit temperatures to Celsius. (*Hint*: One possible site you can use to determine these conversions is http://home.clara.net/brianp/, then click on the Temperature link.)
c. Think about how to create an Excel equation that will perform the conversion.
d. Create column and row titles using Table B-3 to get started.
e. In the appropriate cell, create an equation that calculates the conversion of a Fahrenheit temperature to a Celsius temperature.
f. Copy the equation, then paste it in the remaining Celsius cells.
g. Enter your name in a worksheet cell.
h. Save and print your work.

TABLE B-3

Temperature Conversions

Season	Fahrenheit	Celsius
Spring	62	
Winter	68	
Summer	75	
Fall	70	

Excel 2002 | Practice

▶ Visual Workshop

Create a worksheet similar to Figure B-23 using the skills you learned in this unit. Save the workbook as **Annual Budget** in the drive and folder where your Project Files are stored. Enter your name in cell A13, then preview and print the worksheet.

FIGURE B-23

	A	B	C	D	E	F
1	Computer Consultants, Inc.					
2						
3		Hardware	Software	Training	Contracts	Total
4	Quarter 1	86600	14200	6100	21000	127900
5	Quarter 2	96000	16800	5000	24600	142400
6	Quarter 3	78300	14600	9000	21000	122900
7	Quarter 4	100600	24900	6500	30600	162600
8	Total	361500	70500	26600	97200	
9						
10	1.7					
11	Increase	614550	119850	45220	165240	

Excel 2002

Unit C

Formatting
a Worksheet

Objectives

- Format values
- Use fonts and font sizes
- Change attributes and alignment
- Adjust column widths
- Insert and delete rows and columns
- Apply colors, patterns, and borders
- Use conditional formatting
- Check spelling

You can use Excel formatting features to make a worksheet more attractive, to make it easier to read, or to emphasize key data. You do this by using different colors and fonts for the cell contents, adjusting column and row widths, and inserting and deleting columns and rows. The marketing managers at MediaLoft have asked Jim Fernandez to create a workbook that lists advertising expenses for all MediaLoft stores. Jim has prepared a worksheet for the New York City store containing this information, which he can adapt later for use in other stores. He asks you to use formatting to make the worksheet easier to read and to call attention to important data.

Excel 2002 — Unit C

Formatting Values

If you enter a value in a cell and you don't like the way the data appears, you can adjust the cell's format. **Formatting** determines how labels and values appear in cells, such as boldface, italic, with or without dollar signs or commas, and the like. Formatting changes only the way a value or label appears; it does not alter cell data in any way. To format a cell, first select it, then apply the formatting. You can format cells and ranges before or after you enter data. ✒ The Marketing department has requested that Jim begin by listing the New York City store's advertising expenses. Jim developed a worksheet that lists advertising invoices. He entered all the information and now wants you to format some of the labels and values. Because some of the changes might also affect column widths, you make all formatting changes before widening the columns.

Steps

1. **Start Excel, open the Project File EX C-1 from the drive and folder where your Project Files are stored, then save it as Ad Expenses**
   The store advertising worksheet appears in Figure C-1. You can display numeric data in a variety of ways, such as with decimals or leading dollar signs. Excel provides a special format for currency, which adds two decimal places and a dollar sign.

   > **QuickTip**
   > Recall that to save a workbook in a different location, you click File on the menu bar, click Save As, click the Save in list arrow and navigate to a new drive or folder, type a new filename if necessary, then click Save.

2. **Select the range E4:E32, then click the Currency Style button $ on the Formatting toolbar**
   Excel adds dollar signs and two decimal places to the Cost data. Excel automatically resizes the column to display the new formatting. Another way to format dollar values is to use the comma format, which does not include the $ sign.

3. **Select the range G4:I32, then click the Comma Style button on the Formatting toolbar**
   The values in columns G, H, and I display the comma format. You can also format percentages by using the Formatting toolbar.

   > **QuickTip**
   > Select any range of contiguous cells by clicking the top-left cell, pressing and holding [Shift], then clicking the bottom-right cell. Add a row to the selected range by continuing to hold down [Shift] and pressing [↓], add a column by pressing [→].

4. **Select the range J4:J32, click the Percent Style button % on the Formatting toolbar, then click the Increase Decimal button on the Formatting toolbar to show one decimal place**
   The % of Total column is now formatted with a percent sign (%) and one decimal place. You decide that you prefer the percentages rounded to the nearest whole number.

5. **Click the Decrease Decimal button**
   You can also apply a variety of formats to dates in a worksheet.

6. **Select the range B4:B31, click Format on the menu bar, click Cells, then if necessary click the Number tab**
   The Format Cells dialog box opens with the Number tab in front and the Date category already selected. See Figure C-2.

7. **Select the format 14-Mar-01 in the Type list box, then click OK**
   The dates in column B appear in the format you selected. You decide you don't need the year to appear in the Inv. Due column.

   > **QuickTip**
   > The 3-14-01 format displays a single-digit day (such as 5/9/03) just as 9-May-03 does. The format below it displays the same day as 5/09/03.

8. **Select the range C4:C31, click Format on the menu bar, click Cells, click 14-Mar in the Type list box, then click OK**
   Compare your worksheet to Figure C-3.

9. **Click the Save button on the Standard toolbar**

EXCEL C-2   FORMATTING A WORKSHEET

FIGURE C-1: Advertising expense worksheet

FIGURE C-2: Format Cells dialog box

- Number categories
- Date format types
- Sample of selected date type
- Displays single digit months and dates without a preceding zero

FIGURE C-3: Worksheet with formatted values

Date formats appear without year

Clues to Use

Using the Format Painter

You can "paint" a cell's format into other cells by using the Format Painter button on the Standard toolbar. This is similar to using copy and paste to copy information, but instead of copying cell contents, you copy only the cell format. Select the cell containing the desired format, then click . The pointer changes to . Use this pointer to select the cell or range you want to contain the new format. You can paint a cell's format onto multiple cells by double-clicking , then clicking each cell that you want to paint with . When you are finished painting formats, you can turn off the Format Painter by pressing [Esc] or by clicking again.

FORMATTING A WORKSHEET EXCEL C-3

Using Fonts and Font Sizes

Excel 2002 — Unit C

A **font** is the name for a collection of characters (letters, numerals, symbols, and punctuation marks) with a similar, specific design. The **font size** is the physical size of the text, measured in units called points. A **point** is equal to 1/72 of an inch. The default font in Excel is 10-point Arial. You can change the font, the size, or both of any worksheet entry or section by using the Format command on the menu bar or by using the Formatting toolbar. Table C-1 shows several fonts in different sizes. Now that the data is formatted, Jim wants you to change the font and size of the labels and the worksheet title so that they stand out more from the data.

Steps

1. Press **[Ctrl][Home]** to select cell A1

2. Click **Format** on the menu bar, click **Cells**, then click the **Font tab** in the Format Cells dialog box
   See Figure C-4.

   > **QuickTip**
   > You can also open the Format Cells dialog box by right-clicking selected cells, then clicking Format Cells.

3. Scroll down the **Font list** to see an alphabetical listing of the fonts available on your computer, click **Times New Roman** in the Font list box, click **24** in the Size list box, then click **OK**
   The title font appears in 24-point Times New Roman, and the Formatting toolbar displays the new font and size information. You can also change a font and increase the font size by using the Formatting toolbar. The column headings should stand out more from the data.

4. Select the range **A3:J3**, then click the **Font list arrow** [Arial] on the Formatting toolbar
   Notice that the fonts on this font list actually look like the font they represent.

5. Click **Times New Roman** in the Font list, click the **Font Size** list arrow [10], then click **14** in the Font Size list
   Compare your worksheet to Figure C-5. Notice that some of the column headings are now too wide to appear fully in the column. Excel does not automatically adjust column widths to accommodate cell formatting; you have to adjust column widths manually. You'll learn to do this in a later lesson.

6. Click the **Save button** on the Standard toolbar

TABLE C-1: Types of fonts

font	12 point	24 point	font	12 point	24 point
Arial	Excel	Excel	Playbill	Excel	Excel
Comic Sans MS	Excel	Excel	Times New Roman	Excel	Excel

FIGURE C-4: Font tab in the Format Cells dialog box

- Currently selected font
- Available fonts may differ on your computer
- Effects options
- Type a custom font size or select from the list
- Font style options
- Sample of selected font and formatting

FIGURE C-5: Worksheet with formatted title and labels

- Font and size of active cell or range
- Column headings now 14-point Times New Roman
- Title after changing to 24-point Times New Roman

Clues to Use

Inserting Clip Art

You can add clips to your worksheets to make them look more professional. A **clip** is an individual media file, such as art, sound, animation, or a movie. **Clip art** refers to images such as a corporate logo, a picture, or a photo; Excel comes with many clips that you can use. To add clip art to your worksheet, click Insert on the menu bar, point to Picture, then click Clip Art. The Insert Clip Art task pane appears. Here you can search for clips by typing one or more **keywords** (words related to your subject) in the Search text box, then clicking Search. Clips that relate to your keywords appear in the Clip Art task pane, as shown in Figure C-6. Click the image you want. (If you have a standard Office installation and have a dial-up Internet connection, you will have fewer images available.) You can also add your own images to a worksheet by clicking Insert on the menu bar, pointing to Picture, then clicking From File. Navigate to the file you want, then click Insert. To resize an image, drag its lower right corner. To move an image, drag it to a new location.

FIGURE C-6: Results of search on keyword "magic"

Excel 2002

FORMATTING A WORKSHEET EXCEL C-5

Changing Attributes and Alignment

Excel 2002 Unit C

Attributes are styling formats such as bold, italics, and underlining that you can apply to affect the way text and numbers look in a worksheet. You can also change the **alignment** of labels and values in cells to be left, right, or center. You can apply attributes and alignment options from the Formatting toolbar or from the Alignment tab of the Format Cells dialog box. See Table C-2 for a list and description of the available attribute and alignment toolbar buttons. Now that you have applied new fonts and font sizes to his worksheet labels, Jim wants you to further enhance the worksheet's appearance by adding bold and underline formatting and centering some of the labels.

Steps

1. **Press [Ctrl][Home] to move to cell A1, then click the Bold button B on the Formatting toolbar**
   The title appears in bold.

2. **Select the range A3:J3, then click the Underline button U on the Formatting toolbar**
   Excel underlines the text in the column headings in the selected range.

   > **QuickTip**
   > Overuse of any attribute can be distracting and make a workbook less readable. Be consistent, adding emphasis the same way throughout.

3. **Click cell A3, click the Italics button I on the Formatting toolbar, then click B**
   The word "Type" appears in boldface italic type. Notice that the Bold, Italics, and Underline buttons are selected.

4. **Click I**
   Excel removes italics from cell A3 but the bold and underline formatting attributes remain.

   > **QuickTip**
   > Use formatting shortcuts on any selected range: [Ctrl][B] to bold, [Ctrl][I] to italicize, and [Ctrl][U] to underline.

5. **Select the range B3:J3, then click B**
   Bold formatting is added to the rest of the labels in the column headings. The title would look better if it were centered over the data columns.

6. **Select the range A1:J1, then click the Merge and Center button on the Formatting toolbar**
   The Merge and Center button creates one cell out of the 10 cells across the row, then centers the text in that newly created large cell. The title "MediaLoft NYC Advertising Expenses" is centered across the 10 columns you selected. You can change the alignment within individual cells using toolbar buttons; you can split merged cells into their original components by selecting the merged cells, then clicking .

   > **QuickTip**
   > To clear all formatting, click Edit on the menu bar, point to Clear, then click Formats.

7. **Select the range A3:J3, then click the Center button on the Formatting toolbar**
   Compare your screen to Figure C-7. Although they may be difficult to read, notice that all the headings are centered within their cells.

8. **Click the Save button on the Standard toolbar**

Clues to Use

Rotating and indenting cell entries

In addition to applying fonts and formatting attributes, you can rotate or indent cell data within a cell to further change its appearance. You can rotate text within a cell by altering its alignment. To change alignment, select the cells you want to modify, click Format on the menu bar, click Cells, then click the Alignment tab. Click a position in the Orientation box, or type a number in the degrees text box to change from the default horizontal alignment, then click OK. You can indent cell contents using the Increase Indent button on the Formatting toolbar, which moves cell contents to the right one space, or the Decrease Indent button , which moves cell contents to the left one space.

► EXCEL C-6 FORMATTING A WORKSHEET

FIGURE C-7: Worksheet with formatting attributes applied

Callouts:
- Center button
- Title centered across columns
- Formatting buttons outlined
- Column headings centered, bolded, and underlined

TABLE C-2: Attribute and Alignment buttons on the Formatting toolbar

button	description	button	description
B	Bolds text		Aligns text on the left side of the cell
I	Italicizes text		Centers text horizontally within the cell
U	Underlines text		Aligns text on the right side of the cell
	Adds lines or borders		Centers text across columns, and combines two or more selected adjacent cells into one cell

---

Clues to Use

Using AutoFormat

Excel has 17 predefined worksheet formats to make formatting easier and to give you the option of consistently styling your worksheets. AutoFormats are designed for worksheets with labels in the left column and top rows, and totals in the bottom row or right column. To use AutoFormat, select the data to be formatted—or place your mouse pointer anywhere within the range to be selected (Excel can automatically detect a range of cells)—click Format on the menu bar, click AutoFormat, select a format from the sample boxes, as shown in Figure C-8, then click OK.

FIGURE C-8: AutoFormat dialog box

Samples of available formats

FORMATTING A WORKSHEET   EXCEL C-7

Excel 2002

Excel 2002 Unit C

Adjusting Column Widths

As you continue formatting a worksheet, you might need to adjust column widths to accommodate a larger font size or style. The default column width is 8.43 characters wide, a little less than one inch. With Excel, you can adjust the column width for one or more columns by using the mouse or the Column command on the Format menu. Table C-3 describes the commands available on the Format Column menu. ➥ Jim notices that some of the labels in column A have been truncated and don't fit in the cells. He asks you to adjust the widths of the columns so that the labels appear in their entirety.

Steps

1. **Position the pointer on the line between the column A and column B headings**
   The **column heading** is the gray box at the top of each column containing a letter. The pointer changes to ↔, as shown in Figure C-9. You position the pointer on the right edge of the column that you are adjusting. The Yellow Pages entries are the widest in the column.

2. **Click and drag the ↔ pointer to the right until the column displays the Yellow Pages entries fully**
   The **AutoFit** feature lets you use the mouse to resize a column so it automatically accommodates the widest entry in a cell.

3. **Position the pointer on the column line between columns B and C headings until it changes to ↔, then double-click**
   Column B automatically widens to fit the widest entry, in this case, the column label.

4. **Use AutoFit to resize columns C, D, and J**
   You can also use the Column Width command on the Format menu to adjust several columns to the same width.

5. **Select the range F5:I5**
   Columns can be adjusted by selecting any cell in the column.

6. **Click Format on the menu bar, point to Column, then click Width**
   The Column Width dialog box appears. Move the dialog box, if necessary, by dragging it by its title bar so you can see the selected columns. The column width measurement is based on the number of characters in the Normal font (in this case, Arial).

7. **Type 11 in the Column Width text box, then click OK**
   The column widths change to reflect the new setting. See Figure C-10.

8. **Click the Save button 💾 on the Standard toolbar**

QuickTip
To reset columns to the default width, click the column headings to select the columns, click Format on the menu bar, point to Column, click Standard Width, then click OK.

Trouble?
If "######" appears after you adjust a column of values, the column is too narrow to display the contents. Increase the column width until the values appear.

TABLE C-3: Format Column commands

command	description	command	description
Width	Sets the width to a specific number of characters	Unhide	Unhide(s) column(s)
AutoFit Selection	Fits to the widest entry	Standard Width	Resets width to default widths
Hide	Hide(s) column(s)		

FIGURE C-9: Preparing to change the column width

Resize pointer between columns A and B

Row 2 heading

Column D heading

FIGURE C-10: Worksheet with column widths adjusted

Columns widened to display text

Columns widened to same width

Clues to Use

Specifying row height

The Row Height command on the Format menu allows you to customize row height to improve readability. Row height is calculated in points, the same units of measure used for fonts. The row height must exceed the size of the font you are using. Normally, you don't need to adjust row heights manually. If you format something in a row to be a larger point size, Excel will adjust the row to fit the largest point size in the row. You can also adjust row height by placing the ✥ pointer under the row heading and dragging to the desired height.

FORMATTING A WORKSHEET EXCEL C-9

Inserting and Deleting Rows and Columns

As you modify a worksheet, you might find it necessary to insert or delete rows and columns to keep your worksheet current. For example, you might need to insert rows to accommodate new inventory products or remove a column of yearly totals that are no longer necessary. Jim has already improved the appearance of his worksheet by formatting the labels and values in the worksheet. Now he decides to improve the overall appearance of the worksheet by inserting a row between the last row of data and the totals. Jim has located a row of inaccurate data and an unnecessary column that he wants you to delete.

Steps

1. **Right-click cell A32, then click Insert**
   The Insert dialog box opens. See Figure C-11. You can choose to insert a column or a row, or you can shift the data in the cells in the active column right or in the active row down. An additional row between the last row of data and the totals will visually separate the totals.

   > **QuickTip**
   > Inserting or deleting rows or columns can cause problems in formulas that contain absolute cell references. After adding rows or columns to a worksheet, be sure to proof your formulas.

2. **Click the Entire row option button, then click OK**
   A blank row appears between the totals and the Billboard data. Excel inserts rows above the cell pointer and inserts columns to the left of the cell pointer. When you insert a new row, the contents of the worksheet shift down from the newly inserted row. The formula result in cell E33 has not changed. When you insert a new column, the contents of the worksheet shift to the right from the point of the new column. To insert a single row, you can also right-click the row heading immediately below where you want the new row, then click Insert. To insert multiple rows, drag across row headings to select the same number of rows as you want to insert. The Insert Options button appears beside cell A33. When you place over, you can click the list arrow and select from the following options: Format Same As Above, Format same As Below, or Clear Formatting.

3. **Click the row 27 heading**
   Hats from Mass Appeal Inc. will no longer be part of the advertising campaign. All of row 27 is selected, as shown in Figure C-12.

   > **QuickTip**
   > Use the Edit menu, or right-click the selected row and click Delete, to remove a selected row. Pressing [Delete] removes the contents of a selected row; the row itself remains.

4. **Click Edit in the menu bar, then click Delete**
   Excel deletes row 27, and all rows below this shift up one row.

5. **Click the column J heading**
   The percentage information is calculated elsewhere and is no longer necessary in this worksheet.

6. **Click Edit in the menu bar, then click Delete**
   Excel deletes column J. The remaining columns to the right shift left one column.

7. **Click the Save button on the Standard toolbar**

FIGURE C-11: Insert dialog box

Click here to insert a row

FIGURE C-12: Worksheet with row 27 selected

Row 27 heading

Inserted row

Insert Options button may appear in a different location, or may not be visible

Adding and editing comments

Much of your Excel work may be in collaboration with teammates with whom you share worksheets. You can share ideas with other worksheet users by adding comments within selected cells. To include a comment in a worksheet, click the cell where you want to place the comment, click Insert on the menu bar, then click Comment. A resizable text box containing the computer's user name opens where you can type your comments. A small, red triangle appears in the upper-right corner of a cell containing a comment. If the comments are not already displayed, workbook users can point to the triangle to display the comment. To see all worksheet comments, as shown in Figure C-13, click View on the menu bar, then click Comments. To edit a comment click the cell containing the comment, click Insert on the menu bar, then click Edit Comment. To delete a comment, right-click the cell containing the comment, then click Delete Comment.

FIGURE C-13: Comments in worksheet

Excel 2002

FORMATTING A WORKSHEET EXCEL C-11

Applying Colors, Patterns, and Borders

You can use colors, patterns, and borders to enhance the overall appearance of a worksheet and to make it easier to read. You can add these enhancements by using the Patterns or Borders tabs in the Format Cells dialog box or by using the Borders and Color buttons on the Formatting toolbar. You can apply color or patterns to the background of a cell, to a range, or to cell contents. You can also apply borders to all the cells in a worksheet or only to selected cells to call attention to individual or groups of cells. See Table C-4 for a list of border buttons and their functions. Jim asks you to add a pattern, a border, and color to the title of the worksheet to give it a more professional appearance.

1. Press **[Ctrl][Home]** to select cell **A1**, then click the **Fill Color list arrow** on the Formatting toolbar
   The color palette appears.

   > **QuickTip**
   > Use color sparingly. Too much color can divert the reader's attention from the worksheet data.

2. Click the **Turquoise** color (fourth row, fifth column)
   Cell A1 has a turquoise background, as shown in Figure C-14. Cell A1 spans columns A through I because of the Merge and Center command used for the title.

3. Click **Format** on the menu bar, then click **Cells**
   The Format Cells dialog box opens.

4. Click the **Patterns tab** if it is not already displayed
   See Figure C-15. A high contrast between foreground and background increases the readability of cell contents.

5. Click the **Pattern list arrow**, click the **Thin Diagonal Crosshatch pattern** (third row, last column), then click **OK**
   A border also enhances a cell's appearance. Unlike underlining, which is a text formatting tool, borders extend the width of the cell.

   > **QuickTip**
   > You can also draw cell borders using the mouse pointer. Click the Borders list arrow on the Formatting toolbar. Click Draw Borders, then drag to create borders or boxes.

6. Click the **Borders list arrow** on the Formatting toolbar, then click the **Thick Bottom Border** (second row, second column) on the Borders palette
   It can be difficult to view a border in a selected cell.

7. Click cell **A3**
   The border is a nice enhancement. Font color can also help distinguish information in a worksheet.

   > **QuickTip**
   > The default color on the Fill Color and Font Color buttons changes to the last color you selected.

8. Select the range **A3:I3**, click the **Font Color list arrow** on the Formatting toolbar, then click **Blue** (second row, third column from the right) on the palette
   The text changes color, as shown in Figure C-16.

9. Click the **Print Preview button** on the Standard toolbar, preview the first page, click **Next** to preview the second page, click **Close** on the Print Preview toolbar, then click the **Save button** on the Standard toolbar

EXCEL C-12   FORMATTING A WORKSHEET

FIGURE C-14: Background color added to cell

Cell A1 with turquoise background

FIGURE C-15: Patterns tab in the Format Cells dialog box

Sample of selected color

Pattern list arrow

FIGURE C-16: Worksheet with colors, patterns, and border

TABLE C-4: Border buttons

button	function	button	function	button	function
	No Border		Bottom Double Border		Top and Thick Bottom Border
	Bottom Border		Thick Bottom Border		All Borders
	Left Border		Top and Bottom Border		Outside Borders
	Right Border		Top and Double Bottom Border		Thick Box Border

FORMATTING A WORKSHEET EXCEL C-13

Excel 2002 Unit C

Using Conditional Formatting

Formatting makes worksheets look professional and helps distinguish different types of data. You can have Excel automatically apply formatting depending on specific outcomes in cells. You might, for example, want advertising costs above a certain number to appear in red boldface and lower values to appear in blue. Automatically applying formatting attributes based on cell values is called **conditional formatting**. If the data meets your criteria, Excel applies the formats you specify. Jim wants the worksheet to include conditional formatting so that total advertising costs greater than $175 appear in boldface red type. He asks you to create the conditional format in the first cell in the Total cost column.

Steps

1. **Click cell G4**
   Use the scroll bars if necessary, to make column G visible.

2. **Click Format on the menu bar, then click Conditional Formatting**
   The Conditional Formatting dialog box opens. Depending on the logical operator you've selected (such as "greater than" or "not equal to"), the Conditional Formatting dialog box displays different input boxes. You can define up to three different conditions that let you determine the outcome, and then assign formatting attributes to each one. You define the condition first. The default setting for the first condition is "Cell Value Is" "between."

   > **Trouble?**
   > If the Office Assistant appears, close it by clicking the No, don't provide help now button.

3. **To change the current condition, click the Operator list arrow, then click greater than or equal to**
   Because you changed the operator from "between," which required text boxes for two values, only one value text box now appears. The first condition is that the cell value must be greater than or equal to some value. See Table C-5 for a list of options. The value can be a constant, formula, cell reference, or date. That value is set in the third box.

4. **Click the Value text box, then type 175**
   Now that you have assigned the value, you need to specify what formatting you want for cells that meet this condition.

5. **Click Format, click the Color list arrow, click Red (third row, first column), click Bold in the Font style list box, click OK, compare your settings to Figure C-17, then click OK to close the Conditional Formatting dialog box**
   The value in cell G4, 325.55, is formatted in bold red numbers because it is greater than 175, meeting the condition to apply the format. You can copy conditional formats the same way you would copy other formats.

6. **With cell G4 selected, click the Format Painter button on the Standard toolbar, then drag to select the range G5:G30**

7. **Click cell G4**
   Compare your results to Figure C-18. All cells with values greater than or equal to 175 in column G appear in bold red text.

8. **Press [Ctrl][Home] to move to cell A1**

9. **Click the Save button on the Standard toolbar**

EXCEL C-14 FORMATTING A WORKSHEET

FIGURE C-17: Completed Conditional Formatting dialog box

- Operator list arrow
- Click to add additional condition(s)
- Enter value in the value text box
- Click to delete existing condition(s)
- Click to define format of cells that meet the condition

FIGURE C-18: Worksheet with conditional formatting

- Format Painter button
- Results of conditional formatting

TABLE C-5: Conditional formatting options

option	mathematical equivalent	option	mathematical equivalent
Between	X>Y<Z	Greater than	Z>Y
Not between	B≯C≮A	Less than	Y<Z
Equal to	A=B	Greater than or equal to	A≧B
Not equal to	A≠B	Less than or equal to	Z≦Y

CLUES TO USE

Deleting conditional formatting

Because it's likely that the conditions you define will change, you can delete any conditional format you define. Select the cell(s) containing conditional formatting, click Format on the menu bar, click Conditional Formatting, then click Delete. The Delete Conditional Format dialog box opens, as shown in Figure C-19. Select the check boxes for any of the conditions you want to delete, click OK, then click OK again. The previously assigned formatting is deleted—leaving the cell's contents intact.

FIGURE C-19: Delete Conditional Format dialog box

FORMATTING A WORKSHEET   EXCEL C-15

Unit C
Excel 2002

Checking Spelling

A single misspelled word can cast doubt on the validity and professional value of your entire workbook. Excel includes a spelling checker to help you ensure workbook accuracy. The spelling checker scans your worksheet, displays words it doesn't find in its built-in dictionary, and when possible suggests replacements. To check other sheets in a multiple-sheet workbook, you need to display each sheet and run the spelling checker again. Because the built-in dictionary cannot possibly include all the words that each of us needs, you can add words to the dictionary, such as your company name, an acronym, or an unusual technical term. The spelling checker will no longer consider that word misspelled. Any words you've added to the dictionary using Word, Access, or PowerPoint are also available in Excel. Because he will distribute this workbook to the marketing managers, Jim asks you to check its spelling.

Steps

Trouble?
If a language other than English is being used, the Spelling English dialog box will list the name of that language.

1. **Click the Spelling button on the Standard toolbar**
   The Spelling English (U.S.) dialog box opens, as shown in Figure C-21, with MediaLoft selected as the first misspelled word in the worksheet. For any word you have the option to Ignore or Ignore All cases the spell checker flags, or Add the word to the dictionary.

2. **Click Ignore All for MediaLoft**
   The spell checker found the word "cards" misspelled and offers "crabs" as an alternative.

3. **Scroll through the Suggestions list, click cards, then click Change**
   The word "Concepts" is also misspelled and the spell checker suggests the correct spelling.

4. **Click Change**
   When no more incorrect words are found, Excel displays a message indicating that all the words on that worksheet have been checked.

5. **Click OK**

6. **Enter your name in cell A34, then press [Ctrl][Home]**

QuickTip
You can set the Excel AutoCorrect feature to correct spelling as you type. Click Tools on the menu bar, then click AutoCorrect Options.

7. **Click the Save button on the Standard toolbar, then preview the worksheet**

8. **In the Preview window, click Setup, under Scaling click Fit to option button to print the worksheet on one page, click OK, click Print, then click OK**
   Compare your printout to Figure C-22.

9. **Click File on the menu bar, then click Exit to close the workbook without saving changes and exit Excel**

Clues to Use

Using e-mail to send a workbook

You can use e-mail to send an entire workbook from within Excel. To send a workbook as an e-mail message attachment, open the workbook, click File, point to Send to, then click Mail Recipient (as Attachment). You supply the To and (optional) Cc information, as shown in Figure C-20, then click Send. You can also route a workbook to one or more recipients on a routing list. Click File, point to Send to, then click Routing Recipient. Click Create New Contact and enter contact information, then fill in the Routing slip. Depending on your e-mail program and Web browser, you may have to follow a different procedure.

FIGURE C-20: E-mailing an Excel workbook

Workbook is automatically attached to message

EXCEL C-16   FORMATTING A WORKSHEET

FIGURE C-21: Spelling English dialog box

- Misspelled word
- Type replacement word here or click a suggestion
- Click to ignore all occurrences of misspelled word
- Click to add word to dictionary

FIGURE C-22: Completed worksheet

MediaLoft NYC Advertising Expenses

Sales Tax 0.0841

Type	Inv. Date	Inv. Due	Placed with	Cost ea.	Quantity	Ext. Cost	Sales Tax	Total
Newspaper	1-Jan-03	31-Jan	Village Reader	$ 65.11	5	325.55	27.38	352.93
Radio spot	7-Jan-03	6-Feb	WHAT	$ 11.00	15	165.00	13.88	178.88
Subway	20-Jan-03	19-Feb	Advertising Concepts	$ 35.00	30	1,050.00	88.31	1,138.31
Yellow Pages	1-Jan-03	31-Jan	NYNEX	$ 152.94	4	611.76	51.45	663.21
Blow-in cards	13-Jan-03	12-Feb	Advertising Concepts	$ 0.17	230	39.56	3.33	42.89
Magazine	7-Jan-03	6-Feb	Young Upstart	$ 100.92	12	1,211.04	101.85	1,312.89
Pens	5-Jan-03	4-Feb	Mass Appeal, Inc.	$ 0.12	250	30.75	2.59	33.34
Radio spot	15-Jan-03	14-Feb	WHAT	$ 11.00	15	165.00	13.88	178.88
Billboard	12-Jan-03	11-Feb	Advertising Concepts	$ 101.87	20	2,037.40	171.35	2,208.75
Newspaper	25-Jan-03	24-Feb	Village Reader	$ 65.11	6	390.66	32.85	423.51
Newspaper	1-Feb-03	3-Mar	University Voice	$ 23.91	2	47.82	4.02	51.84
T-Shirts	3-Feb-03	5-Mar	Mass Appeal, Inc.	$ 5.67	200	1,134.00	95.37	1,229.37
Yellow Pages	1-Feb-03	3-Mar	NYNEX	$ 152.94	4	611.76	51.45	663.21
Newspaper	1-Mar-03	31-Mar	University Voice	$ 23.91	2	47.82	4.02	51.84
Blow-in cards	28-Feb-03	30-Mar	Advertising Concepts	$ 0.17	275	47.30	3.98	51.28
Magazine	27-Feb-03	29-Mar	Young Upstart	$ 100.92	12	1,211.04	101.85	1,312.89
Subway	22-Feb-03	24-Mar	Advertising Concepts	$ 35.00	30	1,050.00	88.31	1,138.31
Radio spot	1-Feb-03	3-Mar	WHAT	$ 11.00	30	330.00	27.75	357.75
Newspaper	25-Feb-03	27-Mar	Village Reader	$ 65.11	6	390.66	32.85	423.51
Blow-in cards	10-Mar-03	9-Apr	Advertising Concepts	$ 0.17	275	47.30	3.98	51.28
Radio spot	15-Feb-03	17-Mar	WHAT	$ 11.00	25	275.00	23.13	298.13
Pens	15-Mar-03	14-Apr	Mass Appeal, Inc.	$ 0.12	250	30.75	2.59	33.34
Yellow Pages	1-Mar-03	31-Mar	NYNEX	$ 152.94	4	611.76	51.45	663.21
Subway	20-Mar-03	19-Apr	Advertising Concepts	$ 35.00	30	1,050.00	88.31	1,138.31
Newspaper	1-Apr-03	1-May	University Voice	$ 23.91	2	47.82	4.02	51.84
Subway	10-Apr-03	10-May	Advertising Concepts	$ 35.00	30	1,050.00	88.31	1,138.31
Billboard	28-Mar-03	27-Apr	Advertising Concepts	$ 101.87	20	2,037.40	171.35	2,208.75
name				$ 1,321.89	1784	16,047.15	1,349.57	17,396.72

FORMATTING A WORKSHEET EXCEL C-17

Excel 2002 Practice

▶ Concepts Review

Label each element of the Excel worksheet window shown in Figure C-23.

FIGURE C-23

Match each command or button with the statement that describes it.

8. Cells command on the Format menu
9. Delete command on the Edit menu
10. Conditional Formatting
11. 📋
12. $
13. ✓

a. Changes appearance of cell depending on result
b. Erases the contents of a cell
c. Used to check the spelling in a worksheet
d. Used to change the appearance of selected cells
e. Pastes the contents of the Clipboard into the current cell
f. Changes the format to Currency

Select the best answer from the list of choices.

14. Which button increases the number of decimal places in selected cells?
    a.
    b. .00→
    c.
    d. ←.00

15. Each of the following operators can be used in conditional formatting, *except*:
    a. Equal to.
    b. Greater than.
    c. Similar to.
    d. Not between.

16. How many conditional formats can be created in any cell?
    a. 1
    b. 2
    c. 3
    d. 4

17. Which button center-aligns the contents of a single cell?
    a.
    b.
    c.
    d.

FORMATTING A WORKSHEET

Practice

18. Which of the following is an example of the comma format?
    a. $5,555.55
    b. 5555.55
    c. 55.55%
    d. 5,555.55
19. What is the name of the feature used to resize a column to its widest entry?
    a. AutoResize
    b. AutoFormat
    c. AutoFit
    d. AutoAdjust
20. Which feature applies formatting attributes according to cell contents?
    a. Conditional Formatting
    b. Comments
    c. AutoFormat
    d. Merge and Center

▶ Skills Review

1. **Format values.**
    a. Start Excel and open a new workbook.
    b. Enter the information from Table C-6 in your worksheet. Begin in cell A1, and do not leave any blank rows or columns.

    TABLE C-6

    MediaLoft Great Britain
    Quarterly Sales Projection

Department	Average Price	Quantity	Totals
Sports	25	2250	
Computers	40	3175	
History	35	1295	
Personal Growth	25	2065	

    c. Save this workbook as **MediaLoft GB Inventory** in the drive and folder where your Project Files are stored.
    d. Add the bold attribute to the data in the Department column.
    e. Use the Format Painter to paste the format from the data in the Department column to the Department and Totals labels.
    f. Add the italics attribute to the Average Price and Quantity labels.
    g. Apply the Comma format to the Price and Quantity data and reduce the number of decimals in the Quantity column to 0.
    h. Insert formulas in the Totals column (multiply the average price by the Quantity).
    i. Apply the Currency format to the Totals data.
    j. Save your work.
2. **Use fonts and font sizes.**
    a. Select the range of cells containing the column titles.
    b. Change the font of the column titles to Times New Roman.
    c. Increase the font size of the column titles and the title in cell A1 to 14-point.
    d. Resize the columns as necessary.
    e. Select the range of values in the Average Price column.
    f. Format the range using the Currency Style button.
    g. Save your changes.
3. **Change attributes and alignment.**
    a. Select the worksheet title **MediaLoft Great Britain**, then use the Bold button to boldface it.
    b. Use the Merge and Center button to center the title and the Quarterly Sales Projection labels over columns A through D.

FORMATTING A WORKSHEET EXCEL C-19

Excel 2002 | Practice

    c. Select the label **Quarterly Sales Projection**, then apply underlining to the label.
    d. Select the range of cells containing the column titles, then center them.
    e. Return the underlined, merged and centered Quarterly Sales Projection label to its original alignment.
    f. Move the Quarterly Sales Projection label to cell D2 and change the alignment to Align Right.
    g. Save your changes, then preview and print the workbook.

4. **Adjust column widths.**
   a. Use the Format menu to change the size of the Average Price column to **25**.
   b. Use the AutoFit feature to resize the Average Price column.
   c. Use the Format menu to resize the Department column to **18** and the Sold column to **11**.
   d. Change the text in cell C3 to **Sold**, use AutoFit to resize the column, then change the column size to 11.
   e. Save your changes.

5. **Insert and delete rows and columns.**
   a. Insert a new row between rows 4 and 5.
   b. Add MediaLoft Great Britain's newest department—**Children's Corner**—in the newly inserted row. Enter **35** for the average price and **1225** for the number sold.
   c. Add the following comment to cell A5: **New department**.
   d. Add a formula in cell D5 that multiplies the Average Price column by the Sold column.
   e. Add a new column between the Department and Average Price columns with the title **Location**.
   f. Delete the History row.
   g. Edit the comment so it reads "New department. Needs promotion."
   h. Save your changes.

6. **Apply colors, patterns, and borders.**
   a. Add an outside border around the Average Price and Sold data.
   b. Apply a light green background color to the labels in the Department column.
   c. Apply a gold background to the column labels in cells **B3:E3**.
   d. Change the color of the font in the column labels in cells B3:E3 to blue.
   e. Add a 12.5% Gray pattern fill to the title in Row 1. (*Hint*: Use the Patterns tab in the Format Cells dialog box to locate the 12.5% Gray pattern.)
   f. Enter your name in cell A20, then save your work.
   g. Preview and print the worksheet, then close the workbook.

7. **Use conditional formatting.**
   a. Open the Project File EX C-2 from the drive and folder where your Project Files are stored, then save it as **Monthly Operating Expenses**.
   b. Create conditional formatting that changes the monthly data entry to blue if a value is **greater than 2500**, and changes it to red if **less than 700**.
   c. Create a third conditional format that changes the monthly data to green if a value is **between 1000 and 2000**.
   d. Use the Bold button and Center button to format the column headings and row titles.
   e. Make Column A wide enough to accommodate the contents of cells **A4:A9**.
   f. AutoFit the remaining columns.
   g. Use Merge and Center in Row 1 to center the title over columns A–E.
   h. Format the title in cell A1 using 14-point Times New Roman text. Fill the cell with a color and pattern of your choice.
   i. Delete the third conditional format.
   j. Enter your name in cell A20, then apply a green background to it and make the text color yellow.
   k. Use the Edit menu to clear the cell formats from the cell with your name, then save your changes.

8. **Check spelling.**
   a. Check the spelling in the worksheet using the spell checker, correcting any spelling errors.
   b. Save your changes, then preview and print the workbook.
   c. Close the workbook, then exit Excel.

Practice

▶ Independent Challenge 1

Beautiful You, a small beauty salon, has been using Excel for several months. Now that the salon's accounting records are in Excel, the manager would like you to work on the inventory. Although more items will be added later, the worksheet has enough items for you to begin your modifications.

   a. Start Excel, open the Project File EX C-3 from the drive and folder where your Project Files are stored, then save it as **BY Inventory**.
   b. Create a formula that calculates the value of the inventory on hand for each item.
   c. Use an absolute reference to calculate the sale price of each item, using the markup percentage shown.
   d. Add the bold attribute to the column headings.
   e. Make sure all columns are wide enough to display the data and headings.
   f. Add a row under #2 Curlers for **Nail Files**, price paid **$0.25**, sold **individually (each)**, with **59** on hand.
   g. Verify that all the formulas in the worksheet are correct. Adjust any items as needed, check the spelling, then save your work.
   h. Use conditional formatting to call attention to items with a quantity of 25 or fewer on hand. Use boldfaced red text.
   i. Add an outside border around the data in the Item column.
   j. Delete the row with #3 Curlers.
   k. Enter your name in an empty cell, then save the file.
   l. Preview and print the worksheet, close the workbook, then exit Excel.

▶ Independent Challenge 2

You volunteer several hours each week with the Community Action Center. You would like to examine the membership list, and decide to use formatting to make the existing data look more professional and easier to read.

   a. Start Excel, open the Project File EX C-4 from the drive and folder where your Project Files are stored, then save it as **Community Action**.
   b. Remove any blank columns.
   c. Format the Annual Revenue figures using the Currency format.
   d. Make all columns wide enough to fit their data and headings.
   e. Use formatting enhancements, such as fonts, font sizes, and text attributes to make the worksheet more attractive.
   f. Center-align the column labels.
   g. Use conditional formatting so that Number of Employees data greater than 50 employees appears in a contrasting color.
   h. Before printing, preview the file so you know what the worksheet will look like. Adjust any items as necessary, check spelling, enter your name in an empty cell, save your work, then print a copy.
   i. Close the workbook then exit Excel.

Excel 2002 | Practice

▶ Independent Challenge 3

Classic Instruments is a Miami-based company that manufactures high-quality pens and markers. As the finance manager, one of your responsibilities is to analyze the monthly reports from your five district sales offices. Your boss, Joanne Bennington, has just asked you to prepare a quarterly sales report for an upcoming meeting. Because several top executives will be attending this meeting, Joanne reminds you that the report must look professional. In particular, she asks you to emphasize the company's surge in profits during the last month and to highlight the fact that the Northeastern district continues to outpace the other districts.

a. Plan a worksheet that shows the company's sales during the first quarter. Assume that all pens are the same price. Make sure you include:
 - The number of pens sold (units sold) and the associated revenues (total sales) for each of the five district sales offices. The five sales districts include: Northeastern, Midwestern, Southeastern, Southern, and Western
 - Calculations that show month-by-month totals and a three-month cumulative total
 - Calculations that show each district's share of sales (percent of Total Sales)
 - Formatting enhancements to emphasize the recent month's sales surge and the Northeastern district's sales leadership

b. Ask yourself the following questions about the organization and formatting of the worksheet: How will you calculate the totals? What formulas can you copy to save time and keystrokes? Do any of these formulas need to use an absolute reference? How will you show dollar amounts? What information should be shown in bold? Do you need to use more than one font? Should you use more than one point size?

c. Start Excel, then build the worksheet with your own price and sales data. Enter the titles and labels first, then enter the numbers and formulas. You can use the form in Table C-7 to get started.

d. Save the workbook as **Classic Instruments** in the drive and folder where your Project Files are stored.

e. Adjust the column widths as necessary.

f. Change the height of row 1 to 30 points.

g. Format labels and values, and change the attributes and alignment.

h. Use the AutoFormat feature to add color and formatting to the data.

i. Resize columns and adjust the formatting as necessary.

j. Add a column that calculates a 22% increase in sales dollars. Use an absolute cell reference in this calculation.

k. Create a new column named Increased Sales that adds the projected increase to the Total Sales. (*Hint*: Make sure the current formatting is applied to the new information.)

l. Insert a ClipArt image in an appropriate location, adjusting its size and position as necessary.

m. Enter your name in an empty cell.

n. Check the spelling, then save your work.

o. Preview, then print the file in landscape orientation.

p. Close the file then exit Excel.

TABLE C-7

Classic Instruments

1st Quarter Sales Report

Office	Price	January Units Sold	Sales	February Units Sold	Sales	March Units Sold	Sales	Total Units Sold	Sales
Northeastern									
Midwestern									
Southeastern									
Southern									
Western									

Practice

e Independent Challenge 4

After saving for many years, you now have enough funds to take that international trip you have always dreamed about. Your well-traveled friends have told you that you should always have the local equivalent of $100 U.S. dollars in cash with you when you enter a country. You decide to use the Web to determine how much money you will need in each country.

a. Start Excel, open a new workbook, then save it as **Currency Conversions** in the drive and folder where your Project Files are stored.

b. Enter column and row labels using the following table to get started.

Currency Equivalents			
$100 in US dollars			
Country	$1 Equivalent	$100 US	Name of Units
Australia			
Canada			
France			
Germany			
Sweden			
United Kingdom			

c. Go to the Alta Vista search engine at www.altavista.com and locate information on currency conversions. (*Hint*: One possible site where you can determine currency equivalents is www.oanda.com/. Use the Quick Converter.)

d. Find out how much cash is equivalent to **$1** in U.S. dollars for the following countries: **Australia**, **Canada**, **France**, **Germany**, **Sweden**, and the **United Kingdom**. Also enter the name of the currency used in each country.

e. Create an equation that calculates the equivalent of **$100** in U.S. dollars for each country in the list, using an absolute value in the formula.

f. Format the entries in columns B and C using the correct currency unit for each country, with two decimal places. (*Hint*: Use the Numbers tab in the Format cells dialog box; choose the appropriate currency format from the Symbol list, using 2 decimal places. For example, use the **F (French) Standard** format for the France row, and so forth.)

g. Create a conditional format that changes the font attributes of the calculated amount in the "$100 US" column to bold and red if the amount is equals or exceeds **500 units** of the local currency.

h. Merge and center the title over the column headings.

i. Add a background color to the title.

j. Apply the AutoFormat of your choice to the conversion table.

k. Enter your name in an empty worksheet cell.

l. Spell check, save, preview, then print the worksheet.

m. If you have access to an e-mail account, e-mail your workbook to your instructor as an attachment.

n. Close the workbook and exit Excel.

FORMATTING A WORKSHEET   EXCEL C-23

Excel 2002 | Practice

▶ Visual Workshop

Create the worksheet shown in Figure C-24, using skills you learned in this unit. Open the Project File EX C-5 from the drive and folder where your Project Files are stored, then save it as **Projected March Advertising Invoices**. Create a conditional format in the Cost ea. column so that entries greater than 60 appear in red. (*Hint*: The only additional font used in this exercise is Times New Roman. It is 22 points in row 1, and 16 points in row 3.) Spell check the worksheet, then save and print your work.

FIGURE C-24

	A	B	C	D	E	F
1	Projected March Advertising Invoices					
2						
3	Type	Inv Date	Placed with	Cost ea.	Quantity	Ext. Cost
4	Newspaper	01-Mar-03	Village Reader	65.11	5	$ 325.55
5	Radio spot	07-Mar-03	WHAT	11.00	15	$ 165.00
6	Subway	20-Mar-03	Advertising Concepts	35.00	30	$ 1,050.00
7	Yellow Pages	01-Mar-03	NYNEX	152.94	4	$ 611.76
8	Blow-in cards	13-Mar-03	Advertising Concepts	0.17	230	$ 39.56
9	Magazine	07-Mar-03	Young Upstart	100.92	12	$ 1,211.04
10	Pens	05-Mar-03	Mass Appeal, Inc.	0.12	250	$ 30.75
11	Radio spot	15-Mar-03	WHAT	11.00	15	$ 165.00
12	Billboard	12-Mar-03	Advertising Concepts	101.87	20	$ 2,037.40
13	Billboard	28-Mar-03	Advertising Concepts	101.87	20	$ 2,037.40
14						
15	Total			580.01	601	$ 7,673.46

EXCEL C-24   FORMATTING A WORKSHEET

Excel 2002

Unit D

Working
with Charts

Objectives

- ▶ Plan and design a chart
- ▶ Create a chart
- ▶ Move and resize a chart
- ▶ Edit a chart
- ▶ Format a chart
- ▶ Enhance a chart
- ▶ Annotate and draw on a chart
- ▶ Preview and print a chart

Worksheets provide an effective way to organize information, but they are not always the best format for presenting data to others. Information in a selected range or worksheet can easily be displayed as a chart. Charts, often called graphs, allow you to communicate the relationships in your worksheet data in readily understandable pictures. In this unit, you will learn how to create a chart, how to edit a chart and change the chart type, how to add text annotations and arrows to a chart, and how to preview and print a chart. For the annual meeting Jim Fernandez needs you to create a chart showing the six-month sales history for the MediaLoft stores in the eastern division. He wants to illustrate the growth trend in this division.

Excel 2002 Unit D

Planning and Designing a Chart

Before creating a chart, you need to plan the information you want your chart to show and how you want it to look. In early June, the Marketing Department launched a regional advertising campaign for the eastern division. The results of the campaign were increased sales during the fall months. Jim wants his chart for the annual meeting to illustrate the growth trend for sales in MediaLoft's eastern division stores and to highlight this sales increase.

Details

Jim wants you to use the worksheet shown in Figure D-1 and the following guidelines to plan the chart:

▶ **Determine the purpose of the chart and identify the data relationships you want to communicate graphically**

You want to create a chart that shows sales throughout MediaLoft's eastern division from July through December. In particular, you want to highlight the increase in sales that occurred as a result of the advertising campaign.

▶ **Determine the results you want to see, and decide which chart type is most appropriate to use**

Different charts display data in distinctive ways. Some chart types are more appropriate for particular types of data and analyses. How you want your data displayed—and how you want that data interpreted—can help you determine the best chart type to use. Table D-1 describes several different types of charts and indicates when each one is best used. Because you want to compare data (sales in multiple locations) over a time period (the months July through December), you decide to use a column chart.

▶ **Identify the worksheet data you want the chart to illustrate**

You are using data from the worksheet titled "MediaLoft Eastern Division Stores" shown in Figure D-1. This worksheet contains the sales data for the four stores in the eastern division from July through December.

▶ **Sketch the chart, then use your sketch to decide where the chart elements should be placed**

You sketch your chart as shown in Figure D-2. You put the months on the horizontal axis (the **x-axis**) and the monthly sales figures on the vertical axis (the **y-axis**). The x-axis is often called the **category axis** because it often contains the names of data groups, such as months or years. The y-axis is called the **value axis** because it often contains numerical values that help you interpret the size of chart elements. (In a 3-D chart, the y-axis is referred to as the z-axis.) The area inside the horizontal and vertical axes is called the **plot area**. The **tick marks** on the y-axis create a scale of measure for each value. Each value in a cell you select for your chart is a **data point**. In any chart, a **data marker** visually represents each data point, which in this case is a column. A collection of related data points is a **data series**. In this chart, there are four data series (Boston, Chicago, Kansas City, and New York), so you include a **legend** to make it easy to identify them.

FIGURE D-1: Worksheet containing sales data

	A	B	C	D	E	F	G	H
1	MediaLoft Eastern Division Stores							
2	FY 2003 Sales Following Advertising Campaign							
3								
4								
5		July	August	September	October	November	December	Total
6	Boston	15,000	13,000	18,600	22,500	22,300	20,500	$109,600
7	Chicago	17,200	18,200	17,000	19,500	18,500	19,200	$111,900
8	Kansas City	12,100	11,400	15,000	18,100	17,000	16,500	$109,600
9	New York	19,500	16,000	18,800	20,500	22,000	23,000	$ 90,100
10	Total	$ 63,800	$ 58,600	$ 69,400	$ 80,600	$ 79,800	$ 79,200	$421,200
11								

FIGURE D-2: Column chart sketch

Labels on chart:
- Sales begin to rise
- Data point
- Data series
- Tick mark
- Value (y) axis
- Data marker
- Legend
- Plot area
- Category (x) axis

Chart title: MediaLoft Eastern Division Stores
Legend: Boston, Chicago, Kansas City, New York
Y-axis: Sales (in $), 5,000 to 25,000
X-axis: Months — July, August, September, October, November, December

TABLE D-1: Commonly used chart types

type	button	description
Area		Shows how individual volume changes over time in relation to total volume
Bar		Compares distinct object levels over time using a horizontal format; sometimes referred to as a horizontal bar chart in other spreadsheet programs
Column		Compares distinct object levels over time using a vertical format; the Excel default; sometimes referred to as a bar chart in other spreadsheet programs
Line		Compares trends over even time intervals; appears similar to an area chart, but does not emphasize total
Pie		Compares sizes of pieces as part of a whole; used for a single series of numbers
XY (scatter)		Compares trends over uneven time or measurement intervals; used in scientific and engineering disciplines for trend spotting and extrapolation
Combination	none	Combines a column and line chart to compare data requiring different scales of measure

WORKING WITH CHARTS EXCEL D-3

Excel 2002 — Unit D

Creating a Chart

To create a chart in Excel, you first select the range containing the data you want to chart. Once you've selected a range, you can use the Excel Chart Wizard to lead you through the process of creating the chart. Using the worksheet containing the sales data for the eastern division, Jim asks you to create a chart that shows the growth trend that occurred as a result of the advertising campaign.

Steps

QuickTip
When charting any data for a given time period, make sure all series are for the same time period, so you don't misrepresent your data.

1. **Start Excel, open the Project File EX D-1 from the drive and location where your Project Files are stored, then save it as MediaLoft Sales - Eastern Division**
   You want the chart to include the monthly sales figures for each of the eastern division stores, as well as month and store labels. You don't include the Total column and row because the monthly figures make up the totals, and these figures would skew the chart.

Trouble?
You can create a chart from non-contiguous cells by pressing the Option key and selecting each range.

2. **Select the range A5:G9, then click the Chart Wizard button on the Standard toolbar**
   The selected range contains the data you want to chart. The Chart Wizard opens. The Chart Wizard - Step 1 of 4 - Chart Type dialog box lets you choose the type of chart you want to create. The default chart type is a Clustered Column, as shown in Figure D-3. You can see a preview of the chart using your selected data by clicking, then holding the **Press and Hold to View Sample** button.

3. **Click Next to accept Clustered Column, the default chart type**
   The Chart Wizard - Step 2 of 4 - Chart Source Data dialog box lets you choose the data to chart and whether the series appear in rows or columns. You want to chart the effect of sales for each store over the time period. Currently, the rows are accurately selected as the data series, as specified by the Series in option button located under the Data range. Because you selected the data before clicking the Chart Wizard button, Excel converted the range to absolute values and the correct range, =Sheet1!$A$5:$G$9, appears in the Data range text box.

4. **Click Next**
   The Chart Wizard - Step 3 of 4 - Chart Options dialog box shows a sample chart using the data you selected. The store locations (the rows in the selected range) are plotted against the months (the columns in the selected range), and Excel added the months as labels for each data series. A legend shows each location and its corresponding color on the chart. The Titles tab lets you add titles to the chart and its axes. Other tabs let you modify the axes, legend, and other chart elements.

5. **Click the Chart title text box, then type MediaLoft Sales - Eastern Division**
   After a moment, the title appears in the Sample Chart box. See Figure D-4.

6. **Click Next**
   In the Chart Wizard - Step 4 of 4 - Chart Location dialog box, you determine the placement of the chart in the workbook. You can display a chart as an object on the current sheet, on any other existing sheet, or on a newly created chart sheet. A **chart sheet** in a workbook contains only a chart, which is linked to the worksheet data. The default selection—displaying the chart as an object in the sheet containing the data—will help Jim emphasize his point at the annual meeting.

QuickTip
If you want to delete a chart, select it, then press [Delete].

7. **Click Finish**
   The column chart appears and the Chart toolbar opens, either docked or floating, as shown in Figure D-5. Your chart might be in a different location and look slightly different. You will adjust the chart's location and size in the next lesson. The **selection handles**, the small squares at the corners and sides of the chart's border, indicate that the chart is selected. Anytime a chart is selected, as it is now, a blue border surrounds the worksheet data range, a green border surrounds the row labels, and a purple border surrounds the column labels.

8. **Click the Save button on the Standard toolbar**

EXCEL D-4   WORKING WITH CHARTS

FIGURE D-3: First Chart Wizard dialog box

- Selected chart
- Chart types
- Clustered column chart is the default
- Chart subtypes for selected chart
- Description of selected chart subtype

FIGURE D-4: Third Chart Wizard dialog box

- Type the chart title here
- Sample chart
- Title added
- Legend

FIGURE D-5: Worksheet with column chart

- Column labels
- Row labels
- Data range
- Selected chart object
- Chart toolbar title bar
- Title
- Legend
- Selection handles
- Month labels on the x-axis

WORKING WITH CHARTS   EXCEL D-5

Moving and Resizing a Chart

Excel 2002 — Unit D

Charts are graphics, or drawn objects, and are not located in a specific cell or at a specific range address. An **object** is an independent element on a worksheet. You can select an object by clicking within its borders to surround it with selection handles. You can move a selected chart object anywhere on a worksheet without affecting formulas or data in the worksheet. However, any data changed in the worksheet will automatically be updated in the chart. You can resize a chart to improve its appearance by dragging its selection handles. You can even put a chart on another sheet, and it will still reflect the original data. Chart objects contain other objects, such as a title and legend, which you can move and resize. To move an object, select it, then drag it or cut and copy it to a new location. When you select a chart object, the name of the selected object appears in the Chart Objects list box on the Chart toolbar and in the name box. Jim wants you to increase the size of the chart, position it below the worksheet data, then change the position of the legend.

Steps

1. **Make sure the chart is still selected, then position the pointer over the chart**
   The pointer shape indicates that you can move the chart or use a selection handle to resize it. For a table of commonly used chart pointers, refer to Table D-2. On occasion, the Chart toolbar obscures your view. You can dock the toolbar to make it easier to see your work.

   > **QuickTip**
   > The Chart menu only appears on the menu bar when a chart or one of its objects is selected.

2. **If the chart toolbar is floating, click the Chart toolbar's title bar, drag it to the right edge of the status bar until it docks, then release the mouse button**
   The toolbar is docked on the bottom of the screen.

3. **Place ▷ on a blank area near the edge of the chart, press and hold the left mouse button, using ✥, drag it until the upper-left edge of the chart is at the top of row 13 and the left edge of the chart is at the left border of column A, then release the mouse button**
   As you drag the chart, you can see a dotted outline representing the chart's perimeter. The chart appears in the new location.

   > **QuickTip**
   > Resizing a chart doesn't affect the data in the chart, only the way the chart looks on the sheet.

4. **Position the pointer on the right-middle selection handle until it changes to ↔, then drag the right edge of the chart to the right edge of column H**
   The chart is widened. See Figure D-6.

5. **Position the pointer over the top-middle selection handle until it changes to ↕, then drag it to the top of row 12**

6. **If the labels for the months do not fully appear, position the pointer over the bottom middle selection handle until it changes to ↕, then drag down to display the months**
   You can move the legend to improve the chart's appearance. You want to align the top of the legend with the top of the plot area.

7. **Click the legend to select it, then drag the legend upward using ▷ so the top of the legend aligns with the top of the plot area**
   Selection handles appear around the legend when you click it; "Legend" appears in the Chart Objects list box on the Chart toolbar as well as in the name box, and a dotted outline of the legend perimeter appears as you drag. Changing any label will modify the legend text.

   > **QuickTip**
   > Because the chart is no longer selected, the chart toolbar no longer appears.

8. **Click cell A9, type NYC, then click ✓**
   See Figure D-7. The legend changes to the text you entered.

9. **Click the Save button on the Standard toolbar**

EXCEL D-6 WORKING WITH CHARTS

FIGURE D-6: Worksheet with resized and repositioned chart

— Widened to column H

— Docked Chart toolbar

FIGURE D-7: Worksheet with repositioned legend

Repositioned legend

Legend changes to match change in cell A9

TABLE D-2: Commonly used pointers

name	pointer	use	name	pointer	use
Diagonal resizing	↗ or ↘	Change chart shape	**I-beam**	I	Edit chart text from corners
Draw	+	Create shapes	**Move chart**	✥	Change chart location
Horizontal resizing	↔	Change chart shape from left to right	**Vertical resizing**	↕	Changes chart shape from top to bottom

Clues to Use

Identifying chart objects

There are many objects within a chart, such as bars and axes; Excel makes it easy to identify each of them. Placing the mouse pointer over a chart object displays a ScreenTip identifying it, whether the chart is selected or not. If a chart—or any object in it—is selected, the ScreenTips still appear. In addition, the name of the selected chart object appears in the Chart Object list box on the Chart toolbar and in the name box.

WORKING WITH CHARTS — Excel 2002

Excel 2002 Unit D

Editing a Chart

Once you've created a chart, it's easy to modify it. You can change data values in the worksheet, and the chart will automatically be updated to reflect the new data. You can also easily change the type of chart displayed by using the buttons on the Chart toolbar. Jim looks over his worksheet and realizes that he entered the wrong data for the Kansas City store in November and December. After you correct this data, he wants to see how the same data looks using different chart types.

Steps

Trouble?
If you cannot see the chart and data together on your monitor, click View on the menu bar, click Zoom, then click 75%.

1. If necessary, scroll the worksheet so that you can see both the chart and row 8, containing the Kansas City sales figures, then place your mouse pointer over the December data point to display **Series "Kansas City" Point "December" Value: 16,500**

2. Click cell **F8**, type **19000** to correct the November sales figure, press [→], type **20500** in cell **G8**, then click ✓
    The Kansas City columns for November and December reflect the increased sales figures. See Figure D-8. The totals in column H and row 10 are also updated.

3. Select the chart by clicking on a blank area within the chart border, then click the **Chart Type list arrow** on the Chart toolbar
    The chart type buttons appear on the Chart Type palette. Table D-3 describes the principal chart types available.

4. Click the **Bar Chart button** on the palette
    The column chart changes to a bar chart. See Figure D-9. You look at the bar chart, take some notes, then decide to convert it back to a column chart. You now want to see if the large increase in sales would be better presented with a three-dimensional column chart.

QuickTip
As you work with charts, experiment with different formats for your charts until you get just the right look.

5. Click the **Chart Type list arrow**, then click the **3-D Column Chart button** on the palette
    A three-dimensional column chart appears. You notice that the three-dimensional column format is more crowded than the two-dimensional format but gives you a sense of volume.

QuickTip
The chart type button displays the last chart type selected.

6. Click the **Chart Type list arrow**, then click the **Column Chart button** on the palette

7. Click the **Save button** on the Standard toolbar

TABLE D-3: Commonly used chart type buttons

click to display a	click to display a	click to display a	click to display a
area chart	pie chart	3-D area chart	3-D pie chart
bar chart	(XY) scatter chart	3-D bar chart	3-D surface chart
column chart	doughnut chart	3-D column chart	3-D cylinder chart
line chart	radar chart	3-D line chart	3-D cone chart

WORKING WITH CHARTS

FIGURE D-8: Worksheet with new data entered for Kansas City

[Worksheet showing monthly sales data July–December with Total column. Boston: 15,000; 13,000; 18,600; 22,500; 22,300; 20,500; $111,900. Chicago: 17,200; 18,200; 17,000; 19,500; 18,500; 19,200; $109,600. Kansas City: 12,100; 11,400; 15,000; 18,100; 19,000; 20,500; $96,100. NYC: 19,500; 16,000; 18,800; 20,500; 22,000; 23,000; $119,800. Total: $63,800; $58,600; $69,400; $80,600; $81,800; $83,200; $437,400. Clustered column chart titled "MediaLoft Sales - Eastern Division" below.]

Adjusted data points — New data

FIGURE D-9: Bar chart

[Same data table above a horizontal bar chart titled "MediaLoft Sales - Eastern Division" with legend showing NYC, Kansas City, Chicago, Boston and axis labels July, September, November.]

Your chart may show more axis labels — Row and column data are reversed

Rotating a 3-D chart

In a three-dimensional chart, other data series in the same chart can sometimes obscure columns or bars. You can rotate the chart to obtain a better view. Click the chart, click the tip of one of its axes (select the Corners object), then drag the handles until a more pleasing view of the data series appears. See Figure D-10.

FIGURE D-10: 3-D chart rotated with improved view of data series

[3-D column chart of MediaLoft Sales - Eastern Division]

Click to rotate chart

WORKING WITH CHARTS EXCEL D-9

Unit D — Excel 2002

Formatting a Chart

After you've created a chart using the Chart Wizard, you can easily modify its appearance. You can use the Chart toolbar and Chart menu to change the colors of data series and to add or eliminate a legend and gridlines. **Gridlines** are the horizontal and vertical lines in the chart that enable the eye to follow the value on an axis. The Chart toolbar buttons are listed in Table D-4. Jim wants you to make some changes in the appearance of his chart. He wants to see if the chart looks better without gridlines, and he wants to change the color of a data series.

Steps

1. **Make sure the chart is still selected**
   Horizontal gridlines currently extend from the y-axis tick marks across the chart's plot area.

2. **Click Chart on the menu bar, click Chart Options, click the Gridlines tab in the Chart Options dialog box, then click the Major Gridlines check box for the Value (Y) axis to remove the check**
   The gridlines disappear from the sample chart in the dialog box, as shown in Figure D-11.

3. **Click the Major Gridlines check box for the Value (Y) axis to reselect it, then click the Minor Gridlines check box for the Value (Y) axis**
   Both major and minor gridlines appear in the sample. **Minor gridlines** show the values between the tick marks.

4. **Click the Minor Gridlines check box for the Value (Y) axis, then click OK**
   The minor gridlines disappear, leaving only the major gridlines on the Value axis. You can change the color of the columns to better distinguish the data series.

5. **With the chart selected, double-click any light blue column in the NYC data series**
   Handles appear on all the columns in the NYC data series, and the Format Data Series dialog box opens, as shown in Figure D-12.

6. **Click the fuchsia box (fourth row, first column) in the Patterns tab, then click OK**
   All the columns for the series become fuchsia, and the legend changes to match the new color. Compare your finished chart to Figure D-13.

7. **Click the Save button on the Standard toolbar**

> **QuickTip**
> Add labels, values, and percentages to your chart by using the Data Labels tab in the Chart Options dialog box.

TABLE D-4: Chart enhancement buttons

button	use
	Displays formatting dialog box for the selected object on the chart
	Selects chart type (chart type on button changes to last chart type selected)
	Adds/deletes legend
	Creates a data table within the chart
	Charts data by row
	Charts data by column
	Angles selected text downward (clockwise)
	Angles selected text upward (counter clockwise)

WORKING WITH CHARTS

FIGURE D-11: Chart Options dialog box

Sample chart appears without gridlines

FIGURE D-12: Format Data Series dialog box

Sample of selected color

FIGURE D-13: Chart with formatted data series

	July	August	September	October	November	December	Total
Boston	15,000	13,000	18,600	22,500	22,300	20,500	$111,900
Chicago	17,200	18,200	17,000	19,500	18,500	19,200	$109,600
Kansas City	12,100	11,400	15,000	18,100	19,000	20,500	$ 96,100
NYC	19,500	16,000	18,800	20,500	22,000	23,000	$119,800
Total	$ 63,800	$ 58,600	$ 69,400	$ 80,600	$ 81,800	$ 83,200	$437,400

Gridlines make it easy to follow axis values

New data series color

New color appears in legend

Excel 2002

WORKING WITH CHARTS EXCEL D-11

Enhancing a Chart

There are many ways to enhance a chart to make it easier to read and understand. You can create titles for the x-axis and y-axis, add graphics, or add background color. You can even format the text you use in a chart. Jim wants you to improve the appearance of his chart by creating titles for the x-axis and y-axis and adding a drop shadow to the title.

Steps

1. **Click a blank area of the chart to select it, click Chart on the menu bar, click Chart Options, click the Titles tab in the Chart Options dialog box, then type Months in the Category (X) axis text box**
   Descriptive text on the x-axis helps readers understand the chart. The word "Months" appears below the month labels in the sample chart, as shown in Figure D-14.

   > **QuickTip**
   > To edit the text, position the pointer over the selected text box until it changes to I, click, then edit the text.

2. **In the Value (Y) axis text box, type Sales (in $), then click OK**
   A selected text box containing "Sales (in $)" appears rotated 90 degrees to the left of the y-axis. Once the Chart Options dialog box is closed, you can move the Value or Category axis title to a new position by clicking on an edge of the object then dragging it.

3. **Press [Esc] to deselect the Value-axis title**
   Next you decide that a border with a drop shadow will enhance the chart title.

4. **Click the chart title, MediaLoft Sales – Eastern Division, to select it**

   > **QuickTip**
   > The Format button opens a dialog box with the appropriate formatting options for the selected chart element. The ScreenTip for the button changes, depending on the selected object.

5. **Click the Format Chart Title button on the Chart toolbar to open the Format Chart Title dialog box, make sure the Patterns tab is selected, then click the Shadow check box to select it**
   A border with a drop shadow surrounds the title in the Sample area.

6. **Click the Font tab in the Format Chart Title dialog box, click Times New Roman in the Font list, click Bold Italic in the Font style list, click OK, then press [Esc] to deselect the chart title**
   A border with a drop shadow appears around the chart title, and the chart title text is reformatted.

   > **QuickTip**
   > You can also double-click the Category axis title to open the Format Axis Titles dialog box.

7. **Click Months (the Category axis title), click , click the Font tab if necessary, select Times New Roman in the Font list, then click OK**
   The Category axis title appears in the Times New Roman font.

8. **Click Sales (in $) (the Value axis title), click , click the Font tab if necessary, click Times New Roman in the Font list, click OK, then press [Esc] to deselect the title**
   The Value axis title appears in the Times New Roman font. Compare your chart to Figure D-15.

9. **Click the Save button on the Standard toolbar**

EXCEL D-12   WORKING WITH CHARTS

FIGURE D-14: Sample chart with Category (X) axis text

FIGURE D-15: Enhanced chart

Changing text alignment in charts

You can modify the alignment of axis text to make it fit better within the plot area. With a chart selected, double-click the axis text to be modified. The Format Axis dialog box opens. Click the Alignment tab, then change the alignment by typing the number of degrees in the Degrees text box, or by clicking a marker in the Degrees sample box. When you have made the desired changes, click OK.

WORKING WITH CHARTS EXCEL D-13

Annotating and Drawing on a Chart

Excel 2002 — Unit D

You can add arrows and text annotations to point out critical information in your charts. **Text annotations** are labels that you add to a chart to further describe your data. You can draw lines and arrows that point to the exact locations you want to emphasize. Jim wants you to add a text annotation and an arrow to highlight the October sales increase.

Steps

1. **Make sure the chart is selected**
   To call attention to the Boston October sales increase, you can draw an arrow that points to the top of the Boston October data series with the annotation, "Due to ad campaign." With the chart selected, simply typing text in the formula bar creates annotation text.

2. **Type Due to ad campaign, then click the Enter button**
   As you type, the text appears in the formula bar. After you confirm the entry, the text appears in a selected text box within the chart window.

3. **Point to an edge of the text box so that the pointer changes to**

   > **Trouble?**
   > If the pointer changes to I or ↔, release the mouse button, click outside the text box area to deselect it, select the text box, then repeat Step 3.

4. **Drag the text box above the chart, as shown in Figure D-16, then release the mouse button**
   You can add an arrow to point to a specific area or item in a chart by using the Drawing toolbar.

5. **Click the Drawing button on the Standard toolbar**
   The Drawing toolbar appears below the worksheet.

   > **QuickTip**
   > To annotate charts, you can also use the Callout shapes on the AutoShapes menu in the Drawing toolbar.

6. **Click the Arrow button on the Drawing toolbar, then move the pointer over the chart**
   The pointer changes to +, and the status bar displays "Click and drag to insert an AutoShape." When you draw an arrow, the point farthest from where you start will have the arrowhead.

   > **QuickTip**
   > You can also insert text and an arrow in the data section of a worksheet by clicking the Text Box button on the Drawing toolbar, drawing a text box, typing the text, then adding the arrow.

7. **Position + under the t in the word "to" in the text box, press and hold the left mouse button, drag the line to the Boston column in the October sales series, then release the mouse button**
   An arrow appears, pointing to Boston October sales. The arrow is a selected object in the chart; you can resize, format, or delete it just like any other object. Compare your finished chart to Figure D-17.

8. **Click to close the Drawing toolbar**

9. **Click the Save button on the Standard toolbar**

EXCEL D-14 **WORKING WITH CHARTS**

FIGURE D-16: Repositioning text annotation

FIGURE D-17: Completed chart with text annotation and arrow

Clues to Use

Exploding a pie slice

Just as an arrow can call attention to a data series, you can emphasize a pie slice by exploding, or pulling it away from, the pie chart. Once the pie chart is selected, click the pie to select it, click the desired slice to select only that slice, then drag the slice away from the pie, as shown in Figure D-18. After you change the chart type, you may need to adjust arrows within the chart.

FIGURE D-18: Exploded pie slice

WORKING WITH CHARTS EXCEL D-15

Previewing and Printing a Chart

Excel 2002 — Unit D

After you complete a chart, you will often need to print it. Like previewing a worksheet, previewing a chart lets you see what your chart looks like before you print it. You can print a chart by itself or as part of the worksheet. ▶ Jim wants a printed version of the chart for the annual meeting. He wants you to print the worksheet and the chart together, so that the shareholders can see the actual sales numbers for the eastern division stores.

Steps

1. Press **[Esc]** to deselect the arrow and the chart, enter your name in cell **A35**, then press **[Ctrl][Home]**

2. Click the **Print Preview button** on the Standard toolbar
   The Print Preview window opens. You decide the chart and data would make better use of the page if they were printed in **landscape** orientation—that is, with the text running the long way on the page. You will use Page Setup to change the page orientation.

   QuickTip: The preview will show in color if you have a color printer selected.

3. Click **Setup** on the Print Preview toolbar to open the Page Setup dialog box, then click the **Page tab**, if necessary

4. Click the **Landscape option button** in the Orientation section, as shown in Figure D-19, then click **OK**
   Because each page has a default left margin of 0.75", the chart and data will print too far over to the left of the page. You can change this setting using the Margins tab.

5. Click **Setup** on the Print Preview toolbar, click the **Margins tab**, click the **Horizontally check box** (under Center on page), then click **OK**
   The data and chart are positioned horizontally on the page. See Figure D-20.

   QuickTip: The printer you have selected may affect the appearance of the preview screen.

6. Click **Print** to display the Print dialog box, then click **OK**
   The data and chart print, and you are returned to the worksheet. If you want, you can choose to preview (and print) only the chart.

7. Select the **chart**, then click the **Print Preview button**
   The chart appears in the Print Preview window. If you wanted to, you could print the chart by clicking the Print button on the Print Preview toolbar.

8. Click **Close** on the Print Preview toolbar

9. Click the **Save button** on the Standard toolbar, close the workbook, then exit Excel

EXCEL D-16   WORKING WITH CHARTS

FIGURE D-19: Page tab of the Page Setup dialog box

Landscape option button selected

Depending on your printer, your settings may differ

FIGURE D-20: Chart and data ready to print

Centered on page

Orientation changed to landscape

Chart and data will print on one page

Using the Page Setup dialog box for a chart

When a chart is selected, a different Page Setup dialog box opens than when neither the chart nor data is selected. The Center on Page options are not always available. To accurately position a chart on the page, you can click the Margins button on the Print Preview toolbar. Margin lines appear on the screen and show you exactly how the margins will appear on the page. The exact placement appears in the status bar when you press and hold the mouse button on the margin line. You can drag the lines to the exact settings you want.

WORKING WITH CHARTS   EXCEL D-17

Excel 2002 Practice

▶ Concepts Review

Label each element of the Excel chart shown in Figure D-21.

FIGURE D-21

Match each chart type with the statement that describes it.

7. Column
8. Area
9. Pie
10. Combination
11. Line

a. Shows how volume changes over time
b. Compares data as parts of a whole
c. Displays a column and line chart using different scales of measurement
d. Compares trends over even time intervals
e. Compares data over time—the Excel default

Select the best answer from the list of choices.

12. The object in a chart that identifies patterns used for each data series is a:
    a. Data point.
    b. Plot.
    c. Legend.
    d. Range.

▶ EXCEL D-18 WORKING WITH CHARTS

Practice

13. **What is the term for a row or column on a chart?**
    a. Range address
    b. Axis title
    c. Chart orientation
    d. Data series

14. **The orientation of a page whose dimensions are 11" wide by 8½" tall is:**
    a. Sideways.
    b. Longways.
    c. Portrait.
    d. Landscape.

15. **In a 2-D chart, the Value axis is the:**
    a. X-axis.
    b. Z-axis.
    c. D-axis.
    d. Y-axis.

16. **In a 2-D chart, the Category axis is the:**
    a. X-axis.
    b. Z-axis.
    c. D-axis.
    d. Y-axis.

17. **Which pointer is used to resize a chart object?**
    a. I
    b. ↘
    c. ✥
    d. +

▶ Skills Review

1. **Create a chart.**
   a. Start Excel, open a new workbook, then save it as **MediaLoft Vancouver Software Usage** in the drive and folder where your Project Files are stored.
   b. Enter the information from the following table in your worksheet in range A1:F6. Resize columns as necessary.

	Excel	Word	PowerPoint	Access	Publisher
Accounting	27	15	2	7	1
Marketing	13	35	35	15	35
Engineering	25	5	3	1	5
Personnel	15	25	10	10	27
Production	6	5	22	0	25

Excel 2002 | Practice

    c. Save your work.
    d. Select the range containing the data and headings.
    e. Start the Chart Wizard.
    f. In the Chart Wizard, select a clustered column chart, then verify that the series are in rows; add the chart title **Software Usage by Department**, and make the chart an object on the worksheet.
    g. After the chart appears, save your work.

2. Move and resize a chart.
    a. Make sure the chart is still selected.
    b. Move the chart beneath the data.
    c. Resize the chart so it extends to column L.
    d. Move the legend below the charted data. (*Hint*: Change the legend's position by using the Legend tab in the Chart Options dialog box.)
    e. Save your work.

3. Edit a chart.
    a. Change the value in cell B3 to **6**. Notice the change in the chart.
    b. Select the chart.
    c. Resize the chart so the bottom is at row 24.
    d. Use the Chart Type list arrow to change the chart to a 3-D Column Chart.
    e. Rotate the chart to move the data.
    f. Change the chart back to a column chart.
    g. Save your work.

4. Format a chart.
    a. Make sure the chart is still selected.
    b. Use the Chart Options dialog box to turn off the displayed gridlines.
    c. Change the font used in the Category and Value labels to Times New Roman. (*Hint*: Click the axis to select it, then proceed as you would to change an axis title.)
    d. Turn on the major gridlines for the Value axis.
    e. Change the title's font to Times New Roman.
    f. Save your work.

5. Enhance a chart.
    a. Make sure the chart is selected, then select the **Titles tab** in the Chart Options dialog box.
    b. Enter **Software** as the x-axis title.
    c. Enter **Users** as the y-axis title.
    d. Change **Production** in the legend to **Art**. (*Hint*: Change the text entry in the worksheet.)
    e. Add a drop shadow to the title.
    f. Save your work.

Practice

6. **Annotate and draw on a chart.**
   a. Make sure the chart is selected, then create the text annotation **Needs More Users**.
   b. Position the text annotation beneath the title.
   c. Below the text annotation, use the Drawing toolbar to create an arrow similar to the one in Figure D-22 that points to the area containing the Access data.
   d. Save your work.

FIGURE D-22

7. **Preview and print a chart.**
   a. In the worksheet, enter your name in cell A30.
   b. Preview the chart and data.
   c. Change the page orientation to landscape.
   d. Center the page contents horizontally and vertically on the page.
   e. Print the data and chart from the Print Preview window.
   f. Save your work.
   g. Preview only the chart, then print it.
   h. Close the workbook, then exit Excel.

▶ Independent Challenge 1

You are the operations manager for the Springfield, Oregon Theater Group. Each year the group applies to various state and federal agencies for matching funds. For this year's funding proposal, you need to create charts to document the number of productions in previous years.

a. Sketch a sample worksheet on a piece of paper describing how you will create the charts. Which type of chart is best suited for the information you need to display? What kind of chart enhancements do you want to use? Will a 3-D effect make your chart easier to understand?
b. Start Excel, open the Project File EX D-2, then save it as **Springfield Theater Group** in the drive and folder where your Project Files are stored.
c. Create a column chart for the data, accepting all Chart Wizard defaults.
d. Change at least one of the colors used in a data series.
e. Create at least two additional charts for the same data to show how different chart types display the same data. (*Hint*: Move each chart to a new location, then deselect each chart before using the Wizard to create the next one.)
f. After creating the charts, make the appropriate enhancements. Include chart titles, legends, and value and category axis titles, using the suggestions in the following table:

suggested chart enhancements	
Title	Types and Number of Plays
Legend	Year 1, Year 2, Year 3, Year 4
Value axis title	Number of Plays
Category axis title	Play Types

WORKING WITH CHARTS   EXCEL D-21

Excel 2002 | Practice

   g. Add data labels.
   h. Enter your name in a worksheet cell.
   i. Save your work. Before printing, preview the file so you know what the charts will look like. Adjust any items as necessary.
   j. Print the worksheet (charts and data).
   k. Close the workbook, then exit Excel.

▶ Independent Challenge 2

Beautiful You, a small beauty salon, has been using Excel for several months. One of your responsibilities at the Beautiful You Salon is to re-create the company's records using Excel. Another is to convince the current staff that Excel can help them make daily operating decisions more easily and efficiently. To do this, you've decided to create charts using the previous year's operating expenses, including rent, utilities, and payroll. The manager will use these charts at the next monthly meeting.

   a. Decide which data in the worksheet should be charted. Sketch two sample charts. What type of charts are best suited for the information you need to show? What kind of chart enhancements will be necessary?
   b. Start Excel, open the Project File EX D-3 from the drive and folder where your Project Files are stored, then save it as **BY Expense Charts**.
   c. Create a column chart on the worksheet, containing the expense data for all four quarters.
   d. Using the same data, create an area chart and one additional chart using any other appropriate chart type. (*Hint*: move each chart to a new location, then deselect it before using the Wizard to create the next one.)
   e. Add annotated text and arrows to the column chart that highlight any important data or trends.
   f. In one chart, change the color of a data series, then in another chart, use black-and-white patterns only. (*Hint*: use the Fill Effects button in the Format Data Series dialog box. Then display the Patterns tab. Adjust the Foreground color to black and the Background color to white, then select a pattern.
   g. Enter your name in a worksheet cell.
   h. Save your work. Before printing, preview each chart so you know what the charts will look like. Adjust any items as needed.
   i. Print the charts.
   j. Close the workbook, then exit Excel.

▶ Independent Challenge 3

You are working as an account representative at the Bright Light Ad Agency. You have been examining the expenses charged to clients of the firm. The Board of Directors wants to examine certain advertising expenses and has asked you to prepare charts that can be used in this evaluation.

   a. Start Excel, open the Project File EX D-4 from the drive and folder where your Project Files are stored, then save it as **Bright Light**.
   b. Decide what types of charts would be best suited for the data in the range A16:B24. Sketch two sample charts. What kind of chart enhancements will be necessary?
   c. Use the Chart Wizard to create at least three different types of charts that show the distribution of advertising expenses. (*Hint*: Move each chart to a new location, then deselect it before using the Wizard to create the next one.)
   d. Add annotated text and arrows highlighting important data, such as the largest expense.
   e. Change the color of at least one data series.
   f. Add chart titles and Category and Value axis titles. Format the titles with a font of your choice. Place a drop shadow around the chart title.

Practice

g. Enter your name in a worksheet cell.
h. Save your work. Before printing, preview the file so you know what the charts will look like. Adjust any items as needed. Be sure the chart is placed appropriately on the page.
i. Print the charts, close the workbook then exit Excel.

e Independent Challenge 4

Your company, Film Distribution, is headquartered in Montreal, and is considering opening a new office in the U.S. They would like you to begin investigating possible locations. You can use the Web to find and compare median pay scales in specific cities to see how relocating will affect the standard of living for those employees who move to the new office.

a. Start Excel, open a new workbook, then save it as **New Location Analysis** in the drive and folder where your Project Files are located.
b. Connect to the Internet, use your browser to go to homeadvisor.msn.com/pickaplace/comparecities.asp. (If this address is no longer current, go to homeadvisor.msn.com or www.homefair.com, and follow links for **Moving and Relocation**, **Compare Cost of Living**, or similar links to find the information needed for your spreadsheet. You can also use your favorite search engine to locate other sites on cost of living comparisons.)
c. Determine the median incomes for Seattle, San Francisco, Dallas, Salt Lake City, Memphis, and Boston. Record this data on a sheet named Median Income in your workbook. (*Hint*: See the table below for suggested data layout.)

Location	Income
Seattle	
San Francisco	
Dallas	
Salt Lake City	
Memphis	
Boston	

d. Format the data so it looks attractive and professional.
e. Create any type of column chart, with the data series in columns, on the same worksheet as the data. Include a descriptive title.
f. Determine how much an employee would need to earn in Seattle, San Francisco, Dallas, Memphis, and Boston to maintain the same standard of living as if the company chose to relocate to Salt Lake City and pay $75,000. Record this data on a sheet named **Standard of Living** in your workbook.
g. Format the data so it looks attractive and professional.
h. Create any type of chart you feel is appropriate on the same worksheet as the data. Include a descriptive title.
i. Do not display the legends in either chart.
j. Change the color of the data series in the Standard of Living chart to bright green.
k. Remove the major gridlines in the Median Income chart.
l. Format the Value axis in both charts so that the salary income displays a 1000 separator (comma) but no decimal places.
m. Enter your name in a cell in both worksheets.
n. Save the workbook. Preview the chart and change margins as necessary.
o. Print each worksheet, including the data and chart, making setup modifications as necessary.
p. Close the workbook, then exit Excel.

WORKING WITH CHARTS EXCEL D-23

Excel 2002 | **Practice**

▶ Visual Workshop

Modify a worksheet, using the skills you learned in this unit and using Figure D-23 for reference. Open the Project File EX D-5 from the drive and folder where your Project Files are stored, then save it as **Quarterly Advertising Budget**. Create the chart, then change the chart to reflect Figure D-23. Enter your name in cell A13, save, preview, then print your results.

FIGURE D-23

	A	B
1	Quarterly Advertising Budget	
2		
3	Type	Amount
4	Billboard	7,200.00
5	Radio spots	850.00
6	Subway	500.00
7	Yellow Pages	3,200.00
8	Pens	540.00
9	Flyers	600.00
10	Magazine	2,900.00
11	Total	15,790.00

Chart title: **Quarterly Advertising Budget**
Legend: Billboard, Radio spots, Subway, Yellow Pages, Pens, Flyers, Magazine
Annotation: "Increase exposure here" (pointing to exploded Subway slice)

▶ EXCEL D-24 **WORKING WITH CHARTS**

Excel 2002

Unit E

Working
with Formulas and Functions

Objectives

- Create a formula with several operators
- Use names in a formula
- Generate multiple totals with AutoSum
- Use dates in calculations
- Build a conditional formula with the IF function
- Use statistical functions
- Calculate payments with the PMT function
- Display and print formula contents

Without formulas, Excel would simply be an electronic grid with text and numbers. Used with formulas, Excel becomes a powerful data analysis software tool. As you learn how to analyze data using different types of formulas, including those that call for functions, you will discover more ways to use Excel. In this unit, you will gain a further understanding of Excel formulas and learn how to build several Excel functions. Top management at MediaLoft has asked Jim Fernandez to analyze various company data. To do this, Jim creates several worksheets that require the use of formulas and functions. Because management is considering raising salaries for store managers, Jim has asked you to create a report that compares the payroll deductions and net pay for store managers before and after a proposed raise.

Excel 2002

Creating a Formula with Several Operators

You can create formulas that contain a combination of cell references (for example, Z100 and B2), operators (for example, * [multiplication] and - [subtraction]), and values (for example, 99 or 1.56). Formulas can also contain functions. You have used AutoSum to insert the Sum function into a cell. You can also create a single formula that performs several calculations. If you enter a formula with more than one operator, Excel performs the calculations in a particular sequence based on algebraic rules, called the order of precedence (also called the order of operations); that is, Excel performs the operation(s) within the parentheses first, then performs the other calculations in a specific order. See Table E-1. Jim has been given the gross pay and payroll deductions for the monthly payroll and needs to complete his analysis. He has also preformatted, with the Comma style, any cells that are to contain values. He asks you to enter a formula for net pay that subtracts the payroll deductions from gross pay.

Steps

1. **Start Excel if necessary, open the Project File EX E-1 from the drive and folder where your Project Files are stored, then save it as Company Data**
   The first part of the net pay formula will go in cell B11.

2. **Click Edit on the menu bar, click Go To, type B11 in the Reference box, then click OK**
   Cell B11 is now the active cell. The Go To command is especially useful when you want to select a cell in a large worksheet.

   > **Trouble?**
   > If you make a mistake while building a formula, press [Esc] and begin again.

3. **Type =, click cell B6, type -, then click the Insert Function button on the formula bar to open the Insert Function dialog box**
   You type the equal sign (=) to tell Excel that a formula follows. B6 references the cell containing the gross pay, and the minus sign (-) indicates that the next entry, a sum, will be subtracted from cell B6. The Function Wizard begins by displaying the Insert Function dialog box, which allows you to choose from a list of available functions or search for a specific function. See Figure E-1.

4. **Type Sum in the Search for a function text box, click Go, make sure Sum is selected in the Select a function list, then click OK**
   B6:B10 appears in the Number1 text box. You want to sum the range B7:B10.

5. **With the Number1 argument selected in the Function Arguments dialog box, click the Number1 Collapse Dialog box button , select the range B7:B10 in the worksheet, click the Redisplay Dialog Box button , then click OK**
   Collapsing the dialog box allows you to select the worksheet range. The net pay for Payroll Period 1 appears in cell B11.

6. **Copy the formula in cell B11 into cells C11:F11, then return to cell A1**
   The formula in cell B11 is copied to the range C11:F11 to complete row 11. See Figure E-2.

7. **Save the workbook**

EXCEL E-2   WORKING WITH FORMULAS AND FUNCTIONS

FIGURE E-1: Insert Function dialog box

- Type a function description
- Click to start a function search
- Your function listing may be different
- Click to select the highlighted function

FIGURE E-2: Worksheet with copied formulas

TABLE E-1: Sample formulas using parentheses and several operators

formula	order of precedence	calculated result
=10-20/10-5	Divide 20 by 10; subtract the result from 10, then subtarct 5	3
=(10-20)/10-5	Subtract 20 from 10; divide that by 10; then subtract 5	-6
=(10*2)*(10+2)	Multiply 10 by 2; add 10 to 2; then multiply the results	240

Clues to Use

Using Paste Special to paste formulas and values and to perform calculations

You can use the Paste Special command to quickly enter formulas and values or even to perform quick calculations. Click the cell(s) containing the formula or value you want to copy, click the Copy button on the Standard toolbar, then right-click the cell where you want the result to appear. In the pop-up menu, choose Paste Special, choose the feature you want to paste, then click OK.

WORKING WITH FORMULAS AND FUNCTIONS EXCEL E-3

Excel 2002

Using Names in a Formula

Excel 2002 — Unit E

To reduce errors and make your worksheet easier to follow, you can assign names to cells and ranges. You can also use names in formulas to make formulas easier to build. For example, the formula Revenue-Cost is much easier to understand than the formula A2-D3. When used in formulas, names become absolute cell references by default. Names can use uppercase or lowercase letters as well as digits. After you name a cell or range, you can use the name on any sheet in the workbook. If you move a named cell or range, its name moves with it. Jim wants to include a formula that calculates the percentage of monthly gross pay the managers would actually take home (their net pay) if they received a 7% raise. He asks you to name the cells you'll use in the calculation.

Steps

1. **Click cell F6, click the name box on the formula bar to select the active cell reference, type Gross_with_Raise, then press [Enter]**

   The name assigned to cell F6, Gross_with_Raise, appears in the name box. Note that you must type underscores instead of spaces between words. Cell F6 is now named Gross_with_Raise to refer to the monthly gross pay amount that includes the 7% raise. The name box displays as much of the name as fits (Gross_with_...). The net pay cell needs a name.

   QuickTip: You can also assign names to ranges of cells. Select the range, click the name box, then type in the range name. You can also name a range by pointing to Name on the Insert menu then choosing Define to provide the name.

2. **Click cell F11, click the name box, type Net_with_Raise, then press [Enter]**

   The new formula will use names instead of cell references.

3. **Click cell F13, type =Net_with_Raise/Gross_with_Raise, then click the Enter button on the formula bar (make sure you begin the formula with an equal sign)**

   Notice that as you finish typing each name, the name changes color to match the outline around the cell reference. The formula bar now shows the new formula, and the result, 0.735, appears in the cell. You can also insert names in a formula by clicking Insert on the menu bar, pointing to Name, then clicking Paste. If you want to replace existing formula references with the corresponding names you have added, click Insert on the menu bar, point to Name, click Apply, click the name or names, then click OK. Cell F13 needs to be formatted in Percent style.

   QuickTip: You can use the Label Ranges dialog box (Insert menu, Name submenu, Label command) to designate existing column or row headings as labels. Then instead of using cell references for the column or row in formulas, you can use the labels. (If this feature is not turned on, go to Tools/Options/Calculation tab/Accept labels in formulas.)

4. **Select cell F13 if necessary, click Format on the menu bar, click Style, click the Style name list arrow, click Percent, then click OK**

   The result shown in cell F13, 74%, is rounded to the nearest whole percent, as shown in Figure E-3. A **style** is a combination of formatting characteristics, such as bold, italic, and underlined. You can use the Style dialog box instead of the Formatting toolbar to apply styles. You can also use it to remove styles: select the cell that has a style and select Normal in the Style name list. To define your own style (such as bold, italic, and 14 point), select a cell, format it using the Formatting toolbar, open the Style dialog box and type a name for your style, then click Add. Later, you can apply all those formatting characteristics by applying your new style from the dialog box.

5. **Add your name to cell A20, save the workbook, then preview and print the worksheet**

   QuickTip: To delete a cell or range name, click Insert on the menu bar, point to Name, then click Define. Select the name, click Delete, then click OK.

EXCEL E-4 WORKING WITH FORMULAS AND FUNCTIONS

FIGURE E-3: Worksheet formula that includes cell names

Name box → F13, =Net_with_Raise/Gross_with_Raise
Formula with cell names

	A	B	C	D	E	F
1	MediaLoft					
2	Payroll Deductions for Store Managers					
3						
4						
5		Payroll Period 1	Payroll Period 2	Monthly Total	Proposed Monthly Raise	Monthly Total (with raise)
6	Gross Pay	2,025.00	2,025.00	4,050.00	283.50	4,333.50
7	Federal income tax	283.50	283.50	567.00	39.69	606.69
8	Social Security	151.88	151.88	303.75	21.26	325.01
9	CA Disability	20.25	20.25	40.50	2.84	43.34
10	State income tax	81.00	81.00	162.00	11.34	173.34
11	Net Pay	1,488.38	1,488.38	2,976.75	208.37	3,185.12
12						
13	Proposed raise:	7%		Percent mgrs take home:		74%
14						

Cell named Gross_with_Raise — *Result of calculation* — *Cell named Net_with_Raise*

Clues to Use

Producing a list of names

You might want to verify the names you have in a workbook and the cells they reference. To paste a list of names in a workbook, select a blank cell that has several blank cells beside and beneath it. Click Insert on the menu bar, point to Name, then click Paste. In the Paste Name dialog box, click Paste List. Excel produces a list of names that includes the sheet name and the cell or range the name identifies. See Figure E-4.

FIGURE E-4: Worksheet with pasted list of names

	A	B	C	D	E	F
1	MediaLoft				Gross_with_Raise	=Payroll!$F$6
2	Payroll Deductions for Store Managers				Net_with_Raise	=Payroll!$F$11
3						

Pasted list of names in workbook — *Sheet location*

WORKING WITH FORMULAS AND FUNCTIONS EXCEL E-5

Excel 2002 Unit E

Generating Multiple Totals with AutoSum

In most cases, the result of a function is a value derived from a single calculation. You have used AutoSum to produce a total of a single range of numbers; you can also use it to total multiple ranges. If you include blank cells to the right or at the bottom of a selected range, AutoSum will generate several totals and enter the results in the blank cells. You can have Excel generate grand totals of worksheet subtotals by selecting a range of cells and using the AutoSum function. Maria Abbott, MediaLoft's general sales manager, has given Jim a worksheet summarizing store sales. He asks you to complete the worksheet totals.

Steps

Trouble?
If you select the wrong combination of cells, click on a single cell and begin again.

1. **Make the Sales sheet active, select range B5:E9, press and hold [Ctrl], then select range B11:E15**
   To select nonadjacent cells, you must press and hold [Ctrl] while selecting the additional cells. Compare your selections with Figure E-6. The totals will appear in the last line of each selection.

2. **Click the AutoSum button Σ on the Standard toolbar**
   When the selected range you want to sum (B5:E9 and B11:E15, in this example) includes a blank cell with data values above it, AutoSum enters the total in the blank cell.

3. **Select the range B5:F17, then click Σ**
   Whenever the selected range you want to sum includes a blank cell in the bottom row or right column, AutoSum enters the total in the blank cell. In this case, Excel ignores the data values and totals only the sums. Although Excel generates totals when you click the AutoSum button, it is a good idea to check the results.

4. **Click cell B17**
   The formula bar reads =SUM(B15,B9). See Figure E-7. When generating grand totals, Excel references the cells contained in SUM functions with a comma separator between cell references. Excel uses commas to separate multiple arguments in all functions, not just in SUM.

5. **Enter your name into cell A20, save the workbook, then preview and print the worksheet**

Clues to Use

Quick calculations with AutoCalculate

To view a total quickly without entering a formula, just select the range you want to sum, and the answer appears in the status bar next to SUM=. You also can perform other quick calculations, such as averaging or finding the minimum value in a selection. To do this, right-click the AutoCalculate area in the status bar and select from the list of options. The option you select remains in effect and in the status bar until you make another selection. See Figure E-5.

FIGURE E-5: Using AutoCalculate

Sum of current selection — AutoCalculate area — List of AutoCalculate options

---

EXCEL E-6   WORKING WITH FORMULAS AND FUNCTIONS

FIGURE E-6: Selecting nonadjacent ranges using [Ctrl]

	A	B	C	D	E
1	MediaLoft				
2	2002 Sales Summary				
3					
4	**MediaLoft East**	Qtr 1	Qtr 2	Qtr 3	Qtr 4
5	Boston	$ 158,000	$ 168,000	$ 162,000	$ 184,000
6	Chicago	184,000	252,000	255,000	260,000
7	Kansas City	159,000	209,000	230,000	245,000
8	New York	190,000	235,000	243,000	251,000
9	Total				
10	**MediaLoft West**				
11	Houston	$ 82,000	$ 119,000	$ 153,000	$ 192,000
12	San Diego	68,000	99,000	157,000	189,000
13	San Francisco	112,000	153,000	192,000	228,000
14	Seattle	96,000	135,000	189,000	202,000
15	Total				
16					
17	Grand Total				
18					

Cell B11: 82000

FIGURE E-7: Completed worksheet

B17: =SUM(B15,B9)

	A	B	C	D	E	F
1	MediaLoft					
2	2002 Sales Summary					
3						
4	**MediaLoft East**	Qtr 1	Qtr 2	Qtr 3	Qtr 4	Total
5	Boston	$ 158,000	$ 168,000	$ 162,000	$ 184,000	$ 672,000
6	Chicago	184,000	252,000	255,000	260,000	951,000
7	Kansas City	159,000	209,000	230,000	245,000	843,000
8	New York	190,000	235,000	243,000	251,000	919,000
9	Total	$ 691,000	$ 864,000	$ 890,000	$ 940,000	$ 3,385,000
10	**MediaLoft West**					
11	Houston	$ 82,000	$ 119,000	$ 153,000	$ 192,000	$ 546,000
12	San Diego	68,000	99,000	157,000	189,000	513,000
13	San Francisco	112,000	153,000	192,000	228,000	685,000
14	Seattle	96,000	135,000	189,000	202,000	622,000
15	Total	$ 358,000	$ 506,000	$ 691,000	$ 811,000	$ 2,366,000
16						
17	Grand Total	$ 1,049,000	$ 1,370,000	$ 1,581,000	$ 1,751,000	$ 5,751,000
18						

Comma separates multiple arguments

WORKING WITH FORMULAS AND FUNCTIONS

Using Dates in Calculations

Excel 2002

If you enter dates in a worksheet in a format that Excel recognizes as a date, you can sort them and perform date calculations. When you enter an Excel date format, Excel converts it to a serial number so it can be used in calculations. A date's serial number is the number of days it is from January 1, 1900. Excel assigns the serial number of "1" to January 1, 1900 and counts up from there; the serial number of January 1, 2003, for example, is 37,622. Jim's next task is to calculate the due date and age of each invoice on the worksheet. He reminds you to enter the worksheet dates in a format that Excel recognizes, so he can use date calculations.

Steps

1. **Make the Invoice sheet active, click cell C4, click the Insert Function button on the formula bar, type Date in the Search for a function text box, click Go, click Date in the Select a function list, then click OK**
   The calculations will be based on a current date of 4/1/03, the date that Jim is revising his worksheet.

   Trouble?
   If the year appears with four digits instead of two, your system administrator may have set a four-digit year display. You can continue with the lesson.

2. **Enter 2003 in the Year text box, enter 4 in the month text box, enter 1 in the Day text box, then click OK**
   The date appears in cell C4 as 4/1/03. The Date function uses the format DATE(year, month, day). You want to enter a formula that calculates the invoice due date, which is 30 days from the invoice date. The formula adds 30 days to the invoice date.

3. **Click cell E7, type =, click cell B7, type +30, then click the Enter button on the formula bar**
   Excel calculates the result by converting the 3/1/03 invoice date to a serial date number, adding 30 to it, then automatically formatting the result as the date 3/31/03, as shown in Figure E-8. You can use the same formula to calculate the due dates of the other invoices.

   QuickTip
   You can also perform time calculations in Excel. For example, you can enter an employee's starting and ending time, then calculate how long he or she worked. You must enter time in an Excel time format.

4. **Drag the fill handle to copy the formula in cell E7 into cells E8:E13**
   Relative cell referencing adjusts the copied formula to contain the appropriate cell references. Now you are ready to enter the formula that calculates the age of each invoice. You do this by subtracting the invoice date from the current date. Because each invoice age formula must refer to the current date, you must make cell C4, the current date cell, an absolute reference in the formula.

5. **Click cell F7, type =, click cell C4, press [F4] to add the absolute reference symbols ($), type -, click B7, then click**
   The formula bar displays the formula $C$4-B7. The numerical result, 31, appears in cell F7 because there are 31 days between 3/1/03 and 4/1/03. You can use the same formula to calculate the age of the remaining invoices.

   QuickTip
   You can also insert the current date into a worksheet by using the TODAY() function. The NOW() function inserts the current date and time into a cell.

6. **Drag the fill handle to copy the formula in F7 to the range F8:F13, then return to cell A1**
   The age of each invoice appears in column F, as shown in Figure E-9.

7. **Save the workbook**

EXCEL E-8   WORKING WITH FORMULAS AND FUNCTIONS

FIGURE E-8: Worksheet with formula for invoice due date

Formula is invoice date +30

Formula result automatically calculated as date

FIGURE E-9: Worksheet with copied formulas

Age of each invoice

Clues to Use

Custom number and date formats

When you use numbers and dates in worksheets or calculations, you can use built-in Excel formats or create your own. For example, 9/1/03 uses the Excel format m/d/yy, but you could change it to the format d-mmm, or 1-Sep. The value $3,789 uses the number format $#,### where # represents positive numbers. To apply number formats, click Format on the menu bar, click Cells, then click the Number tab. In the category list, click a category, then specify the exact format in the list or scroll box to the right. To create a custom format, click Custom in the category list, then click a format that resembles the one you want. In the Type box, edit the symbols until they represent the format you want, then click OK. See Figure E-10.

FIGURE E-10: Custom formats on the Number tab in the Format Cells dialog box

Custom formats category

Edit these symbols to customize this format

Custom formats

WORKING WITH FORMULAS AND FUNCTIONS

Excel 2002
Building a Conditional Formula with the IF Function

You can build a conditional formula using an IF function. A **conditional formula** is one that makes calculations based on stated conditions. For example, you can build a formula to calculate bonuses based on a person's performance rating. If a person is rated a 5 (the stated condition) on a scale of 1 to 5, with 5 being the highest rating, he or she receives 10% of his or her salary as a bonus; otherwise, there is no bonus. A condition that can be answered with a true or false response is called a **logical test**. The IF function has three parts, separated by commas: a condition or logical test, an action to take if the logical test or condition is true, then an action to take if the logical test or condition is false. Another way of expressing this is: IF(test_cond,do_this,else_this). Translated into an Excel IF function, the formula to calculate bonuses would look something like this: IF(Rating=5,Salary*0.10,0). The translation would be: If the rating equals 5, multiply the salary by 0.10 (the decimal equivalent of 10%), then place the result in the selected cell; if the rating does not equal 5, place a 0 in the cell. When entering the logical test portion of an IF statement, you typically use some combination of the comparison operators listed in Table E-2. You are almost finished with the invoice worksheet. To complete it, you need to use an IF function that calculates the number of days each invoice is overdue.

Steps

1. **Click cell G7, click the Insert Function button on the formula bar, enter Conditional in the Search for a function text box, click Go, click IF in the Select a function list, then click OK**
   You want the function to calculate the number of days overdue as follows: If the age of the invoice is greater than 30, calculate the days overdue (Age of Invoice - 30), and place the result in cell G7; otherwise, place a 0 (zero) in the cell.

2. **Enter F7>30 in the Logical_test text box**
   The symbol (>) represents "greater than". So far, the formula reads: If Age of Invoice is greater than 30 (in other words, if the invoice is overdue). The next part of the function tells Excel the action to take if the invoice is over 30 days old.

3. **Enter F7-30 in the Value_if_true text box**
   This part of the formula is what you want Excel to do if the logical test is true (that is, if the age of the invoice is over 30). Continuing the translation of the formula, this part means: Take the Age of Invoice value and subtract 30. The last part of the formula tells Excel the action to take if the logical test is false (that is, if the age of the invoice is 30 days or less).

4. **Enter 0 in the Value_if_false text box, then click OK**
   The function is complete, and the result, 1 (the number of days overdue), appears in cell G7. See Figure E-11.

5. **Copy the formula in cell G7 into cells G8:G13 and return to cell A1**
   Compare your results with Figure E-12.

6. **Save the workbook**

EXCEL E-10 WORKING WITH FORMULAS AND FUNCTIONS

FIGURE E-11: Worksheet with IF function

Logical test
Action taken if test is true
Action taken if test is false
Invoice age in F7 is 31, so result is 31-30, or 1

FIGURE E-12: Completed worksheet

TABLE E-2: Comparison operators

operator	function	operator	function
<	Less than	<=	Less than or equal to
>	Greater than	>=	Greater than or equal to
=	Equal to	<>	Not equal to

Clues to Use

Correcting circular references

A cell with a circular reference contains a formula that refers to its own cell location. If you accidentally enter a formula with a circular reference, a warning box will open alerting you to the problem. Click OK to display the Circular Reference toolbar or HELP to open a Help window explaining how to find the circular reference. In simple formulas, a circular reference is easy to spot. To correct it, edit the formula to remove any reference to the cell where the formula is located.

[Handwritten note: You can't type in a formula in a cell that refers to that same cell.]

WORKING WITH FORMULAS AND FUNCTIONS EXCEL E-11

Excel 2002
Using Statistical Functions

Excel offers several hundred worksheet functions. A small group of these functions calculates statistics such as averages, minimum values, and maximum values. See Table E-3 for a brief description of these commonly used functions. Now that you have experience using the Function Wizard, you'll type in a few of the more common functions. Jim wants to present summary information about open accounts payable. To do this, he asks you to add some statistical functions to the worksheet. You begin by using the MAX function to calculate the maximum value in a range.

Steps

1. **Click cell D19, type =MAX(, select range G7:G13, then press [Enter]**
   Excel automatically adds the closing parenthesis. The age of the oldest invoice (or maximum value in range G7:G13) is 57 days, as shown in cell D19. Jim needs to know the largest dollar amount among the outstanding invoices.

2. **In cell D20, type =MAX(, select range D7:D13, then press [Enter]**
   The largest outstanding invoice, of 1550.00, is shown in cell D20. The MIN function finds the smallest dollar amount and the age of the newest invoice.

   Trouble?
   If your results do not match those shown here, check your formulas and make sure you did not type a comma following each open parenthesis. The formula in cell D20, for example, should be =MAX(D7:D13).

3. **In cell D21, type =MIN(, select range D7:D13, then press [Enter]; in cell D22, type =MIN(, select range F7:F13, then press [Enter]**
   The smallest dollar amount owed is 55.00, as shown in cell D21, and the newest invoice is 10 days old. The COUNT function calculates the number of invoices by counting the number of entries in column A.

4. **In cell D23, click the Insert Function button *fx* on the formula bar to open the Insert Function dialog box**

   QuickTip
   If you don't see the desired function in the Function name list, scroll to display more function names.

5. **Click the Select a category list arrow, choose Statistical, then in the Select a function box, click COUNT**
   After selecting the function name, notice that the description of the COUNT function reads, "Counts the number of cells that contain numbers..." Because the invoice numbers are formatted in General rather than in the Number format, they are considered text entries, not numerical entries, so the COUNT function will not work. There is another function, COUNTA, that counts the number of cells that are not empty and therefore can be used to count the number of invoice number entries.

6. **Under Select a function, click COUNTA, then click OK**
   The Function Arguments dialog box opens and automatically references the range above the active cell as the first argument (in this case, range D19:D22, which is not the range you want to count). See Figure E-13. You need to select the correct range of invoice numbers.

   QuickTip
   Instead of using the Collaspe dialog box button, you can click the desired worksheet cell to insert a cell address.

7. **With the Value1 argument selected in the Function Arguments dialog box, click the Value1 Collapse Dialog Box button, select range A7:A13 in the worksheet, click the Redisplay Dialog Box button, click OK, then return to cell A1**
   Cell D23 confirms that there are seven invoices. Compare your worksheet with Figure E-14.

8. **Enter your name in cell A26, save the workbook, then print the worksheet**

EXCEL E-12   **WORKING WITH FORMULAS AND FUNCTIONS**

FIGURE E-13: Formula Palette showing COUNTA function

- Click to pick a different function
- Default range is incorrect
- Collapse Dialog Box button
- Result of the COUNTA function

FIGURE E-14: Worksheet with invoice statistics

- Number of invoices in A7:A13

TABLE E-3: Commonly used statistical functions

function	worksheet action	function	worksheet action
AVERAGE	Calculates an average value	**MAX**	Finds the largest value
COUNT	Counts the number of values	**MIN**	Finds the smallest value
COUNTA	Counts the number of nonblank entries	**MEDIAN**	Finds the middle value

WORKING WITH FORMULAS AND FUNCTIONS EXCEL E-13

Calculating Payments with the PMT Function

Excel 2002 — Unit E

PMT is a financial function that calculates the periodic payment amount for money borrowed. For example, if you want to borrow money to buy a car, the PMT function can calculate your monthly payment on the loan. Let's say you want to borrow $15,000 at 8.5% interest and pay the loan off in five years. The Excel PMT function can tell you that your monthly payment will be $311.38. The parts of the PMT function are: PMT(rate, nper, pv, fv, type). See Figure E-15 for an illustration of a PMT function that calculates the monthly payment in the car loan example. For several months, MediaLoft management has been discussing the expansion of the San Diego store. Jim has obtained quotes from three different lenders on borrowing $27,000 to begin the expansion. He obtained loan quotes from a commercial bank, a venture capitalist, and an investment banker. He wants you to summarize the information, using the Excel PMT function.

Steps

1. **Make the Loan sheet active, click cell E5, click the Insert Function button on the formula bar, enter PMT in the Search for a function text box, click Go, click PMT in the Select a function list if necessary, then click OK**

2. **Move the Function Arguments dialog box to display row 5 of the worksheet; with the cursor in the Rate text box, click cell C5 on the worksheet, type /12, then press [Tab]**

3. **With the cursor in the Nper text box, click cell D5; click the PV text box, click cell B5, then click OK**

    > **QuickTip**
    > You must be consistent about the units you use for rate and nper. If you express nper as the number of monthly payments, then you must express the interest rate as a monthly rate.

    You must divide the annual interest by 12 because you are calculating monthly, not annual, payments. The FV and Type are optional arguments. Note that the payment of ($587.05) in cell E5 appears in red, indicating that it is a negative amount. Excel displays the result of a PMT function as a negative value to reflect the negative cash flow the loan represents to the borrower. To show the monthly payment as a positive number, you place a minus sign in front of the PV cell reference in the function.

4. **Edit cell E5 so it reads =PMT(C5/12,D5,-B5), then click ✓**

    A positive value of $587.05 now appears in cell E5. See Figure E-16. You can use the same formula to generate the monthly payments for the other loans.

5. **With cell E5 selected, drag the fill handle to fill the range E6:E7**

    > **QuickTip**
    > You can cut, copy, and paste functions from one worksheet area to another or from one workbook to another.

    A monthly payment of $883.95 for the venture capitalist loan appears in cell E6. A monthly payment of $1,270.98 for the investment banker loan appears in cell E7. The loans with shorter terms have much higher payments. You will not know the entire financial picture until you calculate the total payments and total interest for each lender.

6. **Click cell F5, type =E5*D5, then press [Tab]; in cell G5, type =F5-B5, then click ✓**

7. **Copy the formulas in cells F5:G5 into the range F6:G7, then return to cell A1**

    You can experiment with different interest rates, loan amounts, or terms for any one of the lenders; the PMT function generates a new set of values automatically. Compare your results with those in Figure E-17.

8. **Enter your name in cell A13, save the workbook, then preview and print the worksheet**

EXCEL E-14 **WORKING WITH FORMULAS AND FUNCTIONS**

FIGURE E-15: Example of PMT function for car loan

$$\text{PMT}(.085/12, 60, 15000) = \$311.38$$

- Interest rate per period (rate)
- Number of payments (nper)
- Present value of loan amount (pv)
- Monthly payment calculated

FIGURE E-16: PMT function calculating monthly loan payment

- Annual interest rate ÷ 12 months
- Loan term
- Loan amount (preceded by a minus sign)
- Monthly payment calculated

FIGURE E-17: Completed worksheet

Clues to Use

Calculating future value with the FV function

You can use the FV (Future Value) function to determine the amount of money a given monthly investment will amount to, at a given interest rate after a given number of payment periods. The syntax is similar to that of the PMT function: FV(rate,nper,pmt,pv,type). For example, suppose you want to invest $1,000 every month for the next 12 months into an account that pays 12% a year, and you want to know how much you will have at the end of 12 months (that is, its future value). You would enter the function FV(.01,12,-1000), and Excel would return the value $12,682.50 as the future value of your investment. As with the PMT function, the units for the rate and nper must be consistent. If you made monthly payments on a three-year loan at 6% annual interest, you would use the rate .06/12 and 36 periods (12*3). The arguments pv and type are optional; pv is the present value, or the total amount the series of payments is worth now. If you omit it, Excel assumes the pv is 0. The "type" argument indicates when the payments are made; 0 is the end of the period, and 1 is the beginning of the period.

WORKING WITH FORMULAS AND FUNCTIONS

Displaying and Printing Formula Contents

Excel 2002

Excel usually displays the result of formula calculations in the worksheet area and displays formula contents for the active cell in the formula bar. However, you can instruct Excel to display the formulas directly in the worksheet cells in which they were entered. You can document worksheet formulas by first displaying the formulas, then printing them. These formula printouts are valuable paper-based worksheet documentation. Because formulas are often longer than their corresponding values, landscape orientation is the best choice for printing formulas. *Jim wants you to produce a formula printout to submit with the worksheet.*

Steps

1. **Click Tools on the menu bar, click Options, then click the View tab**
   The View tab of the Options dialog box appears, as shown in Figure E-18.

2. **Under Window options, click the Formulas check box to select it, then click OK**
   The columns widen and retain their original formats.

3. **Scroll horizontally to bring columns E through G into view**
   Instead of displaying formula results in the cells, Excel shows the actual formulas and automatically adjusts the column widths to accommodate them.

   > **QuickTip**
   > Move the Formula Auditing toolbar if necessary.

4. **Click the Print Preview button on the Standard toolbar**
   The status bar reads Preview: Page 1 of 2, indicating that the worksheet will print on two pages. You want to print it on one page and include the row number and column letter headings.

5. **Click Setup in the Print Preview window, then click the Page tab**

   > **QuickTip**
   > All Page Setup options—such as Landscape orientation, Fit to scaling—apply to the active worksheet and are saved with the workbook.

6. **Under Orientation, click the Landscape option button; then under Scaling, click the Fit to option button and note that the wide and tall check boxes contain the number "1".**
   Selecting Landscape instructs Excel to print the worksheet sideways on the page. The Fit to option ensures that the document is printed on a single page.

   > **QuickTip**
   > To print row and column labels on every page of a multiple-page worksheet, click the Sheet tab, and fill in the Rows to repeat at top and the Columns to repeat at left in the Print titles section.

7. **Click the Sheet tab, under Print click the Row and column headings check box to select it, click OK, then position the Zoom pointer over column A and click**
   The worksheet formulas now appear on a single page, in landscape orientation, with row (number) and column (letter) headings. See Figure E-19.

8. **Click Print in the Print Preview window, then click OK**
   After you retrieve the printout, you want to return the worksheet to displaying formula results. You can do this easily by using a key combination.

9. **Press [Ctrl][`] to redisplay formula results**
   [Ctrl][`] (grave accent mark) toggles between displaying formula results and displaying formula contents.

10. **Save the workbook, then close it and exit Excel**
    The completed figure for the payroll worksheet is displayed in Figure E-3; the completed sales worksheet is displayed in Figure E-7; and the completed invoice worksheet is shown in Figure E-14.

▶ EXCEL E-16 **WORKING WITH FORMULAS AND FUNCTIONS**

FIGURE E-18: View tab of the Options dialog box

Select this option to view formulas

FIGURE E-19: Print Preview window

Column headings

Row headings

Clues to Use

Setting margins and alignment when printing part of a worksheet

You can set custom margins to print smaller sections of a worksheet. Select the range you want to print, click File on the menu bar, click Print, under Print what click Selection, then click Preview. In the Print Preview window, click Setup, then click the Margins tab. See Figure E-20. Double-click the margin numbers and type new ones. Use the Center on page check boxes to center the range horizontally or vertically. If you plan to print the range again, save the view after you print: Click View on the menu bar, click Custom Views, click Add, then type a view name and click OK.

FIGURE E-20: Margins tab in the Page Setup dialog box

WORKING WITH FORMULAS AND FUNCTIONS   EXCEL E-17

Excel 2002 Practice

▶ Concepts Review

Label each element of the Excel screen shown in Figure E-21.

FIGURE E-21

Match each term with the statement that best describes its function.

8. Style
9. COUNTA
10. test_cond
11. COUNT
12. pv

a. Part of the IF function in which the conditions are stated
b. Function used to count the number of numerical entries
c. Part of the PMT function that represents the loan amount
d. Function used to count the number of nonblank entries
e. A combination of formatting characteristics

▶ EXCEL E-18   WORKING WITH FORMULAS AND FUNCTIONS

Practice

Select the best answer from the list of choices.

13. To generate a positive payment value when using the PMT function, you must:
    a. Enter the function arguments as positive values.
    b. Enter the function arguments as negative values.
    c. Enter the amount being borrowed as a negative value.
    d. Enter the interest rate divisor as a negative value.

14. When you enter the rate and nper arguments in a PMT function, you must:
    a. Multiply both units by 12.
    b. Be consistent in the units used.
    c. Divide both values by 12.
    d. Use monthly units instead of annual units.

15. To express conditions such as less than or equal to, you can use a(n):
    a. IF function.
    b. Comparison operator.
    c. AutoCalculate formula.
    d. PMT function.

16. Which of the following statements is false?
    a. $#,### is an Excel number format.
    b. You can create custom number and date formats in Excel.
    c. You can use only existing number and date formats in Excel.
    d. m/d/yy is an Excel date format.

▶ Skills Review

1. **Create a formula with several operators.**
    a. Start Excel, open the Project File EX E-2 from the drive and folder where your Project Files are stored, then save the workbook as **Manager Bonuses**.
    b. On the Bonuses worksheet, select cell **C15** using the Go To command.
    c. Enter the formula **C13+(C14*7)**.
    d. Use the Paste Special command to paste the values and formats in B4:B10 to G4:G10, then save your work.

2. **Use names in a formula.**
    a. Name cell C13 **Dept_Bonus**.
    b. Name cell C14 **Project_Bonus**.
    c. Select the range **C4:C10** and name it **Base_Pay**.
    d. In cell E4, enter the formula **Dept_Bonus*D4+Project_Bonus**.
    e. Copy the formula in cell E4 into the range E5:E10.
    f. Format range E4:E10 with the Comma style, using the Style dialog box.
    g. Select the range **E4:E10** and name it **Bonus_Total**.
    h. In cell F4, enter a formula that sums Base_Pay and Bonus_Total.
    i. Copy the formula in cell F4 into the range F5:F10.
    j. Format range F4:F10 with the Comma style, using the Style dialog box.
    k. Save your work.

WORKING WITH FORMULAS AND FUNCTIONS

Excel 2002 | Practice

3. **Generate multiple totals with AutoSum.**
   a. Select range **E4:F11**.
   b. Enter the totals using AutoSum.
   c. Format range E11:F11 with the Currency style, using the Style dialog box.
   d. Enter your name in cell A18, save your work, then preview and print this worksheet.

4. **Use dates in calculations.**
   a. Make the Merit Pay sheet active.
   b. In cell D6, enter the formula **B6+183**.
   c. Copy the formula in cell D6 into the range D7:D14.
   d. Use the NOW function to insert the date and time in cell A3, widening the column as necessary.
   e. In cell E18, enter the text **Next Pay Date**, and, in cell G18, use the Date function to enter the date **10/1/03**. (*Hint*: You must enter the year as 2003. You can format it as a two-digit year using the Modify button on the Style dialog box and choosing Date in the Category list on the Number tab.)
   f. Save your work.

5. **Build a conditional formula with the IF function.**
   a. In cell F6, use the Function Wizard to enter the formula **IF(C6=5,E6*0.05,0)**.
   b. Copy the formula in cell F6 into the range F7:F14.
   c. Apply the comma format with no decimal places to F6:F14.
   d. Select the range **A4:G4** and delete the cells, using the Delete command on the Edit menu. Shift the remaining cells up.
   e. Repeat the procedure to delete the cells A15:G15.
   f. Use the Cells command on the Insert menu to insert a cell between Department Statistics and Average Salary, moving the remaining cells down.
   g. Check your formulas to make sure the cell references have been updated.
   h. Save your work.

6. **Use statistical functions.**
   a. In cell C18, enter a function to calculate the average salary in the range E5:E13 with no decimal places. Use dragging to select the cells.
   b. In cell C19, enter a function to calculate the largest bonus in the range F5:F13.
   c. In cell C20, enter a function to calculate the lowest performance rating in the range C5:C13.
   d. In cell C21, enter a function to calculate the number of entries in range A5:A13.
   e. Enter your name into cell A28, then save, preview, and print the worksheet.

7. **Calculate payments with the PMT function.**
   a. Make the Loan sheet active.
   b. In cell B9, use the Function Wizard to enter the formula **PMT(B5/12,B6,-B4)**.
   c. In cell B10, enter the formula **B9*B6**.
   d. AutoFit column B, if necessary.
   e. In cell B11, enter the formula **B10-B4**.
   f. Enter your name in cell A15, then save, preview, and print the worksheet.

8. **Display and print formula contents.**
   a. Use the View tab in the Options dialog box to display formulas.
   b. Adjust the column widths as necessary.
   c. Save, preview, and print this worksheet in landscape orientation with the row and column headings.
   d. Redisplay the formula results in the worksheet.
   e. Close the workbook, then exit Excel.

▶ Independent Challenge 1

As manager of Mike's Ice Cream Parlor, you have been asked to create a worksheet that totals the monthly sales of all store products. Your monthly report should include the following:

- Sales totals for the current month for each product
- Sales totals for the last month for each product
- The percent change in sales from last month to this month

To document the report further, you decide to include a printout of the worksheet formulas.

   a. Start Excel, open the Project File EX E-3 from the drive and folder where your Project Files are stored, then save it as **Mike's Sales**.
   b. Use the TODAY function to enter today's date in cell A3. Create and apply a custom format for the date entry.
   c. Complete the headings for weeks 2 through 4. Enter totals for each week, and current month totals for each product. Calculate the percent change in sales from last month to this month. (*Hint*: The formula in words would be (Current Month-Last Month)/Last Month.)
   d. After you enter the percent change formula for regular ice cream, copy the formula down the column and format the column with the Percent style.
   e. Apply a comma format with no decimal places to all numbers and totals.
   f. Enter your name into cell A15, then save, preview, and print the worksheet on a single page. If necessary, print in landscape orientation. If you make any page setup changes, save the worksheet again.
   g. Display and print the worksheet formulas, then print the formulas on one page with row and column headings.
   h. Close the workbook without saving the changes for displaying formulas, then exit Excel.

▶ Independent Challenge 2

You are an auditor with a certified public accounting firm. Fly Away, a manufacturer of skating products, has contacted you to audit its financial records. The management at Fly Away is considering opening a branch in Great Britain and needs its records audited to prepare the business plan. The managers at Fly Away have asked you to assist them in preparing their year-end sales summary as part of this audit. Specifically, they want to add expenses and show the percent of annual expenses that each expense category represents. They also want to show what percent of annual sales each expense category represents. You should include a formula calculating the difference between sales and expenses and another formula calculating expenses divided by sales. The expense categories and their respective dollar amounts are as follows: Building Lease $46,000; Equipment $208,000; Office $25,000; Salary $355,000; Taxes $310,000. Use these expense amounts to prepare the year-end sales and expenses summary for Fly Away.

   a. Start Excel, open the Project File EX E-4 from the drive and folder where your Project Files are stored, then save the workbook as **Fly Away Sales**.
   b. Name the cell containing the formula for total annual expenses **Annual_Expenses**. Use the name Annual_Expenses in cell C12 to create a formula calculating percent of annual expenses. Copy this formula as appropriate and apply the Percent style. Make sure to include a formula that sums all the values for percent of annual expenses, which should equal 100%.

Excel 2002 | Practice

c. Enter a formula calculating the percent of annual sales each expense category represents. Use the name **Annual_Sales** in the formula and format it appropriately. Copy this formula as appropriate and apply the Percent style. Make sure to include a formula that sums all the values for percent of annual sales.

d. Enter the formula calculating Net Profit, using the names Annual_Sales and Annual_Expenses.

e. Enter the formula for Expenses as a percent of sales, using the names Annual_Sales and Annual_Expenses.

f. Format the cells using the Currency, Percent, or Comma style as appropriate. Widen the columns as necessary to display cell contents.

g. Set the top and bottom margins at 4 inches and center the worksheet horizontally so the worksheet will print on two pages. *(Hint:* Use the Margins tab on the Page Setup dialog box.)

h. Print the first row containing the company name on each page. (*Hint*: Use the Sheet tab on the Page Setup dialog box and specify row 1 to repeat at the top.)

i. Enter your name into cell A22, then save, preview, and print the worksheet. Save any page setup changes you make.

j. Close the workbook then exit Excel.

▶ Independent Challenge 3

As the owner of Custom Fit, a general contracting firm specializing in home-storage projects, you are facing yet another business challenge at your firm. Because jobs are taking longer than expected, you decide to take out a loan to purchase some new power tools. According to your estimates, you need a $7,000 loan to purchase the tools. You check three loan sources: the Small Business Administration (SBA), your local bank, and a consortium of investors. The SBA will lend you the money at 8% interest, but you have to pay it off in three years. The local bank offers you the loan at 8.75% interest over four years. The consortium offers you a 7.75% loan, but they require you to pay it back in two years. To analyze all three loan options, you decide to build a tool loan summary worksheet. Using the loan terms provided, build a worksheet summarizing your options.

a. Start Excel, open a new workbook, then save it as **Custom Fit Loan Options** in the drive and folder where your Project Files are stored.

b. Enter today's date in cell A3, using the TODAY function.

c. Enter labels and worksheet data. You need headings for the loan source, loan amount, interest rate, term or number of payments, monthly payment, total payments, and total interest. Fill in the data provided for the three loan sources.

d. Enter formulas as appropriate: a PMT formula for the monthly payment, a formula calculating the total payments based on the monthly payment and term values, and a formula for total interest based on the total payments and the loan amount.

e. Format the worksheet as desired.

f. Enter your name in cell A14, then save, preview, and print the worksheet on a single page using landscape orientation. Print the worksheet formulas showing row and column headings. Do not save the worksheet with the formula settings.

g. Close the workbook then exit Excel.

Independent Challenge 4

The MediaLoft management wants to start IRAs for its employees. The company plans to deposit $2,000 in the employees' accounts at the beginning of each year. You have been asked to research current rates at financial institutions. You will use the Web to find the information.

a. Go to the AltaVista search engine at www.altavista.com and enter "IRA rates" in the Search box. You can also use Yahoo, Excite, Infoseek or another search engine of your choice. Find IRA rates offered by three institutions for a $2,000 minimum deposit, then write down the institution name, the rate, and the minimum deposit in the table below.

b. Start Excel, open a new workbook, then save it as **IRA Rates** in the drive and folder where your Project Files are stored.

c. Enter the column headings, row headings, and research results from the table below into your IRA Rates workbook.

IRA Institution	Rate	Minimum Deposit	Number of Years	Amount Deposited (Yearly)	Future Value
			35	2000	
			35	2000	
			35	2000	
Highest Rate					
Average Rate					
Highest Future Value					

d. Use the FV function to calculate the future value of a $2,000 yearly deposit over 35 years for each institution, making sure it displays as a positive number. Assume that the payments are made at the beginning of the period, so the Type argument equals 1.

e. Use Excel functions to enter the highest rate, the average rate, and the highest future value into the workbook.

f. Enter your name in cell A15, then save, preview, and print the worksheet on a single page.

g. Display and print the formulas for the worksheet on a single page using landscape orientation. Do not save the worksheet with the formulas displayed.

h. Close the workbook then exit Excel.

Excel 2002 | Practice

▶ Visual Workshop

Create the worksheet shown in Figure E-22. (Hint: Enter the items in range C9:C11 as labels by typing an apostrophe before each formula.) Enter your name in row 15, and save the workbook as **Car Payment Calculator**. Preview, then print, the worksheet.

FIGURE E-22

	A	B	C
1	Car Loan Payment Calculator		
2			
3			
4	Loan Amount	25000	
5	Interest Rate	7.8%	
6	Term	60	months
7			
8			Formulas In Column B
9	Monthly Payment	$504.52	=PMT(B5/12,B6,-B4)
10	Total Payments	$30,271.22	=B9*B6
11	Total Interest	$5,271.22	=B10-B4

▶ EXCEL E-24   **WORKING WITH FORMULAS AND FUNCTIONS**

Excel 2002

Unit F

Managing
Workbooks and Preparing Them for the Web

Objectives

- Freeze columns and rows
- Insert and delete worksheets
- Consolidate data with 3-D references
- Hide and protect worksheet areas
- Save custom views of a worksheet
- Control page breaks and page numbering
- Create a hyperlink between Excel files
- Save an Excel file as a Web page

In this unit you will learn several Excel features to help you manage and print workbook data. You will also learn how to prepare workbooks for publication on the World Wide Web. MediaLoft's accounting department asks Jim Fernandez to design a timecard summary worksheet to track salary costs for hourly workers. He asks you to design a worksheet using some employees from the MediaLoft Houston store. When the worksheet is complete, the accounting department will add the rest of the employees and place it on the MediaLoft intranet site for review by store managers. Jim wants you to save the worksheet in HTML format for viewing on the site.

Freezing Columns and Rows

Excel 2002 — Unit F

As rows and columns fill up with data, you might need to scroll through the worksheet to add, delete, modify, and view information. Looking at information without row or column labels can be confusing. In Excel, you can temporarily freeze columns and rows, which enables you to view separate areas of your worksheets at the same time. **Panes** are the columns and rows that **freeze**, or remain in place, while you scroll through your worksheet. Freezing rows and columns is especially useful when you're dealing with large worksheets. Jim needs to verify the total hours worked, hourly pay rate, and total pay for salespeople Paul Cristifano and Virginia Young. Because the worksheet is becoming more difficult to read as its size increases, Jim wants you to freeze the column and row labels.

Steps

1. **Start Excel if necessary, open the Project File EX F-1 from the drive and folder where your Project Files are stored, then save it as Timecard Summary**

2. **Scroll through the Monday worksheet to view the data, then click cell D6**
   You move to cell D6 because Excel freezes the columns to the left and the rows above the cell pointer. You want to freeze columns A, B, and C as well as rows 1 through 5. By doing so, you will be able to see each employee's last name, first name, and timecard number on the screen when you scroll to the right, and you will also be able to read the labels in rows 1 through 5.

3. **Click Window on the menu bar, then click Freeze Panes**
   A thin line appears along the column border to the left of the active cell, and another line appears along the row above the active cell, indicating that columns A through C and rows 1 through 5 are frozen.

4. **Scroll to the right until columns A through C and L through O are visible**
   Because columns A, B, and C are frozen, they remain on the screen; columns D through K are temporarily hidden from view. Notice that the information you are looking for in row 13 (last name, total hours, hourly pay rate, and total pay for Paul Cristifano) is readily available. Paul's data appears to be correct, but you still need to verify Virginia Young's information.

5. **Scroll down until row 26 is visible**
   In addition to columns A through C, rows 1 through 5 remain on the screen. See Figure F-1. Jim jots down the information for Virginia Young. Even though a pane is frozen, you can click in the frozen area of the worksheet and edit the contents of the cells there, if necessary.

6. **Press [Ctrl][Home]**
   Because the panes are frozen, the cell pointer moves to cell D6, not A1.

7. **Click Window on the menu bar, then click Unfreeze Panes**
   The panes are unfrozen.

8. **Return to cell A1, then save the workbook**

▶ EXCEL F-2   MANAGING WORKBOOKS AND PREPARING THEM FOR THE WEB

FIGURE F-1: Scrolled worksheet with frozen rows and columns

Break in row numbers due to frozen rows 1–5

Break in column letters due to frozen columns A–C

Splitting the worksheet into multiple panes

Excel provides a way to split the worksheet area into vertical and/or horizontal panes, so that you can click inside any one pane and scroll to locate information in that pane while the other panes remain in place. See Figure F-2. To split a worksheet area into multiple panes, drag the split box (the small box at the top of the vertical scroll bar or at the right end of the horizontal scroll bar) in the direction you want the split to appear. To remove the split, move the mouse over the split until the pointer changes to a double pointed arrow, then double-click.

FIGURE F-2: Worksheet split into two horizontal panes

Upper pane

Lower pane

Horizontal split box

Vertical split box

MANAGING WORKBOOKS AND PREPARING THEM FOR THE WEB · EXCEL F-3

Inserting and Deleting Worksheets

Excel 2002 — Unit F

You can insert and delete worksheets in a workbook at any time. For example, because new workbooks open with only three sheets available (Sheet1, Sheet2, and Sheet3), you need to insert at least one more sheet if you want to have four quarterly worksheets in an annual financial budget workbook. You can do this by using commands on the menu bar or shortcut menu. Jim was in a hurry when he added the sheet tabs to the Timecard Summary workbook. He wants you to insert a sheet for Thursday and delete the sheet for Sunday because Houston workers do not work on Sundays.

Steps

1. **Click the Friday sheet tab, click Insert on the menu bar, then click Worksheet**
   Excel inserts a new sheet tab labeled Sheet1 to the left of the Friday sheet.

   > **QuickTip**
   > You can copy a selected worksheet by clicking Edit on the menu bar, then clicking Move or Copy Sheet. Choose the sheet the copy will precede, then select the Create a copy check box.

2. **Double-click the Sheet1 tab and rename it Thursday**
   Now the tabs read Monday, Tuesday, Wednesday, Thursday, Friday, and Saturday. The tab for the Weekly Summary is not visible. You still need to delete the Sunday worksheet.

3. **Right-click the Sunday sheet tab, then click Delete on the shortcut menu shown in Figure F-3**
   The shortcut menu allows you to insert, delete, rename, move, or copy sheets; select all the sheets; change tab color; and view any Visual Basic programming code in a worksheet.

4. **Move the mouse pointer over any tab scrolling button, then right-click**
   Excel opens a menu of the worksheets in the active workbook. Compare your list with Figure F-4.

   > **QuickTip**
   > You can scroll several tabs at once by pressing [Shift] while clicking one of the middle tab scrolling buttons.

5. **Return to the Monday sheet, then save the workbook**

Clues to Use

Previewing and printing multiple worksheets

To preview and print multiple worksheets, press and hold down [Ctrl] and click the tabs for the sheets you want to print, then click the Preview or Print button. In Print Preview, the multiple worksheets will appear as separate pages in the Preview window, which you can display by clicking Next and Previous. To preview and print an entire workbook, click File on the menu bar, click Print, click to select the Entire Workbook option button, then click Preview. In the Preview window, you can page through the entire workbook. (Blank worksheets will not appear as pages in Print Preview.) When you click Print, the entire workbook will print.

EXCEL F-4 MANAGING WORKBOOKS AND PREPARING THEM FOR THE WEB

FIGURE F-3: Worksheet shortcut menu

Click to delete selected sheet

FIGURE F-4: Workbook with worksheets menu

Active worksheet

Right-click any tab scrolling button to display the menu of worksheets

Menu of worksheets

Clues to Use

Specifying headers and footers

As you prepare a workbook for others to view, it is helpful to provide as much data as possible about the worksheets such as the number of pages, who created it, and when. You can do this easily in a **header** or **footer**, information that prints at the top or bottom of each printed page. Headers and footers are visible on the screen only in Print Preview. To add a header, for example, click View on the menu bar, click Header and Footer, then click Custom Header. You will see a dialog box similar to that in Figure F-5. Both the header and the footer are divided into three sections, and you can enter information in any or all of them. You can type information, such as your name, and click the icons to enter the page number, total pages, date, time, file path, filename, or sheet name. You can insert a picture by clicking the Insert Picture icon, and you can format the picture by clicking the Format picture icon and selecting formatting options. When you click an icon, Excel inserts a symbol in the footer section containing an ampersand (&) and the element name in brackets. When you are finished, click OK, click the Print Preview button on the Header/Footer tab to see your header and footer, then click Close.

FIGURE F-5: Header dialog box

Click these icons to insert information into header sections

Symbol for date

Symbol for page number

MANAGING WORKBOOKS AND PREPARING THEM FOR THE WEB — EXCEL F-5

Consolidating Data with 3-D References

Excel 2002 — Unit F

When you want to summarize similar data that exists in different sheets or workbooks, you can combine and display it in one sheet. For example, you might have departmental sales figures on four different store sheets that you want to consolidate on one summary sheet showing total departmental sales for all stores. The best way to consolidate data is to use cell references to the various sheets on a consolidation, or summary, sheet. Because they reference other sheets that are usually behind the summary sheet, such references effectively create another dimension in the workbook and are called **3-D references**. You can reference data in other sheets and in other workbooks. Referencing cells is a better method than retyping calculated results because the data values on which calculated totals depend might change. If you reference the values instead, any changes to the original values are automatically reflected in the consolidation sheet. Although Jim does not have timecard data for the remaining days of the week, he wants you to test the Weekly Summary sheet that will consolidate the timesheet data. He asks you to do this by creating a reference from the total pay data in the Monday sheet to the Weekly Summary sheet. You will freeze panes to improve the view of the worksheet before initiating the reference between them.

Steps

1. **On the Monday sheet, click cell D6, click Window on the menu bar, click Freeze Panes, then scroll horizontally to bring columns L through O into view**

2. **Right-click a tab scrolling button, then click Weekly Summary**
   Because the Weekly Summary sheet (which is the consolidation sheet) will contain the reference, the cell pointer must reside there when you initiate the reference. A **simple reference** displays the contents of another cell.

   > **QuickTip**
   > If you have difficulty referencing cells between sheets, press [Esc] and begin again.

3. **While in the Weekly Summary sheet, click cell C6, type =, activate the Monday sheet, click cell O6, then click the Enter button ✓ on the formula bar**
   The Weekly Summary sheet becomes active, and formula bar reads =Monday!O6. See Figure F-6. *Monday* references the Monday sheet. The ! (exclamation point) is an **external reference indicator,** meaning that the cell referenced is outside the active sheet; O6 is the actual cell reference in the external sheet. The result, $34.20, appears in cell C6 of the Weekly Summary sheet, showing the reference to the value in cell O6 of the Monday sheet.

4. **In the Weekly Summary sheet, copy cell C6 into cells C7:C26**
   Excel copies the contents of cell C6 with its relative reference to the Monday sheet data. You can test a reference by changing one cell value on which the reference is based and seeing if the reference changes.

5. **Activate the Monday sheet, edit cell L6 to read 6:30 PM, then activate the Weekly Summary sheet**
   Cell C6 now shows $42.75. Changing Beryl Arenson's "time out" from 5:30 to 6:30 increased her pay from $34.20 to $42.75. This makes sense because Beryl's hours went from four to five, and her hourly salary is $8.55. The reference to Monday's total pay was automatically updated in the Weekly Summary sheet. See Figure F-7.

6. **Enter your name in the left section of the footer, preview the worksheet, then print it**

7. **Activate the Monday sheet, unfreeze the panes, then save the workbook**

EXCEL F-6 MANAGING WORKBOOKS AND PREPARING THEM FOR THE WEB

FIGURE F-6: Worksheet showing referenced cell

Sheet referenced — *Cell referenced*
External reference indicator
Referenced value

FIGURE F-7: Weekly Summary worksheet with updated reference

Updated value — *Copied values also reference the Monday sheet*

Linking data between workbooks

Just as you can reference data between cells in a worksheet and between sheets, you can reference data between workbooks dynamically so that changes made in referenced cells in one workbook are reflected in the consolidation sheet in the other workbook. This dynamic referencing is called **linking**. To link a single cell between workbooks, open both workbooks, select the cell to receive the linked data, type = (the equal sign), select the cell in the other workbook containing the data to be linked, then press [Enter]. Excel automatically inserts the name of the referenced workbook in the cell reference. For example if the linked data is contained in cell C7 of worksheet New in the Products workbook, the cell entry will read ='[Product.xls]New'!$C$7. To perform calculations, enter formulas on the consolidation sheet using cells in the supporting sheets. If you are linking more than one cell, you can copy the linked data to the Clipboard, select the upper-left cell in the workbook to receive the link, click Edit on the menu bar, click Paste Special, then click Paste Link.

MANAGING WORKBOOKS AND PREPARING THEM FOR THE WEB

Hiding and Protecting Worksheet Areas

Excel 2002 — Unit F

Worksheets can contain sensitive information that you don't want others to view or alter. To protect such information, Excel gives you two options. You can **hide** the formulas in selected cells (or rows, columns, or entire sheets), and you can **lock** selected cells, in which case other people will be able to view the data (values, numbers, labels, formulas, etc.) in those cells but not to change it. See Table F-1 for a list of options you can use to protect a worksheet. You set the lock and hide options in the Format Cells dialog box. Excel locks all cells by default but this protection is not in effect until you activate the Excel protection feature via the Tools menu. A common worksheet protection strategy is to unlock cells in which data will be changed, sometimes referred to as the **data entry area**, and to lock cells in which the data should not be changed. Then, when you protect the worksheet, the unlocked areas can still be changed. Because Jim will assign someone to enter the sensitive timecard information into the worksheet, he wants you to hide and lock selected areas of the worksheet.

Steps

1. **On the Monday sheet, select the range I6:L27, click Format on the menu bar, click Cells, then click the Protection tab**
   You include row 27, even though it does not contain data, in the event that new data is added to the row later. Notice that the Locked box in the Protection tab is already checked, as shown in Figure F-8. The Locked check box is selected by default, meaning that all the cells in a new workbook start out locked. (Note, however, that cell locking is not applied unless the protection feature is also activated. The protection feature is inactive by default.)

2. **Click the Locked check box to deselect it, then click OK**
   Excel stores time as a fraction of a 24-hour day. In the formula for total pay, hours must be multiplied by 24. This concept might be confusing to the data entry person, so you hide the formulas.

3. **Select range O6:O26, click Format on the menu bar, click Cells, click the Protection tab, click the Hidden check box to select it, then click OK**
   The data remains the same (unhidden and unlocked) until you set the protection in the next step.

4. **Click Tools on the menu bar, point to Protection, then click Protect Sheet**
   The Protect Sheet dialog box opens. The default options allow you to protect the worksheet while allowing users to select locked or unlocked cells only. You choose not to use a password.

5. **Click OK**
   You are ready to test the new worksheet protection.

6. **Click cell O6**
   The formula bar is empty because of the hidden formula setting.

7. **In cell O6, type T to confirm that locked cells cannot be changed, then click OK**
   When you attempt to change a locked cell, a message box reminds you of the protected cell's read-only status. See Figure F-9.

8. **Click cell I6, type 9, and notice that Excel allows you to begin the entry, press [Esc] to cancel the entry, then save the workbook**
   Because you unlocked the cells in columns I through L before you protected the worksheet, you can make changes to these cells. Jim is satisfied that the Time In and Time Out data can be changed as necessary.

> **QuickTip**
> To turn off worksheet protection, click Tools on the menu bar, point to Protection, then click Unprotect Sheet. If prompted for a password, type the password, then click OK.

FIGURE F-8: Protection tab in Format Cells dialog box

Click to remove checkmark

FIGURE F-9: Reminder of protected cell's read-only status

TABLE F-1: Options for hiding and protecting worksheet elements

task	menu commands
Hide/Unhide a column	Format, Column, Hide or Unhide
Hide/Unhide a formula	Format, Cells, Protection tab, select/deselect Hidden check box
Hide/Unhide a row	Format, Row, Hide or Unhide
Hide/Unhide a sheet	Format, Sheet, Hide or Unhide
Protect workbook	Tools, Protection, Protect Workbook, assign optional password
Protect worksheet	Tools, Protection, Protect Sheet, assign optional password
Unlock/Relock cells	Format, Cells, Protection tab, deselect/select Locked check box

Note: Some of the hide and protect options do not take effect until protection is enabled.

CLUES TO USE

Changing workbook properties

You can also password-protect an entire workbook from being opened or modified by changing its file properties. Click File on the menu bar, click Save As, click Tools, then click General Options. Specify the password(s) for opening or modifying the workbook. To remove a workbook password, you can double-click the asterisks in the Password to open or Password to modify text boxes and press [Delete]. You can also use this dialog text box to offer users an option to open the workbook in read-only format so that users can open but not change it. Another way to make an entire workbook read-only is to right-click Start on the Taskbar, then click Explore (or Explore All Users). Locate and right-click the filename, click Properties, click the General tab, then, in the Attributes section, select the Read-only check box.

MANAGING WORKBOOKS AND PREPARING THEM FOR THE WEB

Saving Custom Views of a Worksheet

A **view** is a set of display and/or print settings that you can name and save, then access at a later time. By using the Excel Custom Views feature, you can create several different views of a worksheet without having to create separate sheets. For example, if you often switch between portrait and landscape orientations when printing different parts of a worksheet, you can create two views with the appropriate print settings for each view. You set the display and/or print settings first, then name the view. Because Jim will generate several reports from his data, he asks you to save the current print and display settings as a custom view. To better view the data, he wants you to use the Zoom box to display the entire worksheet on one screen.

Steps

1. **With the Monday sheet active, select range A1:O28, click the Zoom list arrow on the Standard toolbar, click Selection, then press [Ctrl][Home] to return to cell A1**
   Excel adjusts the display magnification so that the data selected fits on one screen. See Figure F-10. After selecting the **Zoom box**, you can also pick a magnification percentage from the list or type the desired percentage.

2. **Click View on the menu bar, then click Custom Views**
   The Custom Views dialog box opens. Any previously defined views for the active worksheet appear in the Views box. In this case, Jim had created a custom view named Generic containing default print and display settings. See Figure F-11.

   > **QuickTip**
   > To delete views from the active worksheet, select the view in the Views list box, then click Delete.

3. **Click Add**
   The Add View dialog box opens, as shown in Figure F-12. Here, you enter a name for the view and decide whether to include print settings and hidden rows, columns, and filter settings. You want to include the selected options.

4. **In the Name box, type Complete Daily Worksheet, then click OK**
   After creating a custom view of the worksheet, you return to the worksheet area. You are ready to test the two custom views. In case the views require a change to the worksheet, it's a good idea to turn off worksheet protection.

5. **Click Tools on the menu bar, point to Protection, then click Unprotect Sheet**

6. **Click View on the menu bar, then click Custom Views**
   The Custom Views dialog box opens, listing both the Complete Daily Worksheet and Generic views.

   > **Trouble?**
   > If you receive the message "Some view settings could not be applied," repeat Step 5 to ensure that worksheet protection is turned off.

7. **Click Generic in the Views list box, click Show, preview the worksheet, then close the Preview window**
   The Generic custom view returns the worksheet to the Excel default print and display settings. Now you are ready to test the new custom view.

8. **Click View on the menu bar, click Custom Views, click Complete Daily Worksheet in the Views list box, then click Show**
   The entire worksheet fits on the screen.

9. **Return to the Generic view, then save your work**

FIGURE F-10: Selected data fitted to one screen

Zoom box showing current magnification

FIGURE F-11: Custom Views dialog box

Existing custom views appear here

Click to create new view

FIGURE F-12: Add View dialog box

Type name of view here

Creating a workspace

If you work with several workbooks at a time, you can group them so you can open them in one step by creating a **workspace**, a file with an .xlw extension. Then, instead of opening each workbook individually, you can open the workspace. To create a workspace, open the workbooks you wish to group and locate and size them as you would like them to appear. Click File on the menu bar, click Save Workspace, type a name for the workspace file, then click Save. Remember, however, that the workspace file does not contain the workbooks themselves, so you still have to save any changes you make to the original workbook files. To open the workbooks in the workspace automatically when you start Excel, place the workspace file in your XLStart folder (C:\Program Files\Microsoft Office\Office\XLStart).

MANAGING WORKBOOKS AND PREPARING THEM FOR THE WEB

Controlling Page Breaks and Page Numbering

Excel 2002 — Unit F

The vertical and horizontal dashed lines in worksheets indicate page breaks. Excel automatically inserts a page break when your worksheet data doesn't fit on one page. These page breaks are **dynamic**, which means they adjust automatically when you insert or delete rows and columns and when you change column widths or row heights. Everything to the left of the first vertical dashed line and above the first horizontal dashed line is printed on the first page. You can override the automatic breaks by choosing the Page Break command on the Insert menu. Table F-2 describes the different types of page breaks you can use. Jim wants another report displaying no more than half the hourly workers on each page. To accomplish this, he asks you to insert a manual page break.

Steps

1. **Click cell A16, click Insert on the menu bar, then click Page Break**
   A dashed line appears between rows 15 and 16, indicating a horizontal page break. See Figure F-13. After you set page breaks, it's a good idea to preview each page.

2. **Preview the worksheet, then click Zoom**
   Notice that the status bar reads "Page 1 of 4" and that the data for the employees up through Charles Gallagher appears on the first page. Jim decides to place the date in the footer.

3. **While in the Print Preview window, click Setup, click the Header/Footer tab, click Custom Footer, click the Right section box, click the Date button**

4. **Click the Left section box, type your name, then click OK**
   Your name, the page number, and the date appear in the Footer preview area.

5. **In the Page Setup dialog box, click OK, and while still in Print Preview, check to make sure that all the pages show your name, the page numbers, and the date, click Close, save the workbook, then print the worksheet**

6. **Click View on the menu bar, click Custom Views, click Add, type Half and Half, then click OK**
   Your new custom view has the page breaks and all current print settings.

7. **Make sure cell A16 is selected, then click Insert on the menu bar and click Remove Page Break**
   Excel removes the manual page break above or to the left of the active cell.

8. **Save the workbook**

TABLE F-2: Page break options

type of page break	where to position cell pointer
Both horizontal and vertical page breaks	Select the cell below and to the right of the gridline where you want the breaks to occur
Only a horizontal page break	Select the cell in column A that is directly below the gridline where you want the page to break
Only a vertical page break	Select a cell in row 1 that is to the right of the gridline where you want the page to break

▶ EXCEL F-12 MANAGING WORKBOOKS AND PREPARING THEM FOR THE WEB

FIGURE F-13: Worksheet with horizontal page break

Dashed line indicates horizontal break after row 15

FIGURE F-14: Page Break Preview window

Drag page break lines to change page breaks

Using Page Break Preview

You can view and change page breaks manually by clicking View on the menu bar, then clicking Page Break Preview, or clicking Page Break Preview in the Print Preview window. (If you see a Welcome to Page Break Preview dialog box, click OK to close it.) Drag the page break lines to the desired location. See Figure F-14. To exit Page Break Preview, click View on the menu bar, then click Normal.

MANAGING WORKBOOKS AND PREPARING THEM FOR THE WEB   EXCEL F-13

Creating a Hyperlink Between Excel Files

As you manage the content and appearance of your workbooks, you may want the workbook user to view information in another workbook. It might be nonessential information or data that is too detailed to place in the workbook itself. In these cases, you can create a **hyperlink**, an object (a filename, a word, a phrase, or a graphic) in a worksheet that, when you click it, will display, or "jump to," another worksheet, called the **target**. The target can also be a document or a site on the World Wide Web. Hyperlinks are navigational tools between worksheets and are not used to exchange information. For example, in a worksheet that lists customer invoices, at each customer's name, you might create a hyperlink to an Excel file containing payment terms for each customer. Jim wants managers who view the Timecard Summary workbook to be able to view the pay categories for MediaLoft store employees. He asks you to create a hyperlink at the Hourly Pay Rate column heading. Users will click the hyperlink to view the Pay Rate worksheet.

Steps

1. **Display the Monday worksheet**

2. **Click Edit, click Go To, type N5** (the cell containing the text Hourly Pay Rate), then click **OK**

3. **Click the Insert Hyperlink button** on the Standard toolbar, then click **Existing File or Web Page**, if it is not already selected

   The Insert Hyperlink dialog box opens. See Figure F-15. The icons under "Link to" on the left side of the dialog box let you specify the type of location you want the link to jump to: an existing file or Web page, a place in the same document, a new document, or an e-mail address. Because Jim wants users to display a document he has created, the first icon, Existing File or Web Page, is correct.

   > **QuickTip**
   > To remove a hyperlink or change its target, right-click it, point to Hyperlink, then click Remove Hyperlink or Edit Hyperlink.

4. **Click the Look in list arrow** to navigate to the location where your Project Files are stored, then click **Pay Rate Classifications** in the file list

   The filename you selected appears in the Address text box. This is the document users will see when they click this hyperlink. You can also specify the ScreenTip that users will see when they hold the pointer over the hyperlink.

5. **Click ScreenTip, type Click here to see MediaLoft pay rate classifications, click OK, then click OK again**

   Cell N5 now contains underlined blue text, indicating that it is a hyperlink. After you create a hyperlink, you should check it to make sure that it jumps to the correct destination.

6. **Move the pointer over the Hourly Pay Rate text**, view the ScreenTip, then click once

   Notice that when you move the pointer over the text, the pointer changes to, indicating that it is a hyperlink, and the ScreenTip appears. After you click, the Pay Rate Classifications worksheet appears. See Figure F-16. The Web toolbar appears beneath the Standard and Formatting toolbars.

   > **QuickTip**
   > If you link to a Web page you must open a connection to the Internet to test the link.

7. **Click the Back button** on the Web toolbar, save the workbook, then print the worksheet

Using hyperlinks to navigate large worksheets

Hyperlinks are useful in navigating large worksheets or workbooks. You can create a hyperlink from a cell to another cell in the same worksheet, a cell in another worksheet, or a defined name anywhere in the workbook. Under "Link to" in the Insert Hyperlink dialog box, click Place in This Document. Then type the cell reference and indicate the sheet, or select a named location.

MANAGING WORKBOOKS AND PREPARING THEM FOR THE WEB

FIGURE F-15: Insert Hyperlink dialog box

Locations a hyperlink can jump to

Click here to browse to Hyperlink target

FIGURE F-16: Target document

Web toolbar

Back button

Finding and replacing data and formats

You can easily change worksheet data by using the find-and-replace feature in Excel. Click Edit on the menu bar, click Replace, enter the text you want to find, press [Tab], then enter the text you want to replace it with. Use the Find Next, Find All, Replace, and Replace All buttons to find and replace any or all occurrences of the specified text. You can specify a data format for your search criteria by clicking the Options button, clicking the Format list arrow, and selecting a format.

MANAGING WORKBOOKS AND PREPARING THEM FOR THE WEB EXCEL F-15

Saving an Excel File as a Web Page

One way to share Excel data is to place, or **publish**, it over a network or on the Web so that others can access it using their Web browsers. The network can be an **intranet**, which is an internal network site used by a particular group of people who work together. If you post an entire workbook, users can click worksheet tabs to view each sheet. You can make the workbook interactive, meaning that users can enter, format, and calculate data. To publish an Excel document to an intranet or the Web, you must first save it as an **HTML (Hypertext Markup Language)** document, so it can be interpreted by a Web browser. Jim asks you to save the entire Timecard Summary workbook in HTML format so he can publish it on the MediaLoft intranet for managers to use.

Steps

QuickTip
You can use the Save As option on the File menu to save a workbook in formats that can be opened in earlier versions of Excel as well as in databases and other spreadsheet programs.

1. **Click File on the menu bar, then click Save as Web Page**
   The Save As dialog box opens. By default, the Entire Workbook option button is selected, which is what Jim wants. However, he wants the title bar of the Web page to be more descriptive than the filename.

2. **Click Change Title**
   The Set Page Title dialog box opens.

3. **Type MediaLoft Houston Timecard Summary, then click OK**
   The new title appears in the Page title area. The Save as type list box indicates that the workbook will be saved as a Web page, which is in HTML format. See Figure F-17.

QuickTip
To avoid problems when publishing your pages to a Web server, it is best to use lowercase characters, omit special characters and spaces, and limit your filename to eight characters.

4. **Change the filename to timesum, then click the Save in list arrow to navigate to the drive and folder where your Project Files are stored**

5. **Click Save**
   A dialog box appears, indicating that the custom views you saved earlier will not be part of the HTML file.

6. **Click Yes**
   Excel saves the workbook as an HTML file in the folder location you specified in the Save As dialog box, and in the same place creates a folder in which it places associated files, such as a file for each worksheet. To make the workbook available to others, you would publish all these files on an intranet or Web server. When the save process is complete, the original XLS file closes and the HTML file opens on your screen.

7. **Click File on the menu bar, click Web Page Preview, then maximize the browser window**
   The workbook opens in your default Web browser, which could be Internet Explorer or Netscape, showing you what it would look like if you opened it on an intranet or on the Web. See Figure F-18. The Monday worksheet appears as it would if it were on a Web site or intranet, with tabs at the bottom of the screen for each sheet.

8. **Click the Weekly Summary Sheet tab then print the worksheet using your browser**

9. **Close the Web browser window, then close the timesum workbook and the Pay Rate Classifications workbook**

FIGURE F-17: Save As dialog box

- New title appears here
- Indicates that saved file will be in HTML format
- Click here to modify the title of the Web page

FIGURE F-18: Workbook in Web page preview

- Your screen will differ if you are using a different browser
- New title appears in the title bar
- Sheet tabs allow users to view other sheets in their browser

Clues to Use

Holding Web discussions

You can attach a discussion comment to an Excel worksheet that you will save as an HTML document. This allows people viewing your worksheet on the Web to review and reply to your comments. To insert a discussion comment in Excel, click Tools on the menu bar, point to Online Collaboration, then click Web Discussions. This will display the Web Discussions Toolbar. See Figure F-19. You can add comments that others can view on the Web by clicking the Insert Discussion about the Workbook button on the Web Discussions Toolbar. Your comments, which are stored on a discussion server, will appear with the worksheet when it is saved and published as a Web document. People viewing your worksheet on the Web can reply by clicking the Discuss button on the Standard Buttons toolbar in Internet Explorer to display the Discussions Toolbar. Then they can click the Insert Discussion in the Document button. *Note*: You must specify a discussion server to use this feature.

FIGURE F-19: Web Discussion toolbar

- Web Discussion Toolbar

MANAGING WORKBOOKS AND PREPARING THEM FOR THE WEB

Excel 2002 Practice

▶ Concepts Review

Label each element of the Excel screen shown in Figure F-20.

FIGURE F-20

Match each of the terms with the statement that describes its function.

8. Dashed line
9. Hyperlink
10. 3-D reference
11.
12.

a. Inserts a picture into header or footer.
b. Uses values from different worksheets or workbooks
c. Indicates a page break
d. Inserts a code to print the sheet name in a header or footer
e. A navigational tool for use between worksheets or workbooks

Practice

Select the best answer from the list of choices.

13. You can save frequently used display and print settings by using the _____ feature.
    a. HTML
    b. View menu
    c. Custom Views
    d. Save command

14. You can group several workbooks in a _____ so they can be opened together rather than individually.
    a. Workgroup
    b. Workspace
    c. Consolidated workbook
    d. Work unit

15. You can specify data formats in the Find and Replace dialog box by clicking the _____ button.
    a. Format
    b. Options >>
    c. Data
    d. Tools

▶ Skills Review

1. **Freeze columns and rows.**
   a. Start Excel, open the Project File EX F-2 from the drive and folder where your Project Files are stored, then save it as **San Francisco Budget**.
   b. Activate the 2003 sheet, then freeze columns A and B and rows 1 through 3 for improved viewing. (*Hint*: Click cell C4 prior to issuing the Freeze Panes command.)
   c. Scroll until columns A and B and F through H are visible.
   d. Press **[Ctrl][Home]** to return to cell C4.
   e. Unfreeze the panes.

2. **Insert and delete worksheets.**
   a. With the 2003 sheet active, use the sheet shortcut menu to insert a new sheet to its left.
   b. Delete the 2002 sheet, rename the new sheet 2005 and move it after the 2004 sheet.
   c. Add a custom footer to the 2003 sheet with your name on the left side and the page number on the right side.
   d. Add a custom header with the worksheet name on the left side.
   e. Save and preview the worksheet, compare your results to Figure F-21, then print it.

3. **Consolidate data with 3-D references.**
   a. In cell C22, enter a reference to cell G7.
   b. In cell C23, enter a reference to cell G18.
   c. Activate the 2004 worksheet.
   d. In cell C4, enter a reference to cell C4 on the 2003 worksheet.

FIGURE F-21

MANAGING WORKBOOKS AND PREPARING THEM FOR THE WEB

Excel 2002 | Practice

   e. In the 2004 worksheet, copy the contents of cell C4 into cells C5:C6.
   f. Preview the 2004 worksheet, then use the Setup button to add your name to the footer.
   g. Print the 2004 worksheet, then save your work.

4. **Hide and protect worksheet areas.**
   a. On the 2003 sheet, unlock the expense data in the range C10:F17.
   b. On the 2003 sheet, hide the percent of total formulas in column H and the cash flow formulas in row 20.
   c. Protect the sheet without using a password.
   d. To make sure the other cells are locked, attempt to make an entry in cell D4. You should see the error message displayed in Figure F-22.
   e. Change the first quarter mortgage expense to $3,900.
   f. Verify the formulas in column H and row 20 are hidden.
   g. Unprotect the worksheet.
   h. Save the workbook.

FIGURE F-22

[Microsoft Excel dialog box: "The cell or chart you are trying to change is protected and therefore read-only. To modify a protected cell or chart, first remove protection using the Unprotect Sheet command (Tools menu, Protection submenu). You may be prompted for a password."]

5. **Save custom views of a worksheet.**
   a. Set the zoom on the 2003 worksheet so that all the data fits on your screen.
   b. Make this a new view called **Entire 2003 Budget**.
   c. Use the Custom Views dialog box to return to Generic view. (*Note*: Using custom views may affect your headers, footers, and page orientation.)
   d. Save the workbook.

6. **Control page breaks and page numbering.**
   a. Insert a page break above cell A10.
   b. Save the view as **Halves**.
   c. Save the workbook.

7. **Create a hyperlink between Excel files.**
   a. On the 2003 worksheet, make cell A9 a hyperlink to the file **Expense Details**.
   b. Test the link, then print the Expense Details worksheet.
   c. Edit the hyperlink in cell A9, adding a ScreenTip that reads **Click here to see expense assumptions**.
   d. Return to the San Francisco Budget worksheet by using the Web toolbar.
   e. On the 2004 worksheet, enter the text **Based on 2003 budget** in cell A2.
   f. Make the text in cell A2 a hyperlink to cell A1 in the 2003 worksheet. (*Hint*: Use the Place in This Document button and note the cell reference in the Type the cell reference text box.)
   g. Test the hyperlink.
   h. Save the workbook and protect it with the password **pass**.
   i. Close and reopen the workbook to test the password.
   j. Remove the password and save the workbook again.

8. **Save an Excel file as a Web page.**
   a. If you have access to a Web discussion server, attach a discussion comment to the 2003 worksheet with your name and the date you reviewed the budget. (If you don't have access to discussion server, proceed to step b.)

► EXCEL F-20   MANAGING WORKBOOKS AND PREPARING THEM FOR THE WEB

Practice

b. Save the entire budget workbook as a Web page with a title bar that reads **Our Budget** and the file named **sfbudget**.
c. Preview the Web page in your browser. If your browser doesn't open automatically, check your taskbar.
d. Test the worksheet tabs in the browser to make sure they work.
e. Print the 2003 worksheet from your browser.
f. Close your browser.
g. Return to Excel, close the HTML document and the Expense Details workbook, then exit Excel.

▶ Independent Challenge 1

As a new employee at SoftSales, a computer software retailer, you are responsible for tracking the sales of different product lines and determining which computer operating system generates the most software sales each month. Although sales figures vary from month to month, the format in which data is entered does not. You decide to create a worksheet tracking sales across platforms by month. Use a separate worksheet for each month and create data for three months. Use your own data for the number of software packages sold in the Windows and Macintosh columns for each product.

a. Start Excel, create a new workbook, then save it as **Software Sales Summary** in the drive and folder where your Project Files are stored.
b. Create three worksheets to hold software sales information for the months of January, February, and March. Use Table F-3 as a guide to enter row and column labels, your own data, and formulas for the totals.
c. Create a summary sheet that totals the information in all three sheets.
d. Add headers to all four worksheets that includes your name, the sheet name, and the date.
e. Format the worksheet appropriately.
f. Save the workbook, preview and print the four worksheets, then exit Excel.

TABLE F-3

	Windows	Macintosh	Total
Games Software			
Combat Flight Simulator			
Safari			
NASCAR Racing			
Total			
Business Software			
Word Processing			
Spreadsheet			
Presentation			
Graphics			
Page Layout			
Total			
Utilities			
Antivirus			
File Recovery			
Total			

Excel 2002

MANAGING WORKBOOKS AND PREPARING THEM FOR THE WEB

Excel 2002 | Practice

▶ Independent Challenge 2

You own PC Assist, a software training company located in Montreal, Canada. You have added several new entries to the August check register and are ready to enter September's check activity. Because the sheet for August will include much of the same information you need for September, you decide to copy it. Then you will edit the new sheet to fit your needs for the September check activity. You will use sheet referencing to enter the beginning balance and beginning check number. Using your own data, you will complete five checks for the September register.

   a. Start Excel, open the Project File EX F-3 from the drive and folder where your Project Files are stored, then save it as **Update to Check Register**. The expense amounts in the worksheet include the Goods and Services tax (GST)/(TPS), the Harmonized Sales Tax (HST)/(TVH), and the Quebec sales tax (TVQ).
   b. Delete Sheet 2 and Sheet 3, then create a worksheet for September by copying the August sheet and renaming it.
   c. With the September sheet active, delete the data in range A6:E24.
   d. To update the balance at the beginning of the month, use sheet referencing from the last balance entry in the August sheet.
   e. Generate the first check number. (*Hint*: Use a formula that references the last check number in August and adds one.)
   f. Enter data for five checks using September 2003 dates. For the check number, use the number above it and add 1.
   g. Add a footer to both sheets that includes your name on the left side of the printout and the system date on the right side. Add a header for the worksheets that displays the sheet name centered on the printout. (*Hint*: Select both sheets using the Shift key, then apply the header and footer)
   h. Save the workbook.
   i. Use the Find and Replace dialog box to change the beginning balance for August from **20000** to **25000**, formatted as a number with two decimal places. (*Hint*: The Options >> button will allow you to change the data format)
   j. Select both worksheets, preview the entire workbook, then close the Preview window.
   k. Print the September worksheet in landscape orientation on a single page.
   l. Save and close the workbook, then exit Excel.

▶ Independent Challenge 3

You are a college student with two roommates. Each month you receive your long-distance telephone bill. Because no one wants to figure out who owes what, you split the bill three ways. You are sure that one of your roommates makes most of the long-distance calls. To make the situation more equitable, you decide to create a spreadsheet to track the long-distance phone calls each month. You will create a workbook with a separate sheet for each roommate and track the following information for each month's long-distance calls: date of call, time of call (AM or PM), call minutes, location called, state called, area code, phone number, and call charge. Then you will total the charges for each roommate and create a summary sheet of all three roommates' charges for the month. Since your roommate is working with an older version of Excel, you'll also save the workbook in a format he can open.

   a. Start Excel, create a new workbook, then save it as **Monthly Long Distance** in the drive and folder where your Project Files are stored.
   b. Enter column headings and row labels to track each call.
   c. Use your own data, entering at least three long-distance calls for each roommate.
   d. Create totals for minutes and charges on each roommate's sheet.
   e. Create a summary sheet that shows each name and uses cell references to display the total minutes and total charges for each person.
   f. On the summary sheet, create a hyperlink from each person's name to cell A1 of their respective worksheet. Enter your name on all worksheet footers, then save the workbook.
   g. Create a workbook with the same type of information for the two people in the apartment next door. Save it as **Next Door**.

Practice

h. Use linking to create a 3-D reference that displays the neighbors' totals on your summary sheet so your roommates can compare their expenses with the neighbors'.
i. Create a workspace that groups the workbooks Monthly Long Distance and Next Door. Name the workspace **Phonebill**. (*Hint*: Save Workspace is an option on the File menu.)
j. Change the workbook properties of the Next Door workbook to Read-only.
k. Save the Monthly Long Distance Excel file again in Microsoft Excel 5.0 worksheet format. Name the workbook **Monthly Long Distance-5**. (*Hint*: Use the Save As command on the file menu.) Notice that the links don't work in Excel 5.0.
l. Close your browser then close any open files and exit Excel.

e Independent Challenge 4

Lynne Watson, the creative director at WebProductions, a web design company, is considering purchasing digital cameras for the New York and Montreal offices. You have been asked to research this purchase by comparing features and current prices in US and Canadian currencies. Lynne would like you to prepare a worksheet containing the following information about each camera: Product Description, Manufacturer, Platform (MacOS, Windows), Max Resolution, Image Capacity, and Price in both US and Canadian currencies. You decide to investigate online vendors for this information. You will also use an online currency converter to display the price information in Canadian currency.

a. Find features and pricing for five digital cameras that you think would be appropriate for commercial images. Go to the Alta Vista search engine at www.altavista.com or Yahoo at www.yahoo.com and use their shopping directories. You can also use Excite, Hotbot, Infoseek, or another search engine of your choice. Use your search engine to find a currency converter site, then convert the prices you found from the online vendors into Canadian currency.
b. Start Excel, create a new workbook, then save it as **Camera Research** in the drive and folder where your Project Files are stored.
c. Enter the information you found on the Web in the table below. The image capacity and price information may include ranges of values.

Description	Manufacturer	Platform	Max Resolution	Image Capacity	Price $USD	Price $CAD

d. Enter the information from the table into your Camera Research workbook. Name the worksheet **Online Vendors**.
e. Add a custom header that displays the sheet name centered on the printout.
f. Add a custom footer that includes your name on the left side of the printout.
g. Make the cells in the Manufacturer column hyperlinks to the manufacturer's Web site. Save the workbook.
h. Save the workbook with the name **camera** in HTML format for management's use and preview it in your Web browser.
i. Print the worksheet from your browser.
j. Exit your browser then close any open files and exit Excel.

Excel 2002 | Practice

▶ Visual Workshop

Create the worksheet shown in Figure F-23, then save it as **Martinez.xls**. Enter your name in the footer, save the workbook and print the worksheet. Then save the workbook as a Web page using the name **martinez.htm**. Preview the worksheet in your Web browser, then print the sheet from the browser. Notice that the text in cell A1 is a hyperlink to the Our History worksheet; the graphic is from the Clip Gallery. If you don't have this graphic, substitute the graphic of your choice.

FIGURE F-23

Cell A1: Martinez Agency (hyperlink with tooltip "Click here for a short history of our agency")

Row 12: Supplying the finest in acting talent to the movie industry

	Name	M/F	Age	Role types
14	Name	M/F	Age	Role types
15	Mary Allen	M	32	Dramatic
16	Shelly Connoly	F	24	Ingenue
17	Barbara Bradley	F	54	Grandmother
18	Michael Freedman	M	46	Dad
19	Bill Jones	M	23	Dramatic
20	Shirly Smith	F	35	Dramatic
21	Nick Blackwell	M	19	Teen idol
22	Barry Nolton	M	35	Dad
23	Deborah Sanders	F	46	Mom
24	Aaron Atkins	M	66	Grandfather

Sheet tabs: Top Actors / Our History / Sheet3

▶ EXCEL F-24 **MANAGING WORKBOOKS AND PREPARING THEM FOR THE WEB**

Excel 2002

Unit G

Automating
Worksheet Tasks

Objectives

- ▶ Plan a macro
- ▶ Record a macro
- ▶ Run a macro
- ▶ Edit a macro
- ▶ Use shortcut keys with macros
- ▶ Use the Personal Macro Workbook
- ▶ Add a macro as a menu item
- ▶ Create a toolbar for macros

A **macro** is a set of instructions that performs tasks in the order you specify. You create macros to automate frequently performed Excel tasks that require a series of steps. For example, if you usually enter your name and date in a worksheet footer, you can record the keystrokes in an Excel macro that enters the text and inserts the current date automatically. In this unit, you will plan and design a simple macro, then record and run it. Then you will edit the macro. You will also assign shortcut keys to a macro, store a macro in the Personal Macro Workbook, add a macro option to the Tools menu, and create a new toolbar for macros. Jim wants you to create a macro for the Accounting Department. The macro will automatically insert text that will identify the worksheet as an Accounting Department document.

Planning a Macro

Excel 2002 — Unit G

You create macros for tasks that you perform on a regular basis. For example, you can create a macro to enter and format text or to save and print a worksheet. To create a macro, you record the series of actions or write the instructions in a special programming language. Because the sequence of actions is important, you need to plan the macro carefully before you record it. You use the Macro command on the Tools menu to record, run, and modify macros. ✎ Jim wants you to create a macro for the Accounting Department that inserts the text "Accounting Department" in the upper-left corner of any worksheet. You work with him to plan the macro using the following guidelines:

Details

▶ **Assign the macro a descriptive name**
The first character of a macro name must be a letter; the remaining characters can be letters, numbers, or underscores. Spaces are not allowed in macro names; use underscores in place of spaces. (Press [Shift][-] to enter an underscore character.) Jim wants you to name the macro "DeptStamp". See Table G-1 for a list of macros Jim might create to automate other tasks.

▶ **Write out the steps the macro will perform**
This planning helps eliminate careless errors. Jim writes a description of the macro he wants, as shown in Figure G-1.

▶ **Decide how you will perform the actions you want to record**
You can use the mouse, the keyboard, or a combination of the two. Jim wants you to use both the mouse and the keyboard.

▶ **Practice the steps you want Excel to record, and write them down**
Jim wrote down the sequence of actions he wants you to include in the macro.

▶ **Decide where to locate the description of the macro and the macro itself**
Macros can be stored in an unused area of the active workbook, in a new workbook, or in the Personal Macro Workbook, a special workbook used only for macro storage. Jim wants you to store the macro in a new workbook.

TABLE G-1: Possible macros and their descriptive names

description of macro	descriptive name
Enter a frequently used proper name, such as Jim Fernandez	JimFernandez
Enter a frequently used company name, such as MediaLoft	CompanyName
Print the active worksheet on a single page, in landscape orientation	FitToLand
Turn off the header and footer in the active worksheet	HeadFootOff
Show a frequently used custom view, such as a generic view of the worksheet, setting the print and display settings back to the Excel defaults	GenericView

▶ EXCEL G-2   AUTOMATING WORKSHEET TASKS

FIGURE G-1: Paper description of planned macro

Macro to create stamp with the department name

Name: DeptStamp

Description: Adds a stamp to the top left of the worksheet, identifying it as an Accounting Department worksheet

Steps:
1. Position the cell pointer in cell A1.
2. Type Accounting Department, then click the Enter button.
3. Click Format on the menu bar, then click Cells.
4. Click Font tab, under Font style click Bold, under Underline click Single, and under Color click Red, then click OK.

Macros and viruses

When you open an Excel workbook that has macros, you will see a message asking you if you want to enable or disable macros. This is because macros can contain viruses, destructive software programs that can damage your computer files. If you know your workbook came from a trusted source, click Enable macros. If you are not sure of the workbook's source, click Disable macros. If you disable the macros in a workbook, you will not be able to use them. For more information about macro security and security levels type "About macro security" in the Type a question for help text box.

Unit G
Excel 2002

Recording a Macro

The easiest way to create a macro is to record it using the Excel Macro Recorder. You turn the Macro Recorder on, name the macro, enter the keystrokes and select the commands you want the macro to perform, then stop the recorder. As you record the macro, each action is translated into program code you can later view and modify. You can take as long as you want to record the macro; a recorded macro contains only your actions, not the amount of time you took to record it. Jim wants you to create a macro that enters a department stamp in cell A1 of the active worksheet. You create this macro by recording your actions.

Steps

Trouble?
If the task pane is not visible, click View on the menu bar, then click Task Pane. You can also open a blank workbook by clicking the New button on the Standard toolbar.

1. Start Excel, click the **Blank Workbook button** on the New Workbook task pane, save the blank workbook as **My Excel Macros** in the drive and folder where your Project Files are stored, then close the task pane.
   You are ready to start recording the macro.

2. Click **Tools** on the menu bar, point to **Macro**, then click **Record New Macro**
   The Record Macro dialog box opens. See Figure G-2. The default name Macro1 is selected. You can either assign this name or enter a new name. This dialog box also allows you to assign a shortcut key for running the macro and assign a storage location for the macro.

3. Type **DeptStamp** in the Macro name text box

4. If the "Store macro" in list box does not display "This Workbook", click the **list arrow** and select **This Workbook**

Trouble?
If the Stop Recording toolbar is not displayed, click View, point to Toolbars, then click Stop Recording.

5. If the Description text box does not contain your name, select the existing name, type your own name, then click **OK**
   The dialog box closes. A small Stop Recording toolbar appears containing the Stop Recording button, and the word "Recording" appears on the status bar. Take your time performing the steps below. Excel records every keystroke, menu selection, and mouse action that you make.

6. Press **[Ctrl][Home]**
   When you begin an Excel session, macros record absolute cell references. By beginning the recording in cell A1, you ensure that the macro includes the instruction to select cell A1 as the first step, even if cell A1 is already selected.

7. Type **Accounting Department** in cell A1, then click the **Enter button** on the formula bar

8. Click **Format** on the menu bar, then click **Cells**

9. Click the **Font tab**, in the Font style list box click **Bold**, click the **Underline list arrow** and click **Single**, then click the **Color list arrow** and click **red** (third row, first color on left)
   See Figure G-3.

Trouble?
If your results differ from Figure G-4, clear the contents of cell A1, then slowly and carefully repeat Steps 2 through 10. When prompted to replace the existing macro at the end of Step 5, click Yes.

10. Click **OK**, click the **Stop Recording button** on the Stop Recording toolbar, click **cell D1** to deselect cell A1, then save the workbook
    Compare your results with Figure G-4.

▶ EXCEL G-4 AUTOMATING WORKSHEET TASKS

FIGURE G-2: Record Macro dialog box

Type macro name here

Reflects the computer user's name and the system date

FIGURE G-3: Font tab of the Format Cells dialog box

Stop Recording toolbar

Stop Recording button

Macro will apply these formatting attributes to the text

FIGURE G-4: Accounting Department stamp

AUTOMATING WORKSHEET TASKS EXCEL G-5

Excel 2002

Running a Macro

Excel 2002 — Unit G

Once you record a macro, you should test it to make sure that the actions it performs are correct. To test a macro, you **run**, or execute, it. One way to run a macro is to select the macro in the Macros dialog box, then click Run. Jim asks you to clear the contents of cell A1 then test the DeptStamp macro. After you run the macro in the My Excel Macros workbook, he asks you to test the macro once more from a newly opened workbook.

Steps

1. **Click cell A1, click Edit on the menu bar, point to Clear, click All, then click any other cell to deselect cell A1**
   When you delete only the contents of a cell, any formatting still remains in the cell. By using the Clear All option on the Edit menu, you can be sure that the cell is free of contents and formatting.

2. **Click Tools on the menu bar, point to Macro, then click Macros**
   The Macro dialog box, shown in Figure G-5, lists all the macros contained in the open workbooks. If other people have used your computer, other macros may be listed.

   > **QuickTip**
   > To delete a macro, select the macro name in the Macro dialog box, click Delete, then click Yes to confirm the action.

3. **Make sure DeptStamp is selected, click Run, then deselect cell A1**
   Watch your screen as the macro quickly plays back the steps you recorded in the previous lesson. When the macro is finished, your screen should look like Figure G-6. As long as the workbook containing the macro remains open, you can run the macro in any open workbook.

4. **Click the New button on the Standard toolbar**
   Because the new workbook automatically fills the screen, it is difficult to be sure that the My Excel Macros workbook is still open.

   > **QuickTip**
   > To stop a macro while it is running, press [Esc] then click End.

5. **Click Window on the menu bar**
   A list of open workbooks appears underneath the menu options. The active workbook name (in this case, Book2) appears with a check mark to its left. The My Excel Macros workbook appears on the menu, so you know it's open. See Figure G-7.

6. **Deselect cell A1, click Tools on the menu bar, point to Macro, click Macros, make sure 'My Excel Macros.xls'!DeptStamp is selected, click Run, then deselect cell A1**
   When multiple workbooks are open, the macro name in the Macro dialog box includes the workbook name between single quotation marks, followed by an exclamation point, indicating that the macro is outside the active workbook. Because you only used this workbook to test the macro, you don't need to save it.

   > **Trouble?**
   > If you get a security error message when attempting to run your macro, the security level may be set too high in the workbook. You can enable macros for the workbook by clicking the Macro option on the Tools menu and selecting Security. Set the security level to Medium or Low, then close and reopen the workbook.

7. **Close Book2 without saving changes**
   The My Excel Macros workbook reappears.

▶ EXCEL G-6 AUTOMATING WORKSHEET TASKS

FIGURE G-5: Macro dialog box

Lists macros stored in open workbooks

FIGURE G-6: Result of running DeptStamp macro

DeptStamp macro inserts formatted text in cell A1

FIGURE G-7: Window menu showing the list of open workbooks

Check mark indicates active workbook

Indicates this workbook is still open

Excel 2002

AUTOMATING WORKSHEET TASKS   EXCEL G-7

Excel 2002 Unit G

Editing a Macro

When you use the Macro Recorder to create a macro, the program instructions, called **program code**, are recorded automatically in the Visual Basic for Applications (VBA) programming language. Each macro is stored as a **module**, or program code container, attached to the workbook. After you record a macro, you might need to change it. If you have a lot of changes to make, it might be best to rerecord the macro. If you need to make only minor adjustments, you can edit the macro code directly using the Visual Basic Editor. ✎ Jim wants you to modify his macro to change the point size of the department stamp to 12.

Steps

QuickTip
Another way to start the Visual Basic Editor is to click Tools on the menu bar, point to Macro, then click Visual Basic Editor, or press [Alt][F11].

1. **Make sure the My Excel Macros workbook is open, click Tools on the menu bar, point to Macro, click Macros, make sure DeptStamp is selected, then click Edit**
   The Visual Basic Editor starts, showing the DeptStamp macro steps in a numbered module window (in this case, Module1).

2. **If necessary, maximize the window titled My Excel Macros.xls – [Module1(Code)], then examine the steps in the macro**
   The name of the macro and the date it was recorded appear at the top of the module window. Below that, Excel has translated your keystrokes and commands into macro code. When you open and make selections in a dialog box during macro recording, Excel automatically stores all the dialog box settings in the macro code. For example, the line .FontStyle = "Bold" was generated when you clicked Bold in the Format Cells dialog box. You also see lines of code that you didn't generate directly while recording the DeptStamp macro; for example, .Name = "Arial".

3. **In the line .Size = 10, double-click 10 to select it, then type 12**
   See Figure G-8. Because Module1 is attached to the workbook and not stored as a separate file, any changes to the module are saved automatically when you save the workbook.

4. **In the Visual Basic Editor, click File on the menu bar, click Print, click OK to print the module, then review the printout**

QuickTip
You can return to Excel without closing the module by clicking the View Microsoft Excel button 📊 on the standard toolbar.

5. **Click File on the menu bar, then click Close and Return to Microsoft Excel**
   You want to rerun the DeptStamp macro to make sure the macro reflects the change you made using the Visual Basic Editor.

6. **Click cell A1, click Edit on the menu bar, point to Clear, click All, deselect cell A1, click Tools on the menu bar, point to Macro, click Macros, make sure DeptStamp is selected, click Run, then deselect cell A1**
   Compare your results to Figure G-9. The department stamp is now in 12-point type.

7. **Save the workbook**

▶ EXCEL G-8   AUTOMATING WORKSHEET TASKS

FIGURE G-8: Visual Basic Editor showing Module1

- Name of macro
- Project Explorer with open module selected
- Properties window showing properties for selected objects
- Macro program code
- Comments appear in green preceded by an apostrophe
- Code window

FIGURE G-9: Result of running edited DeptStamp macro

Font size enlarged to 12 pt

Clues to Use

Adding comments to Visual Basic code

With practice, you will be able to interpret the lines of code within your macro. Others who use your macro, however, might want to know the function of a particular line. You can explain the code by adding comments to the macro. Comments are explanatory text added to the lines of code. When you enter a comment, you must type an apostrophe (') before the comment text. Otherwise, the program will try to interpret it as a command. On the screen, comments appear in green after you press [Enter]. See Figure G-8. You also can insert blank lines as comments in the macro code to make the code more readable. To do this, type an apostrophe, then press [Enter].

AUTOMATING WORKSHEET TASKS   EXCEL G-9

Using Shortcut Keys with Macros

Excel 2002 – Unit G

In addition to running a macro from the Macro dialog box, you can run a macro by assigning a shortcut key combination to it. Using shortcut keys to run macros reduces the number of actions required to begin macro playback. You assign shortcut key combinations in the Record Macro dialog box. ➥ Jim also wants you to create a macro called CompanyName to enter the company name into a worksheet. You will assign a shortcut key combination to run the macro.

Steps

1. **Click cell B2**
   You will record the macro in cell B2. You want the macro to enter the company name anywhere in a worksheet. Therefore, you will not begin the macro with an instruction to position the cell pointer, as you did in the DeptStamp macro.

2. **Click Tools on the menu bar, point to Macro, then click Record New Macro**
   The Record Macro dialog box opens. Notice the option Shortcut key: Ctrl+ followed by a blank box. You can type a letter (A–Z) in the Shortcut key text box to assign the key combination of [Ctrl] plus that letter to run the macro. You use the key combination [Ctrl][Shift] plus a letter to avoid overriding any of the Excel [Ctrl] [letter] shortcut keys, such as [Ctrl][C] for Copy.

3. **With the default macro name selected, type CompanyName, click the Shortcut key text box, press and hold [Shift], type C, then, if necessary, replace the name in the Description box with your name**
   Compare your screen with Figure G-10. You are ready to record the CompanyName macro.

4. **Click OK to close the dialog box**
   By default, Excel records absolute cell references in macros. Beginning the macro in cell B2 causes the macro code to begin with a statement to select cell B2. Because you want to be able to run this macro in any active cell, you need to instruct Excel to record relative cell references while recording the macro.

5. **Click the Relative Reference button on the Stop Recording toolbar**
   The Relative Reference button is now selected. See Figure G-11. This button is a toggle and retains the relative reference setting until you click it again to turn it off or you exit Excel.

6. **Type MediaLoft in cell B2, click the Enter button on the formula bar, press [Ctrl][I] to italicize the text, click the Stop Recording button on the Stop Recording toolbar, then deselect cell B2**
   MediaLoft appears in italics in cell B2. You are ready to run the macro in cell A5 using the shortcut key combination.

7. **Click cell A5, press and hold [Ctrl][Shift], type C, then deselect the cell**
   The company name appears in cell A5. See Figure G-12. Because the macro played back in the selected cell (A5) instead of the cell where it was recorded (B2), you know that the macro recorded relative cell references.

8. **Save the workbook**

EXCEL G-10 AUTOMATING WORKSHEET TASKS

FIGURE G-10: Record Macro dialog box with shortcut key assigned

Shortcut to run macro

FIGURE G-11: Stop Recording toolbar with Relative Reference button selected

Relative Reference button selected

FIGURE G-12: Result of running the CompanyName macro

Result of running CompanyName macro in cell A5

Result of recording CompanyName macro in cell B2

AUTOMATING WORKSHEET TASKS   EXCEL G-11

Using the Personal Macro Workbook

Unit G / Excel 2002

You can store commonly used macros in a **Personal Macro Workbook**. The Personal Macro Workbook is always available, unless you specify otherwise, and gives you access to all the macros it contains, regardless of which workbooks are open. The Personal Macro Workbook file is created automatically the first time you choose to store a macro in it. You can add additional macros to the Personal Macro Workbook by saving them there. Jim often likes to add a footer to his worksheets identifying his department, the workbook name, the worksheet name, his name, and the current date. He wants you to create a macro that automatically inserts this footer. Because he wants to use this macro in future worksheets, he asks you to store this macro in the Personal Macro Workbook.

Steps

1. From any cell in the active worksheet, click **Tools** on the menu bar, point to **Macro**, then click **Record New Macro**
   The Record Macro dialog box opens.

2. Type **FooterStamp** in the Macro name text box, click the **Shortcut key text box**, press and hold **[Shift]**, type **F**, then click the **Store macro in list arrow**
   You have named the macro FooterStamp and assigned it the shortcut combination [Ctrl][Shift][F]. Notice that This Workbook is selected by default, indicating that Excel automatically stores macros in the active workbook. See Figure G-13. You also can choose to store the macro in a new workbook or in the Personal Macro Workbook.

   QuickTip
   If you see a message saying that the Personal Macro Workbook needs to be opened, open it, then begin again from Step 1. The Personal Macro Workbook file is usually stored in the Documents and Settings/Administrator/Application Data/Microsoft/Excel/XLSTART folder under the name "Personal.xls" and opens when you open Excel.

3. Click **Personal Macro Workbook**, replace the existing name in the Description text box with your own name, if necessary, then click **OK**
   The recorder is on, and you are ready to record the macro keystrokes. If you are prompted to replace an existing macro named FooterStamp, click Yes.

4. Click **File** on the menu bar, click **Page Setup**, click the **Header/Footer tab** (make sure to do this even if it is already active), click **Custom Footer**, in the Left section box, type **Accounting**; click the **Center section box**, click the **File Name button**, press **[Spacebar]**, type **/**, press **[Spacebar]**, click the **Tab Name button** to insert the sheet name; click the **Right section box**, type your name followed by a comma, press **[Spacebar]**, click the **Date button**, click **OK** to return to the Header/Footer tab
   The footer stamp is set up, as shown in Figure G-14.

   QuickTip
   You can copy or move macros stored in other workbooks to the Personal Macro Workbook by using the Visual Basic Editor.

5. Click **OK** to return to the worksheet, then click the **Stop Recording button** on the Stop Recording toolbar
   You want to ensure that the macro will set the footer stamp in any active worksheet.

6. Activate Sheet2, in cell A1 type **Testing the FooterStamp macro**, press **[Enter]**, press and hold **[Ctrl][Shift]**, then type **F**
   The FooterStamp macro plays back the sequence of commands.

7. Preview the worksheet to verify that the new footer was inserted, then close the Preview window

8. Save the workbook, then print the worksheet
   Jim is satisfied that the FooterStamp macro works in any active worksheet.

FIGURE G-13: Record Macro dialog box showing macro storage options

- Click to store in new blank workbook
- Click to store in Personal Macro Workbook
- Stores macro in active workbook

FIGURE G-14: Header/Footer tab showing custom footer settings

- Workbook name
- Sheet name
- The footer overlap will not appear in the printed document
- Date will reflect your system date

Working with the Personal Macro Workbook

Once you use the Personal Macro Workbook, it opens automatically each time you start Excel so you can add macros to it. By default, the Personal Macro Workbook is hidden as a precautionary measure so you don't accidentally delete anything from it. If you need to delete a macro from the Personal Macro Workbook, click Unhide on the Window menu, click Personal.xls, then click OK.

AUTOMATING WORKSHEET TASKS   EXCEL G-13

Adding a Macro as a Menu Item

Excel 2002 • Unit G

In addition to storing macros in the Personal Macro Workbook so that they are always available, you can add macros as items on the Excel Worksheet menu bar. The **Worksheet menu bar** is the toolbar at the top of the Excel screen. To increase the availability of the FooterStamp macro, Jim decides to add it as an item on the Tools menu. He wants you to add a custom menu item to the Tools menu, then assign the macro to that menu item.

Steps

1. With Sheet2 active, click **Tools** on the menu bar, click **Customize**, click the **Commands tab**, then under Categories, click **Macros**
   See Figure G-15.

   QuickTip
   You may need to reposition the Customize dialog box to make the Tools option on the Worksheet menu bar visible.

2. Click **Custom Menu Item** under Commands, drag the selection to **Tools** on the menu bar (the menu opens), then point just under the last menu option, but do not release the mouse button
   Compare your screen to Figure G-16.

3. Release the mouse button
   Now, Custom Menu Item is the last item on the Tools menu.

4. With the Tools menu still open, right-click **Custom Menu Item**, select the text in the Name box (&Custom Menu Item), type **Footer Stamp**, then click **Assign Macro**
   Unlike a macro name, the name of a custom menu item can have spaces between words like all standard menu items. The Assign Macro dialog box opens.

5. Click **PERSONAL.XLS!FooterStamp** under Macro name, click **OK**, then click **Close**
   You have assigned the FooterStamp macro to the new menu command.

6. Click the **Sheet3 tab**, in cell A1 type **Testing macro menu item**, press **[Enter]**, then click **Tools** on the menu bar
   The Tools menu appears with the new menu option at the bottom. See Figure G-17.

7. Click **Footer Stamp**, preview the worksheet to verify that the footer was inserted, then close the Print Preview window
   The Print Preview window appears with the footer stamp. Because others using your computer might be confused by the macro on the menu, it's a good idea to remove it.

8. Click **Tools** on the menu bar, click **Customize**, click the **Toolbars tab**, click **Worksheet Menu Bar** to highlight it, click **Reset**, click **OK** to confirm, click **Close**, click **Tools** on the menu bar to make sure that the custom item has been deleted, then save the workbook

Clues to Use

Adding a custom menu

You can create a custom menu on an existing toolbar and assign macros to it. To do this, click Tools on the menu bar, click Customize, click the Commands tab, click New Menu in the Categories list, then drag the New Menu from the Commands box to the toolbar. To name the new menu, right-click, then enter a name in the Name box.

FIGURE G-15: Commands tab of the Customize dialog box

FIGURE G-16: Tools menu showing placement of the Custom Menu Item

FIGURE G-17: Tools menu with new Footer Stamp item

AUTOMATING WORKSHEET TASKS   EXCEL G-15

Creating a Toolbar for Macros

Toolbars contain buttons that allow you to access commonly used commands. You can create your own custom toolbars to organize commands so that you can find and use them quickly. Once you create a toolbar, you can add buttons to access Excel commands such as macros. Jim asks you to create a custom toolbar called Macros that will contain buttons to run two of his macros.

Steps

QuickTip

Toolbars you create or customize are available to all workbooks on your computer. You can ensure that a custom toolbar is visible in a specific workbook by attaching the toolbar to the workbook using the Toolbars tab in the Customize dialog box.

1. **With Sheet3 active, click Tools on the menu bar, click Customize, click the Toolbars tab, then click New**
   The New Toolbar dialog box opens, as shown in Figure G-18. Under Toolbar name, a default name of Custom1 is selected.

2. **Type Macros, then click OK**
   Excel adds the new toolbar named Macros to the bottom of the Toolbars list, and a small, empty toolbar named Macros opens. See Figure G-19. You cannot see the entire toolbar name. A toolbar starts out small and expands to fit the buttons you assign to it.

3. **Click the Commands tab in the Customize dialog box, click Macros under Categories, then drag the Custom button over the new Macros toolbar and release the mouse button**
   The Macros toolbar contains one button. You want the toolbar to contain two macros, so you need to add one more button.

4. **Drag the Custom button over the Macros toolbar again**
   With the two buttons in place, you are ready to customize the buttons and assign macros to them.

5. **Right-click the left button on the Macros toolbar, select &Custom Button in the Name box, type Department Stamp, click Assign Macro, click DeptStamp, then click OK**
   With the first toolbar button customized, you are ready to customize the second button.

6. **With the Customize dialog box open, right-click the right button on the Macros toolbar, edit the name to read Company Name, click Change Button Image, click (seventh row, first column), right-click , click Assign Macro, click CompanyName to select it, click OK, then close the Customize dialog box**
   The Macros toolbar appears with the two customized macro buttons.

7. **Move the mouse pointer over on the Macros toolbar to display the macro name (Department Stamp), then click to run the macro; click cell B2, move the mouse pointer over on the Macros toolbar to display the macro name (Company Name), then click to run that macro; deselect the cell**
   Compare your screen with Figure G-20. The DeptStamp macro automatically replaces the contents of cell A1. Because others using your computer might be confused by the new toolbar, it's a good idea to remove it.

8. **Click Tools on the menu bar, click Customize, click the Toolbars tab if necessary, in the Toolbars window click Macros to highlight it, click Delete, click OK to confirm the deletion, then click Close**

9. **Save the workbook, print Sheet 3, then close the document and exit Excel**
   The completed figure for Sheet1 is shown in Figure G-12.

FIGURE G-18: New Toolbar dialog box

Type toolbar name here

FIGURE G-19: Customize dialog box with new Macros toolbar

Check marks indicate toolbars in view

New Macros toolbar

FIGURE G-20: Worksheet showing Macros toolbar with two customized buttons

Click to run DeptStamp macro

Click to run CompanyName macro

AUTOMATING WORKSHEET TASKS EXCEL G-17

Excel 2002 Practice

▶ Concepts Review

Label each element of the Excel screen shown in Figure G-21.

FIGURE G-21

Match each term or button with the statement that describes it.

7. Visual Basic Editor
8. Macro comments
9. Personal Macro Workbook
10. 🔲
11. 😊

a. Statements that appear in green explaining macro code
b. Used to store commonly used macros
c. Used to make changes to macro code
d. Used to record relative cell references
e. Used to add a custom button on a macros toolbar

▶ EXCEL G-18   AUTOMATING WORKSHEET TASKS

Practice

Select the best answer from the list of choices.

12. Which of the following is the best candidate for a macro?
    a. One-button or one-keystroke commands.
    b. Often-used sequences of commands or actions.
    c. Seldom-used commands or tasks.
    d. Nonsequential tasks.

13. When you are recording a macro, you can execute commands by using:
    a. Only the keyboard.
    b. Only the mouse.
    c. Any combination of the keyboard and the mouse.
    d. Only menu commands.

14. Commonly used macros should be stored in:
    a. The Common Macro Workbook.
    b. The Master Macro Workbook.
    c. The Personal Macro Workbook.
    d. The Custom Macro Workbook.

15. Which of the following is *not* true about editing a macro?
    a. You edit macros using the Visual Basic Editor.
    b. A macro cannot be edited and must be recorded again.
    c. You can type changes directly in the existing program code.
    d. You can make more than one editing change in a macro.

16. Why is it important to plan a macro?
    a. Macros won't be stored if they contain errors.
    b. Planning helps prevent careless errors from being introduced into the macro.
    c. It is impossible to edit a macro.
    d. Macros can't be deleted.

17. Macros are recorded with relative references:
    a. Only if the Relative Reference button is selected.
    b. In all cases.
    c. Only if relative references are chosen while recording the macro.
    d. Only if the Absolute Reference button is not selected.

18. You can run macros:
    a. From the Macro dialog box.
    b. From shortcut key combinations.
    c. As items on menus.
    d. Using all of the above.

Excel 2002 | Practice

▶ Skills Review

1. **Record a macro.**
   a. Start Excel, open a new workbook, then save it as **Macros** in the drive and folder where your Project Files are stored. You will record a macro titled **MyAddress** that enters and formats your name, address, and telephone number in a worksheet.
   b. Store the macro in the current workbook.
   c. Record the macro, entering your name in cell A1, your street address in cell A2, your city, state, and ZIP code in cell A3, and your telephone number in cell A4.
   d. Format the information in 12-point Arial bold.
   e. Add a border and make the text red.
   f. Stop the recorder and save the workbook.

2. **Run a macro.**
   a. Clear cell entries and formats in the range affected by the macro.
   b. Run the MyAddress macro in cell A1.
   c. On the worksheet, clear all the cell entries and formats generated by running the MyAddress macro.
   d. Save the workbook.

3. **Edit a macro.**
   a. Open the MyAddress macro in the Visual Basic Editor.
   b. Locate the line of code that defines the font size, then change the size to 16 point.
   c. Edit the Range in the fifth line of macro to A1:D4 to accommodate the increased label size.
   d. Add a comment line that describes this macro.
   e. Save and print the module, then return to Excel.
   f. Test the macro in Sheet1.
   g. Save the workbook.

4. **Use shortcut keys with macros.**
   a. Record a macro called **MyName** in the current workbook that enters your full name in boldface in the selected cell of a worksheet. (*Hint*: You will need to record a relative cell reference).
   b. Assign your macro the shortcut key combination [Ctrl][Shift][Q] and store it in the current workbook.
   c. After you record the macro, clear the cell containing your name that you used to record the macro.
   d. Use the shortcut key combination to run the MyName macro.
   e. Save the workbook.

5. **Use the Personal Macro Workbook.**
   a. Record a new macro called **FitToLand** that sets print orientation to landscape, with content scaled to fit on one page.
   b. Store the macro in the Personal Macro Workbook. If you are prompted to replace the existing FitToLand macro, click Yes.
   c. After you record the macro, activate Sheet2, and enter some test data in row 1 that exceeds one page width.
   d. In the Page Setup dialog box, make sure the orientation is set to portrait and the scaling is 100 percent of normal size.
   e. Run the macro.

Practice

   f. Preview Sheet2 and verify that it's in landscape view and fits on one page.
   g. Save the workbook.

6. **Add a macro as a menu item.**
   a. On the Commands tab in the Customize dialog box, specify that you want to create a Custom Menu Item for macros.
   b. Place the Custom Menu Item at the bottom of the Tools menu.
   c. Rename the Custom Menu Item **Fit to Landscape**.
   d. Assign the macro PERSONAL.XLS!FitToLand to the command.
   e. Go to Sheet3 and make sure the orientation is set to portrait, then enter some test data in column A.
   f. Run the Fit to Landscape macro from the Tools menu.
   g. Preview the worksheet and verify that it is in landscape view.
   h. Reset the Worksheet Menu bar.
   i. Verify that the Fit to Landscape command has been removed from the Tools menu.
   j. Save the workbook.

7. **Create a toolbar for macros.**
   a. With the Macros workbook still open, you will create a new custom toolbar, titled My Info.
   b. Display the Macros command category in the customize dialog box, then drag the Custom Button to the My Info toolbar.
   c. Drag the Custom Button to the My Info toolbar a second time to create another button.
   d. Rename the first button **My Address**, and assign the MyAddress macro to it.
   e. Rename the second button **My Name**, and assign the MyName macro to it.
   f. Change the second button image to one of your choice.
   g. On Sheet3, clear the existing cell data, then test both macro buttons on the My Info toolbar.
   h. Use the Toolbars tab of the Customize dialog box to delete the toolbar named My Info.
   i. Save the workbook, print the worksheet, close the workbook, then exit Excel.

▶ Independent Challenge 1

As a computer-support employee of Boston Accounting Solutions, you need to develop ways to help your fellow employees work more efficiently. Employees have asked for Excel macros that will do the following:

- Delete the current row and insert a blank row
- Delete the current column and insert a blank column
- Place the department name of Accounting in a 14-point red font in cell A1 (The width of A1 should be increased if necessary)

a. Plan and write the steps necessary for each macro.
b. Start Excel, create a new workbook, then save it as **Excel Utility Macros** in the drive and folder where your Project Files are stored.
c. Create a new toolbar called **Helpers**.
d. Create a macro for each employee request described above, name them DeleteRow, DeleteColumn, and DepartmentName, then save them in the Excel Utility Macros workbook.
e. Add comment lines to each module, describing the function of the macro and your name, then return to Excel.
f. Add each macro to the Tools menu.

Excel 2002 | Practice

g. On the Helpers toolbar, install buttons to run the macros.
h. Test each macro by using the Run command, the menu command, and the new buttons.
i. Delete the new toolbar, then reset the Worksheet menu bar.
j. Save the workbook, print the module containing the program code for all three macros, then close the workbook and exit Excel.

▶ Independent Challenge 2

You are an analyst in the Loan Department of Atlantic Bank. Every quarter, you produce a number of single-page quarterly budget worksheets. Your manager has informed you that certain worksheets need to contain a footer stamp indicating that the worksheet was produced in the Loan Department. The footer should also show the current page number out of the total number of pages, (for example, 1 of 5) and the workbook filename. It's tedious to add the footer stamp to the numerous worksheets you produce. You will record a macro to do this.

a. Plan and write the steps to create the macro.
b. Start Excel, create a new workbook, then save it as **Header and Footer Stamp** in the drive and folder where your Project Files are stored.
c. Create the macro described above, name it footerstamp, assign it the shortcut key combination [Ctrl][Shift][F], and store it in the current workbook. Make sure it adds the footer with the department name and the other required information.
d. Add a descriptive comment line to the macro code with your name.
e. Add the macro to the Tools menu.
f. Create a toolbar titled **Stamp**, then add a button to the toolbar to run the macro.
g. Enter the text **Footer Test** in cell A1. Test the macro using the shortcut key combination, the menu command, and the new button.
h. Delete the new toolbar, then reset the Worksheet menu bar.
i. Save the workbook, print the module for the macro, close the module and the workbook, then exit Excel.

▶ Independent Challenge 3

You are an administrative assistant at the Sydney, Australia, branch of Computers Inc. A major part of your job is to create spreadsheets that project sales results in different markets. It seems that you are constantly changing the print settings so that workbooks print in landscape orientation and are scaled to fit on one page. You have decided that it's time to create a macro to streamline this process.

a. Plan and write the steps necessary to create the macro.
b. Start Excel, create a new workbook, then save it as **Computers Inc Macro** in the drive and folder where your Project Files are stored.
c. Create a macro that changes the page orientation to landscape and scales the worksheet to fit on one page.
d. Name the macro **Landscape**, assign it the shortcut key combination [Ctrl][Shift][L], and store it in the current workbook.
e. Add the macro to the Tools menu.
f. Enter the text **Macro test** in cell A1 and add your name. Test the macro using the new menu command.
g. Reset the Worksheet menu bar and change the page orientation back to portrait.
h. Edit the macro to include the company name, Computers Inc, in the center footer and add your name as a comment. Test the macro using the shortcut key combination, making sure the footer was added.

i. Add a custom menu to the standard toolbar and name it **Macros**. Add a custom menu item to the new Macros menu, name the menu option **Page Orientation**, and assign the landscape macro to it.
j. Delete the footer and change the page orientation to portrait, then test the macro using the new menu.
k. Reset the standard toolbar.
l. Save the workbook, print the module for the macro; close the workbook, then exit Excel.

e-Quest Independent Challenge 4

PC Assist, a software training company, has decided to begin purchasing its branch office supplies through online vendors. One of the products the company needs to purchase is toner for the Hewlett-Packard LaserJet 2100 printers in the offices. You have been asked to research vendors and prices on the Web. You will create a workbook to hold office supply vendor information that you can use for various products. You will add a macro to this workbook to find the lowest price of the product, format the information, and add a descriptive footer to the worksheet.

Go to the AltaVista search engine at www.altavista.com and enter **Office Supplies** in the Search box. You can also use Yahoo!, Excite, Infoseek, or another search engine of your choice. You may want to use the shopping directories on the search engines as another source of information. Find three online suppliers of toner for the company's printers and note their prices.

a. Start Excel, open the Project File EX G-1 from the drive and folder where your Project Files are stored, enter your name into cell A15, then save the workbook as **Office Supplies**.
b. Complete the table below with three online suppliers of office products you found in your search.

Office Product	
Vendor	Price
Lowest Price	

c. Enter three vendors and their prices from your table into the Excel worksheet. Enter the Product name **Toner** in the cell next to Office Product.
d. Create a macro named **Toner** in the Office Supplies workbook that can be activated by the [Ctrl][Shift][T] key combination. The macro should do the following:
   • Find the lowest price for the office product and insert it to the right of the Lowest Price label.
   • Boldface the Lowest Price text and the cell to its right that will contain the lowest value.
   • Place a thick box border around all the information.
   • Fill the information area with a light turquoise color.
   • Add a footer with the company name **PC Assist** on the left and the workbook name on the right.
   • Include your name in a comment line.
e. Clear all the formatting, the footer, and the lowest price from the worksheet.
f. Test the macro using the key combination [Ctrl][Shift][T].
g. Save your workbook, print the results of the macro, then open the macro in the Visual Basic Editor and print the macro code.
h. Return to Excel, close the workbook, then exit Excel.

Excel 2002 | Practice

▶ Visual Workshop

Create the macro shown in Figure G-22. (*Hint*: Save a blank workbook as **File Utility Macros**, then create a macro in the current workbook called **SaveClose** that saves a previously named workbook. Finally, include the line **ActiveWorkbook.Close** in the module, as shown in the figure.) Print the module. Test the macro. If the "Macro recorded" comment doesn't contain your name, edit it accordingly.

FIGURE G-22

```
Sub SaveClose()
'
' SaveClose Macro
' Macro recorded 10/31/2003 by Jim Fernandez
'
' Keyboard Shortcut: Ctrl+Shift+C
'
    ActiveWorkbook.Save
    ActiveWorkbook.Close
End Sub
```

Excel 2002

Unit H

Using Lists

Objectives

- Plan a list
- Create a list
- Add records with the data form
- Find records
- Delete records
- Sort a list on one field
- Sort a list on multiple fields
- Print a list

A **database** is an organized collection of related information. Examples of databases include a telephone book, a card catalog, and a roster of company employees. Excel refers to a database as a **list**. Using an Excel list, you can organize and manage worksheet information so that you can quickly find data for projects, reports, and charts. In this unit, you'll learn how to plan and create a list; add, change, find, and delete information in a list; and then sort and print a list.

MediaLoft uses lists to analyze new customer information. Jim Fernandez has asked you to help him build and manage a list of new customers as part of the ongoing strategy to focus on the expenditure of the company's advertising dollars.

Planning a List

When planning a list, consider what information the list will contain and how you will work with the data now and in the future. Lists are organized into records. A **record** contains data about an object or person. Records are rows in the list and are comprised of fields. **Fields** are columns in the list; each field describes a characteristic about the record, such as a customer's last name or street address. Each field has a **field name**, a column label that describes the field. See Table H-1 for additional planning guidelines. Jim has asked you to compile a list of new customers. Before entering the data into an Excel worksheet, you will plan the list using the following guidelines:

Details

▶ Identify the purpose of the list
Determine the kind of information the list should contain. Jim will use the list to identify areas of the country in which new customers live.

▶ Plan the structure of the list
Determine the fields that make up a record. Jim has customer cards that contain information about each new customer. Figure H-1 shows a typical card. Each customer in the list will have a record. The fields in the record correspond to the information on the cards.

▶ Write down the names of the fields
Field names can be up to 255 characters long (the maximum column width), although shorter names are easier to see in the cells. Field names appear in the first row of a list. Jim writes down field names that describe each piece of information shown in Figure H-1.

▶ Determine any special number formatting required in the list
Most lists contain both text and numbers. When planning a list, consider whether any fields require specific number formatting or prefixes. Jim notes that some ZIP codes begin with zero. Because Excel automatically drops a leading zero, Jim must type an apostrophe (') when he enters a ZIP code that begins with 0 (zero). The apostrophe tells Excel that the cell contains a label rather than a value. If a column contains a combination of numbers and text, you should format the field as text. Otherwise, the numbers are sorted first, and the numbers that contain text characters are sorted after that; for example, 11542, 60614, 87105, '01810, '02115. To instruct Excel to sort the ZIP codes properly, Jim enters all ZIP codes with a leading apostrophe and formats the field as text.

FIGURE H-1: Customer record and corresponding field names

Customer record:
- Rodriguez, Virginia → Last Name, First Name
- 123 Main St. → Street Address
- Boston, MA 02007 → City, State, Zip
- 617 → Acode
- Radio → Ad Source
- loves radio personality → Comments

Field names shown at right.

TABLE H-1: Guidelines for planning a list

size and location guidelines	row and column content guidelines
Devote an entire worksheet to your list and list summary information because some list management features can be used on only one list at a time.	Plan and design your list so that all rows have similar items in the same column.
Leave at least one blank column and one blank row between your list and list summary data. Doing this helps Excel select your list when it performs list management tasks such as sorting.	Do not insert extra spaces at the beginning of a cell because that can affect sorting and searching.
Avoid placing critical data to the left or right of the list.	Use the same format for all cells in a column.
	Instead of blank rows or columns between your labels and your data, use formatting to make column labels stand out from the data.

Clues to Use

Using lists versus databases

If your list contains more records than can fit on one worksheet (that is, more than 65,536), you should consider using database software rather than spreadsheet software.

USING LISTS EXCEL H-3

Creating a List

Excel 2002 — Unit H

Once you have planned the list structure, the sequence of fields, and any appropriate formatting, you need to create field names. Table H-2 provides guidelines for naming fields. You are ready to create the list using the field names you wrote down earlier.

Steps

1. Start Excel if necessary, open the Project File EX H-1 from the drive and folder where your Project Files are stored, then save it as **New Customer List**

2. Rename Sheet1 **Practice**, then if necessary maximize the Excel window
   It is a good idea to devote an entire worksheet to your list.

3. Beginning in cell A1 and moving horizontally, enter each field name in a separate cell, as shown in Figure H-2
   Always put field names in the first row of the list. Don't worry if your field names are wider than the cells; you will fix this later.

   > **QuickTip**
   > If the field name you plan to use is wider than the data in the column, you can turn on Wrap Text on the Alignment tab in the Format Cells dialog box to stack the heading in the cell. You can also press [Alt][Enter] to force a line break while entering field names.

4. Select the field headings in range **A1:I1**, then click the **Bold button** on the Formatting toolbar; with range A1:I1 still selected, click the **Borders list arrow**, then click the **Thick Bottom Border** (second column, second row)

5. Enter the information from Figure H-3 in the rows immediately below the field names, using a leading apostrophe (') for all ZIP codes; do not leave any blank rows
   If you don't type an apostrophe, Excel deletes the leading zero (0) in the ZIP code. The data appears in columns organized by field name.

   > **Trouble?**
   > Cells F2:F4 may have a green error indicator in the upper-left corner of the cell, and an error button may appear. This warning is a result of storing the ZIP code numbers as text. To remove the warnings and prevent similar ones in the future, select Options from the Tools menu, click the Error Checking tab, and remove the check next to Number stored as text.

6. Select the range **A1:I4**, click **Format** on the menu bar, point to **Column**, click **AutoFit Selection**, click anywhere in the worksheet to deselect the range, then save the workbook
   Resizing the column widths this way is faster than double-clicking the column divider lines between each pair of columns. Compare your screen with Figure H-4.

TABLE H-2: Guidelines for naming fields

guideline	explanation
Use labels to name fields	Numbers can be interpreted as parts of formulas
Do not use duplicate field names	Duplicate field names can cause information to be incorrectly entered and sorted
Format the field names to stand out from the list data	Use a font, alignment, format, pattern, border, or capitalization style for the column labels that are different from the format of your list data
Use descriptive names	Avoid names that might be confused with cell addresses, such as Q4

FIGURE H-2: Field names entered and formatted in row 1

FIGURE H-3: Cards with customer information

Rodriguez, Virginia
123 Main St.
Boston, MA 02007
617

Radio

loves radio personality

Wong, Sam
2120 Central NE.
San Francisco, CA 93772
415

Newspaper

graphics caught eye

Frei, Carol
123 Elm St.
Salem, MA 01970
978

Newspaper

no comments

FIGURE H-4: List with three records

Leading apostrophe

New records

Clues to Use

Filtering lists using AutoFilter

You can filter a list to show only the rows that meet specific criteria. For example, you might want to display only the records of customers in a certain ZIP code, or only residents of California. (A filter is different from a sort, which rearranges list records.) The AutoFilter feature is the easiest way to apply a filter. To use AutoFilter, click Data on the menu bar, point to Filter, then click AutoFilter. List arrows will appear next to the field names, allowing you to select criteria for a field. For example, if you specify MA as the criteria in a State field, Excel displays only the records where MA is entered as the state.

USING LISTS   EXCEL H-5

Adding Records with the Data Form

You can add records to a list by typing data directly into the cells within the list range. Once the field names are created, you can also use the data form as a quick, easy method of data entry. A **data form** is a dialog box that displays one record at a time. You have entered all the customer records Jim had on his cards, but he receives the names of two additional customers. You decide to use the Excel data form to add the new customer information.

Steps

1. **Make sure the New Customer List file is open, then activate Sheet2 and rename it Working List**
   Working List contains the nearly completed customer list.

2. **Select any cell in the customer list, click Data on the menu bar, then click Form**
   A data form containing the first record appears, as shown in Figure H-5.

3. **Click New**
   A blank data form appears with the insertion point in the first field.

4. **Type Chavez in the Last Name box, then press [Tab] to move the insertion point to the next field**

5. **Enter the rest of the information for Jeffrey Chavez, as shown in Figure H-6**
   Press [Tab] to move the insertion point to the next field, or click in the next field box to move the insertion point there.

   > **Trouble?**
   > If you accidentally press [↑] or [↓] while in a data form and find that you displayed the wrong record, press [↑] or [↓] until you return to the desired record.

6. **Click New to add Jeffrey Chavez's record and open another blank data form, enter the record for Cathy Relman as shown in Figure H-6, then click Close**
   The records that you added with the data form are placed at the end of the list and are formatted in the same way as the previous records.

   > **QuickTip**
   > Excel automatically extends formatting and formulas in lists.

7. **If necessary, scroll down the worksheet to bring rows 46 and 47 into view, check both new records, return to cell A1, then save the workbook**

EXCEL H-6 USING LISTS

FIGURE H-5: Data form showing first record in the list

- Current record number
- Leading apostrophe not visible in data form after records are added
- Total number of records
- Click to open a blank data form for adding a record

FIGURE H-6: Two data forms with information for two new records

- Sheet name
- Identifies this as a new record

USING LISTS EXCEL H-7

Finding Records

Excel 2002 — Unit H

From time to time, you need to locate specific records in your list. You can use the Excel Find command on the Edit menu or the data form to search your list. You can also use the Replace command on the Edit menu to locate and replace existing entries or portions of entries with specified information. Jim wants to be more specific about the radio ad source, so he asks you to replace "Radio" with "KWIN Radio." He also wants to know how many of the new customers originated from the company's TV ads. You begin by searching for those records with the ad source "TV".

Steps

Trouble?
If you receive the message "No list found," select any cell within the list, then repeat Step 1.

1. **Click any cell within the list, click Data on the menu bar, click Form, then click Criteria**
   The data form changes so that all fields are blank and "Criteria" appears in the upper-right corner. See Figure H-7. You want to search for records whose Ad Source field contains the label "TV".

2. **Click in the Ad Source text box, type TV, then click Find Next**
   Excel displays the first record for a customer who learned about the company through its TV ads. See Figure H-8.

QuickTip
You can also use comparison operators when performing a search using the data form. For example, you could specify >50,000 in a Salary field box to return those records in the Salary field with a value greater than $50,000.

3. **Click Find Next until there are no more matching records, then click Close**
   There are six customers whose ad source is TV.

4. **Return to cell A1, click Edit on the menu bar, then click Replace**
   The Find and Replace dialog box opens with the Replace tab selected and the insertion point in the Find what box. See Figure H-9.

5. **Type Radio in the Find what text box, then click the Replace with text box**
   Jim wants you to search for entries containing "Radio" and replace them with "KWIN Radio".

6. **Type KWIN Radio in the Replace with text box**
   Because you notice that there are other list entries containing the word "radio" with a lowercase "r" (in the Comments column), you need to make sure that only capitalized instances of the word are replaced.

QuickTip
Be sure to clear this option for future searches, where you may not want to use it.

7. **Click Options >>, click the Match case check box to select it, click Options <<, then click Find Next**
   Excel moves the cell pointer to the first occurrence of "Radio".

8. **Click Replace All, click OK, then click Close**
   The dialog box closes. Note that in the Comments column, each instance of the word "radio" remains unchanged.

9. **Make sure there are no entries in the Ad Source column that read "Radio", then save the workbook**

Clues To Use

Using wildcards to fine-tune your search

You can use special symbols called **wildcards** when defining search criteria in the data form or Replace dialog box. The question mark (?) wildcard stands for any single character. For example, if you do not know whether a customer's last name is Paulsen or Paulson, you can specify Pauls?n as the search criteria to locate both options. The asterisk (*) wildcard stands for any group of characters. For example, if you specify Jan* as the search criteria in the First Name field, Excel locates all records with first names beginning with Jan (for instance, Jan, Janet, Janice).

EXCEL H-8 USING LISTS

FIGURE H-7: Criteria data form

- Identifies this as a criteria data form
- Type TV here
- Click to restore changes you made in the form
- Click to find previous record that matches criterion
- Click to return to data form
- Click to find next record that matches criterion

FIGURE H-8: Finding a record using the data form

- Record number of the displayed record

FIGURE H-9: Find and Replace dialog box

- Type Radio here
- Type KWIN Radio here
- Click to replace all occurrences of the item in the Find what text box
- Click here to set the Match case option
- Click to find next occurrence of item in Find what text box
- Click to replace current item that matches Find what text box

USING LISTS EXCEL H-9

Deleting Records

Excel 2002 — Unit H

You need to keep your list up to date by removing obsolete records. One way to remove records is to use the Delete button on the data form. You can also delete all records that share something in common—that is, records that meet certain criteria. For example, you can specify a criterion for Excel to find the next record containing ZIP code 01879, then remove the record by using the Delete button. If specifying one criterion does not meet your needs, you can set multiple criteria. Jim notices two entries for Carolyn Smith, and wants you to check the list for additional duplicate entries. You will use the data form to delete the duplicate record.

Steps

1. **Click Data on the menu bar, click Form, then click Criteria**
   The Criteria data form opens.

   > **QuickTip**
   > You can use the data form to edit records as well as to add, search for, and delete them. Just find the desired record and edit the data directly in the appropriate box.

2. **Type Smith in the Last Name text box, press Tab to move the insertion point to the First Name text box, type Carolyn, then click Find Next**
   Excel displays the first record for a customer whose name is Carolyn Smith. You decide to leave the initial entry for Carolyn Smith (record 5 of 46) and delete the second one, once you confirm that it is a duplicate.

3. **Click Find Next**
   The duplicate record for Carolyn Smith, number 40, appears as shown in Figure H-10. You are ready to delete the duplicate entry.

   > **QuickTip**
   > Clicking Restore on the data form will undo your changes when you are adding a new record, as long as you click it before you press Enter or click Close. Restore will not restore deleted record(s).

4. **Click Delete, then click OK to confirm the deletion**
   The duplicate record for Carolyn Smith is deleted, and all the other records move up one row. The data form now shows the record for Julio Manuel.

5. **Click Close to return to the worksheet, scroll down until rows 41–46 are visible, then read the entry in row 41**
   Notice that the duplicate entry for Carolyn Smith is gone and that Manuel Julio moved up a row and is now in row 41. You also notice a record for K. C. Splint in row 43, which is a duplicate entry.

6. **Return to cell A1, and read the record information for K. C. Splint in row 8**
   After confirming the duplicate entry, you decide to delete the row.

7. **Click cell A8, click Edit on the menu bar, then click Delete**
   The Delete dialog box opens, as shown in Figure H-11.

8. **Click the Entire row option button, then click OK**
   You have deleted the entire row. The duplicate record for K. C. Splint is deleted and the other records move up to fill in the gap.

9. **Save the workbook**

EXCEL H-10 USING LISTS

FIGURE H-10: Data form showing duplicate record for Carolyn Smith

Record 40 contains duplicate information for Carolyn Smith

Click to delete current record from list

FIGURE H-11: Delete dialog box

Click to shift remaining cells to fill gap created by deleting cells

Click to delete current row

Click to delete current column

Deleting records using the worksheet

When you delete a record using the data form, you cannot undo your deletion. When you delete a record by deleting its row in the worksheet, however, you can immediately retrieve it; use the Undo command on the Edit menu, click the Undo button, or press [Ctrl][Z].

USING LISTS   EXCEL H-11

Sorting a List on One Field

Usually, you enter records in the order in which they are received, rather than in alphabetical or numerical order. When you add records to a list using the data form, the records are added to the end of the list. Using the Excel sorting feature, you can rearrange the order of the records. You can use the sort buttons on the Standard toolbar to sort records by one field, or you can use the Sort command on the Data menu to perform more advanced sorts. Alternately, you can sort an entire list or any portion of a list, and you can arrange sorted information in ascending or descending order. In ascending order, the lowest value (the beginning of the alphabet, for instance, or the earliest date) appears at the top of the list. In a field containing labels and numbers, numbers come first. In descending order, the highest value (the end of the alphabet or the latest date) appears at the top of the list. In a field containing labels and numbers, labels come first. Table H-3 provides examples of ascending and descending sorts. Because Jim wants to be able to return the records to their original order following any sorts, he wants you to create a new field called Entry Order. You will then perform several single field sorts on the list.

Steps

QuickTip

Before you sort records, it is a good idea to make a backup copy of your list or create a field that numbers the records so you can return them to their original order, if necessary.

1. **In cell J1, enter the column heading and format as shown in Figure H-12, then AutoFit column J**

2. **Type 1 in cell J2, press [Enter], type 2 in cell J3, press [Enter], select cells J2:J3, drag the fill handle to cell J45**
   You are now ready to sort the list in ascending order by last name. You must position the cell pointer within the column you want to sort prior to issuing the sort command.

3. **Return to cell A1, then click the Sort Ascending button on the Standard toolbar**
   Excel rearranges the records in ascending order by last name, as shown in Figure H-13. You can also sort the list in descending order by any field.

Trouble?

If your sort does not perform as intended, press [Ctrl][Z] immediately to undo the sort.

4. **Click cell G1, then click the Sort Descending button on the Standard toolbar**
   Excel sorts the list, placing those records with higher-digit area codes at the top. You are now ready to return the list to original entry order.

5. **Click cell J1, click the Sort Ascending button on the Standard toolbar, then save the workbook**
   The list is back to its original order, and the workbook is saved.

FIGURE H-12: List with Entry Order field added

New field — Entry Order column

Drag fill handle to fill in values

FIGURE H-13: List sorted alphabetically by Last Name

List sorted in ascending order by Last Name

TABLE H-3: Sort order options and examples

option	alphabetic	numeric	date	alphanumeric
Ascending	A, B, C	7, 8, 9	1/1, 2/1, 3/1	12A, 99B, DX8, QT7
Descending	C, B, A	9, 8, 7	3/1, 2/1, 1/1	QT7, DX8, 99B, 12A

USING LISTS EXCEL H-13

Sorting a List on Multiple Fields

Excel 2002 — Unit H

You can sort lists by as many as three fields by specifying **sort keys**, the criteria on which the sort is based. Up to three column headings can be entered in the Sort dialog box to specify the sort criteria. Jim wants you to sort the records alphabetically by state first, then within the state by ZIP code.

Steps

QuickTip
You can specify a capitalization sort by clicking Options in the Sort dialog box, then selecting the Case sensitive box. When you choose this option, lowercase entries precede uppercase entries.

1. **Click Data on the menu bar, then click Sort**
   The Sort dialog box opens, as shown in Figure H-14. You want to sort the list by state and then by ZIP code.

2. **Click the Sort by list arrow, click State, then click the Ascending option button to select it, if necessary**
   The list will be sorted alphabetically in ascending order (A–Z) by the State field. A second sort criterion will sort the entries within each state grouping.

3. **Click the top Then by list arrow, click Zip, then click the Descending option button**
   You could also sort by a third key by selecting a field in the bottom Then by list box.

QuickTip
The Sort warning dialog box will appear if you are sorting a list on a field containing numbers that are formatted as text.

4. **Click OK to perform the sort, click OK on the Sort Warning dialog box, press [Ctrl][Home], then scroll through the list to see the result of the sort**
   The list is sorted alphabetically by state in ascending order, then within each state by ZIP code in descending order. Compare your results with Figure H-15.

5. **Save the workbook**

EXCEL H-14   USING LISTS

FIGURE H-14: Sort dialog box

- First sort field
- Fields on which the sort will be based
- Second sort field
- Third sort field
- Indicates that field name labels will not be included in sort

FIGURE H-15: List sorted by multiple fields

- First sort by state
- Second sort by ZIP code within state

Specifying a custom sort order

You can identify a custom sort order for the field selected in the Sort by box. To do this, click Options in the Sort dialog box, click the First key sort order list arrow, then click the desired custom order. Commonly used custom sort orders are days of the week (Sun, Mon, Tues, Wed, etc.) and months (Jan, Feb, Mar, etc.); alphabetic sorts do not sort these items properly.

USING LISTS EXCEL H-15

Excel 2002 Unit H

Printing a List

If a list is small enough to fit on one page, you can print it as you would any other Excel worksheet. If you have more columns than can fit on a portrait-oriented page, try setting the page orientation to landscape. Because lists often have more rows than can fit on a page, you can define the first row of the list (containing the field names) as the **print title**, which prints at the top of every page. Most lists do not have any descriptive information above the field names on the worksheet. To augment the information contained in the field names, you can use headers and footers to add identifying text, such as the list title or report date. If you want to exclude any fields from your list report, you can hide the selected columns from view so that they do not print. Jim has finished updating his list and would like you to print it. You begin by previewing the list.

Steps

1. **Click the Print Preview button on the Standard toolbar**
   The status bar reads Preview: Page 1 of 2. You want all the fields in the list to fit on a single page, but you'll need two pages to fit all the data.

2. **From the Print Preview window, click Setup, click the Page tab, click the Landscape option button under Orientation, click the Fit to option button under Scaling, double-click the tall box and type 2, click OK**
   The list still does not fit on a single page. Because the records on page 2 appear without column headings, you want to set up the first row of the list, which contains the field names, as a repeating print title.

3. **Click Close to exit the Print Preview window, click File on the menu bar, click Page Setup, click the Sheet tab, click the Rows to repeat at top text box under Print titles, click any cell in row 1, compare your screen to Figure H-16, then click OK**
   When you select row 1 as a print title, Excel automatically inserts an absolute reference to a beginning row to repeat at the top of each page—in this case, the print title to repeat beginning and ending with row 1.

4. **Click the Print Preview button, click Next to view the second page, then click Zoom**
   Setting up a print title to repeat row 1 causes the field names to appear at the top of each printed page. You can save these print settings by creating a custom view.

5. **Click Close, click View on the menu bar, click Custom Views, click Add, enter Print-Title in the Name text box, then click OK**
   This creates a custom view named Print-Title that you can use at any time. You can use the worksheet header to provide information about the list.

6. **Click , click Setup, click the Header/Footer tab, click Custom Header, click the Left section box and enter your name, then click the Center section box and enter MediaLoft -, press [Spacebar], then click the Filename button**

7. **Select the header information in the Center section box, click the Font button, change the font size to 14 and the style to Bold, click OK, click OK again to return to the Header/Footer tab, click OK to preview the list, then click Close**

8. **Save the workbook, print the worksheet, then close the workbook**
   Compare your printed worksheet with Figure H-17.

QuickTip

To print multiple ranges at the same time, click Page Break Preview on the View menu, drag to select the ranges (use [Ctrl] to select nonadjacent areas), click File, point to Print Area, then click Set Print Area. You can view the ranges included in the print area by using Print Preview.

QuickTip

To print more than one worksheet, select each sheet tab while holding down [Shift] or [Ctrl], then click .

EXCEL H-16 USING LISTS

FIGURE H-16: Sheet tab of the Page Setup dialog box

- Indicates that row 1 will appear at top of each printed page
- Indicates which columns will appear at the left of each printed page
- Turns gridline display on or off
- Specifies high or draft quality printing
- Displays row and column headings on printout

FIGURE H-17: Completed list

Setting a print area

There are times when you want to print only part of a worksheet. You can do this in the Print dialog box by choosing Selection under Print what. If you want to print a selected area repeatedly, it's best to define a print area, which will print when you click the Print button on the Standard toolbar. To set a print area, click View on the menu bar, then click Page Break Preview. In the preview window, select the area you want to print. Right-click the area, then select Set Print Area. The print area becomes outlined in a blue border. You can drag the border to extend the print area or add nonadjacent cells to it by selecting them, right-clicking them, then selecting Add to Print Area. To clear a print area, click File on the menu bar, point to Print Area, then click Clear Print Area.

USING LISTS   EXCEL H-17

Excel 2002 Practice

▶ Concepts Review

Label each of the elements of the Excel screen shown in Figure H-18.

FIGURE H-18

Match each term with the statement that best describes it.

6. List
7. Record
8. Database
9. Sort
10. Field name

a. Arrange records in a particular sequence
b. Organized collection of related information in Excel
c. Row in an Excel list
d. Type of software used for lists containing more than 65,536 records
e. Label positioned at the top of the column identifying data

Practice

Select the best answer from the list of choices.

11. Which of the following Excel sorting options do you use to sort a list of employee names in A-to-Z order?
    a. Ascending
    b. Absolute
    c. Alphabetic
    d. Descending
12. Which of the following series is in descending order?
    a. 4, 5, 6, A, B, C
    b. C, B, A, 6, 5, 4
    c. 8, 7, 6, 5, 6, 7
    d. 8, 6, 4, C, B, A
13. To prevent field name labels from being included in a sort, you need to make sure _____ is selected in the Sort dialog box.
    a. Field row
    b. No field row
    c. No header row
    d. Header row
14. When printing a list on multiple pages, you can define a print title containing repeating row(s) to:
    a. Include appropriate fields in the printout.
    b. Include field names at the top of each printed page.
    c. Include the header in list reports.
    d. Exclude from the printout all rows under the first row.

▶ Skills Review

1. **Create a list.**
   a. Create a new workbook, then save it as **MediaLoft New York Employee List** in the drive and folder where your Project files are stored.
   b. In cell A1, enter the title **MediaLoft New York Employees**.
   c. Enter the field names and records, using the information in the following table.

Last Name	First Name	Years	Position	Full/Part Time	Training?
Long	Sarah	3	CD Sales	F	Y
Marino	Donato	2	CD Sales	P	N
Khederian	Jay	4	Video Sales	F	Y
Johnson	Carol	1	Video Sales	F	N
Rabinowicz	Miriam	2	Café Sales	P	Y

   d. Apply bold formatting to the field names.
   e. Center the entries in the Years, Full/Part Time, and Training? fields.
   f. Adjust the column widths to make the data readable.
   g. Enter your name in the footer, save, then print the list.

Excel 2002 | Practice

2. **Add records with the data form.**
   a. Click any record in the list.
   b. Open the data form and add a new record for **David Gitano**, a one-year employee in Book Sales. David is full time and has not completed training.
   c. Add a new record for **George Worley**, the café manager. George is full time, has worked there two years, and has completed training.
   d. Save the file.
3. **Find and delete records.**
   a. Use the Find command to find the record for **Carol Johnson**.
   b. Delete the record.
   c. Save the file.
4. **Sort a list by one field.**
   a. Sort the list alphabetically in ascending order by last name.
   b. Save the file.
5. **Sort a list by multiple fields.**
   a. Sort the list alphabetically in ascending order, first by whether or not the employees have completed training and then by last name.
   b. Save the file.
6. **Print a list.**
   a. Add a header that reads **Employee Information** in the center; format the header in bold.
   b. Set the print area to include the range A1:F8.
   c. Save the workbook, print the print area, then close the workbook.
   d. Exit Excel.

▶ Independent Challenge 1

You own Personalize IT, an advertising firm located in Australia. The firm sells specialty items imprinted with the customer's name and/or logo such as hats, pens, mugs, and T-shirts. Plan and build a list of order information with a minimum of 10 records using the items sold. Your list should contain at least five different customers. (Some customers may place more than one order.) Each record should contain the following fields:

Customer last: Customer last name
Customer first: Customer first name
Item: Item description
Quantity: The number of items purchased
Cost: The item's price

a. Prepare a list plan that states your goal, outlines the data you'll need, and identifies the list elements.
b. Sketch a sample list on a piece of paper, indicating how the list should be built. Which of the data fields will be formatted as labels? As values?
c. Start Excel, create a new workbook, then save it as **Personalize IT** in the drive and folder where your Project Files are stored. Build the list by first entering **Personalize IT** as the worksheet title in cell A1, then enter the following field names in the designated cells:

Cell	Field name
A2	Customer last
B2	Customer first
C2	Item
D2	Quantity
E2	Cost

d. Enter 8 data records using your own data.
e. Add a new record to your list using the data form.
f. Enter **Subtotal** in cell F2, **Total** in cell G2, **Tax** in cell H2, and **.1** in cell I2 (the 10% sales tax).
g. Enter formulas to calculate the subtotal (Quantity*Cost) in cell F3 and the total (including tax) in cell G3. Copy the formulas down the columns.
h. Format the Cost, Subtotal, and Total columns as currency. Adjust the column widths as necessary.
i. Sort the list in ascending order by Item, then by Customer last.
j. Enter your name in the worksheet footer, then save the workbook.
k. Preview the worksheet, print the worksheet on one page, close the workbook, then exit Excel.

▶ Independent Challenge 2

You are taking a class titled Television Shows: Past and Present at a local community college. The instructor has provided you with an Excel list of television programs from the '60s and '70s. She has included fields tracking the following information: the number of years the show was a favorite, favorite character, the show's length in minutes, least favorite character, and comments about the show. The instructor has included data for each show in the list. She has asked you to add a field (column label) and one record (show of your choosing) to the list. Because the list should cover only 30-minute shows, you need to delete any records for shows longer than 30 minutes. Also, your instructor wants you to sort the list by television show and format the list as needed prior to printing. Feel free to change any of the list data to suit your tastes and opinions.

FIGURE H-19

a. Start Excel, open the Project File EX H-2 from the drive and folder where your Project Files are stored, then save it as **Television Shows of the Past**.
b. Add a field called **Rating** in column G. Your worksheet should look like Figure H-19. Complete the Rating field for each record with a value of 1–5 that reflects the rating you would give the television show.
c. Use the data form to add one record to the list. Make sure to enter information in every field.
d. Delete any records having show lengths other than 30. (*Hint*: Use the comparison operator <> in the Show length field to find records not equal to 30.)
e. Make any formatting changes to the list as needed and save the list.
f. Sort the list in ascending order by show name.
g. Enter your name in the worksheet footer, save the workbook, then print the nonadjacent columns Television Show and Rating.

Excel 2002 | Practice

h. Sort the list again, this time in descending order by number of years the show was a favorite.
i. Add a centered header that reads **Television Shows of the Past: '60s and '70s**.
j. Save the workbook, then preview the list and print it on a single page modifying its orientation if necessary.
k. Close the workbook and exit Excel.

▶ Independent Challenge 3

You are the assistant manager at Nite Owl Video in Brisbane, Australia. You have assembled an Excel list of the most popular Australian films your store rents, along with information about the Australian Film Institute (AFI) award they won, the release dates, and the film genres. Your customers have suggested that you prepare an in-store handout listing the films with the information sorted in different ways.

FIGURE H-20

	A	B	C	D
1	Film Name	Release Year	Genre	AFI Award
2	Doing Time for Patsy Cline	1977	Comedy	Cinematography
3	The Castle	1977	Comedy	Screenplay
4	Passion	1998	Drama	Cinematography
5	Bootmen	1999	Drama	Music Score
6	Looking for Alibrandi	1999	Drama	Best Film
7	The Interview	1997	Suspense	Best Film
8	The Boys	1997	Drama	Director
9	Russian Doll	1999	Drama	Screenplay
10	Oscar and Lucinda	1997	Drama	Cinematography
11	Chopper	1999	Drama	Director
12	Kiss or Kill	1997	Thriller	Best Film
13	Two Hands	1998	Comedy	Best Film

a. Start Excel, open the Project File EX H-3 from the drive and folder where your Project Files are stored, then save it as **Best Films**.
b. Format the list using Figure H-20 as a guide.
c. Sort the list in ascending order by Genre. Sort the list again in ascending order by Film Name.
d. Sort the list again using two fields, this time in descending order by the Genre, then in ascending order by Release Year.
e. Enter your name in the worksheet footer, save your work, then print the worksheet.
f. Use the data form to add a record to the list with the following information: Film name: In a Savage Land; Release year: 1998; Genre: Drama; AFI Award: Sound.
g. Use the data form to find and delete the record for the film "Passion."
h. Activate AutoFilter, use it to display only dramas, then print the list.
i. Redisplay all films, then set a print area that includes the range A1:C13.
j. Clear the print area and print the worksheet.
k. Close the workbook and exit Excel.

Practice

e Independent Challenge 4

The Local newspaper you work for has decided to start publishing the top selling MP3 titles. They would like to list the best-selling titles in the genres of Pop and Rock, Jazz, and Latin music. You have been asked to research the best-selling MP3 music along with price information. You will create a workbook to hold the information about the top three titles for each genre. You will add an AutoFilter to the Genre field to make it easier to view titles by the type of music.

a. Go to the AltaVista search engine at www.altavista.com and enter " MP3" in the Search box, then click the direct link to the MP3 site. You can also use Yahoo!, Excite, Infoseek, or another search engine of your choice. (If you prefer, you can enter the URL www.mp3.com directly in your browser.)

b. Complete the table below with the MP3 title information you found in your search.

Title	Artist	Genre	Price

c. Start Excel, open a new workbook enter your name in the worksheet footer, then save the workbook as **MP3 Titles**.

d. Use your table to enter the top three titles for the three music categories along with the Artist and price information into your Excel worksheet. Save the workbook.

e. Add an AutoFilter to the Genre column then use the filter to display only the Jazz records. (*Hint*: To apply a filter to only one column, select the column before applying the AutoFilter.)

f. Print only the records for the Jazz genre, then use the AutoFilter to display all the records.

g. Save the workbook again, set a print area to print only the Title and Artist columns, then print the print area.

h. Clear the print area, save the worksheet, close the workbook, then exit Excel.

USING LISTS   EXCEL H-23

Excel 2002 | Practice

▶ Visual Workshop

Create the worksheet shown in Figure H-21. Save the workbook as **Famous Jazz Performers** in the drive and folder where your Project Files are stored. Once you've entered the field names and records, sort the list using two fields. The first sort should be in ascending order by Contribution to Jazz, and the second sort should be in ascending order by Last Name. Change the page setup so that the list is centered on the page horizontally and the header reads "Famous Jazz Performers". Enter your name in the worksheet footer. Preview and print the list, then save the workbook.

FIGURE H-21

	First Name	Last Name	Contribution to Jazz	Lived	Born In	Comments
1						
2	Benny	Goodman	Clarinetist	1909-86	Chicago, IL	"King of Swing"
3	Louis	Armstrong	Trumpeter, Singer	1900-71	New Orleans, LA	Scat singer
4	Billie	Holiday	Vocalist	1915-59	Baltimore, MD	"Lady Day"
5	Ella	Fitzgerald	Vocalist	1918-96	Newport News, VA	Scat singer
6	Duke	Ellington	Composer, Pianist	1899-1974	Washington, D.C.	Jazz into concert halls
7	Fletcher	Henderson	Band Leader	1898-1952	Cuthbert, GA	Novel song arrangements
8	Coleman	Hawkins	Saxophonist	1904-69	St. Joseph, MO	Bebop style of jazz
9	Count	Basie	Band Leader, Pianist	1904-84	Red Bank, NJ	Influential rhythm section

▶ EXCEL H-24   USING LISTS

Project Files List

Read the following information carefully!

It is very important to organize and keep track of the files you need for this book.

1. Find out from your instructor the location of the Project Files you need and the location where you will store your files.

- To complete many of the units in this book, you need to use Project Files. Your instructor will either provide you with a copy of the Project Files or ask you to make your own copy.
- If you need to make a copy of the Project Files, you will need to copy a set of files from a file server, stand-alone computer, or the Web to the drive and folder where you will be storing your Project Files.
- Your instructor will tell you which computer, drive letter, and folders contain the files you need, and where you will store your files.
- You can also download the files by going to www.course.com. See the inside back cover of the book for instructions on how to download your files.

2. Copy and organize your Project Files.

Floppy disk users

- If you are using floppy disks to store your Project Files, the list on the following pages shows which files you'll need to copy onto your disk(s).
- Unless noted in the Project Files List, you will need one formatted, high-density disk for each unit. For each unit you are assigned, copy the files listed in the **Project File Supplied column** onto one disk.
- Make sure you label each disk clearly with the unit name (e.g., Excel Unit A).
- When working through the unit, save all your files to this disk.

Users storing files in other locations

- If you are using a zip drive, network folder, hard drive, or other storage device, use the Project Files List to organize your files.
- Create a subfolder for each unit in the location where you are storing your files, and name it according to the unit title (e.g., Excel Unit A).
- For each unit you are assigned, copy the files listed in the **Project File Supplied column** into that unit's folder.
- Store the files you modify or create for each unit in the unit folder.

3. Find and keep track of your Project Files and completed files.

- Use the **Project File Supplied column** to make sure you have the files you need before starting the unit or exercise indicated in the **Unit and Location column**.
- Use the **Student Saves File As column** to find out the filename you use when saving your changes to a Project File that was provided.
- Use the **Student Creates File column** to find out the filename you use when saving a file you create new for the exercise.

Unit and Location	Project File Supplied	Student Saves File As	Student Creates File
Excel Unit A			
Lessons	EX A-1.xls	MediaLoft Cafe Budget.xls	
Skills Review	EX A-2.xls	MediaLoft Toronto Cafe.xls	MediaLoft Balance Sheet.xls
Independent Challenge 1	(No files provided or created)		
Independent Challenge 2			Sample Payroll.xls
Independent Challenge 3			Training Workbook.xls
			Template Sample.xls
Independent Challenge 4			New Computer Data.xls
Visual Workshop			Carrie's Camera and Darkroom.xls
Excel Unit B			
Lessons	EX B-1.xls	Author Events Forecast.xls	
Skills Review	EX B-2.xls	Office Furnishings.xls	
Independent Challenge 1			Young Brazilians.xls
Independent Challenge 2	EX B-3.xls	Beautiful You Finances.xls	
Independent Challenge 3			Learn-it-All.xls
Independent Challenge 4			Temperature Conversions.xls
Visual Workshop			Annual Budget.xls
Excel Unit C			
Lessons	EX C-1.xls	Ad Expenses.xls	
Skills Review			MediaLoft GB Inventory.xls
	EX C-2.xls	Monthly Operating Expenses.xls	
Independent Challenge 1	EX C-3.xls	BY Inventory.xls	
Independent Challenge 2	EX C-4.xls	Community Action.xls	
Independent Challenge 3			Classic Instruments.xls
Independent Challenge 4			Currency Conversions.xls
Visual Workshop	EX C-5.xls	Projected March Advertising Invoices.xls	
Excel Unit D			
Lessons	EX D-1.xls	MediaLoft Sales - Eastern Division.xls	
Skills Review			MediaLoft Vancouver Software Usage.xls
Independent Challenge 1	EX D-2.xls	Springfield Theater Group.xls	
Independent Challenge 2	EX D-3.xls	BY Expense Charts.xls	
Independent Challenge 3	EX D-4.xls	Bright Light.xls	
Independent Challenge 4			New Location Analysis.xls
Visual Workshop	EX D-5.xls	Quarterly Advertising Budget.xls	

Unit and Location	Project File Supplied	Student Saves File As	Student Creates File
Excel Unit E			
Lessons	EX E-1.xls	Company Data.xls	
Skills Review	EX E-2.xls	Manager Bonuses.xls	
Independent Challenge 1	EX E-3.xls	Mike's Sales.xls	
Independent Challenge 2	EX E-4.xls	Fly Away Sales.xls	
Independent Challenge 3			Custom Fit Loan Options.xls
Independent Challenge 4			IRA Rates.xls
Visual Workshop			Car Payment Calculator.xls
Excel Unit F			
Lessons	EX F-1.xls	Timecard Summary.xls	
Lessons	Pay Rate Classifications.xls		Student creates hyperlink to this file from Timecard Summary file
Lessons		timesum.htm	Student creates from Timecard Summary file
Skills Review	EX F-2.xls	San Francisco Budget.xls	
Skills Review	Expense Details.xls		Student creates hyperlink to this file from San Francisco Budget file
Skills Review		sfbudget.htm	Student creates from San Francisco Budget file
Independent Challenge 1			Software Sales Summary.xls
Independent Challenge 2	EX F-3.xls	Update to Check Register.xls	
Independent Challenge 3			Monthly Long Distance.xls
Independent Challenge 3			Next Door.xls
Independent Challenge 3			Phonebill.xlw (Workspace file student creates from the Monthly Long Distance and Next Door files.)
Independent Challenge 3			Monthly Long Distance -5.xls
Independent Challenge 4			Camera Research file
Independent Challenge 4		camera.htm	Student creates from Camera Research file
Visual Workshop		Martinez.xls	
Visual Workshop		martinez.htm	
Excel Unit G			
Lessons			My Excel Macros.xls
Skills Review			Macros.xls
Independent Challenge 1			Excel Utility Macros.xls
Independent Challenge 2			Header and Footer Stamp.xls
Independent Challenge 3			Computers Inc Macro.xls

PROJECT FILES 3

Unit and Location	Project File Supplied	Student Saves File As	Student Creates File
Independent Challenge 4	EX G-1.xls		Office Supplies.xls
Visual Workshop			File Utility Macros.xls
Excel Unit H			
Lessons	EX H-1.xls	New Customer List.xls	
Skills Review			MediaLoft New York Employee List.xls
Independent Challenge 1			Personalize IT.xls
Independent Challenge 2	EX H-2.xls	Television Shows of the Past.xls	
Independent Challenge 3	EX H-3.xls	Best Films.xls	
Independent Challenge 4			MP3 Titles.xls
Visual Workshop			Famous Jazz Performers.xls

Excel 2002 Core MOUS Objectives

Below is a list of the Microsoft Office User Specialist program objectives for the Core Excel 2002 skills, showing where each MOUS objective is covered in the Lessons and Practice. For more information on which Illustrated titles meet MOUS certification, please see the inside front cover.

MOUS standardized coding number	Activity	Lesson page where skill is covered	Location in lesson where skill is covered	Practice
Ex2002-1	**Working with Cells and Cell Data**			
Ex2002-1-1	Insert, delete and move cells	EXCEL B-19	Clues to Use	Skills Review
		EXCEL C-6	Step 6	Skills Review, Independent Challenge 4
		EXCEL B-12	Step 7	Skills Review
Ex2002-1-2	Enter and edit cell data including text, numbers, and formulas	EXCEL A-10	Steps 1-7 Step 2 Tip	Skills Review, Independent Challenges 2-4
		EXCEL B-4	Steps 2-9	Skills Review
		EXCEL B-6	Steps 1-6	Skills Review, Independent Challenges 1-4
		EXCEL B-8	Steps 1-5 Clues to Use	Skills Review, Independent Challenges 1-4
		EXCEL B-10	Steps 2-9	Skills Review, Independent Challenge 2
		EXCEL C-2	Steps 2-7	Skills Review, Independent Challenges 1-4
		EXCEL C-3	Clues to Use	Skills Review, Independent Challenges 1-4
		EXCEL E-2	Steps 3-5	Skills Review, Independent Challenges 1, 3, 4
		EXCEL E-8	Steps 1-3	Skills Review, Independent Challenges 1, 3
Ex2002-1-3	Check spelling	EXCEL C-16	Steps 1-5	Skills Review, Independent Challenges 1-4
Ex2002-1-4	Find and replace cell data and formats	EXCEL F-15	Clues to Use	Independent Challenge 2
		EXCEL E-2	Step 2	Skills Review
Ex2002-1-5	Work with a subset of data by filtering lists	EXCEL H-5	Clues to Use	Independent Challenge 4
Ex2002-2	**Managing Workbooks**			
Ex2002-2-1	Manage workbook files and folders	EXCEL A-8	Steps 1-3 Step 4 Tip	Skills Review
Ex2002-2-2	Create workbooks using templates	EXCEL A-9	Clues to Use	Independent Challenge 3
Ex2002-2-3	Save workbooks using different names and file formats	EXCEL A-8	Step 4 Tip	Skills Review
		EXCEL A-8	Steps 4-5	Skills Review, Independent Challenges 1-4
		EXCEL F-16	Steps 1-5; Step 1 Tip	Skills Review, Independent Challenges 3-4

MOUS standardized coding number	Activity	Lesson page where skill is covered	Location in lesson where skill is covered	Practice
Ex2002-3	**Formatting and Printing Worksheets**			
Ex2002-3-1	Apply and modify cell formats	EXCEL C-2	Steps 2-7	Skills Review, Independent Challenges 1-4
		EXCEL C-3	Clues to Use	Skills Review
		EXCEL C-4	Steps 2-5	Skills Review, Independent Challenge 2, Visual Workshop
		EXCEL C-6	Steps 1-7	Skills Review, Independent Challenges 1-4, Visual Workshop
		EXCEL C-12	Steps 1-8	Skills Review, Independent Challenges 1, 4, Visual Workshop
		EXCEL C-14	Steps 2-5	Skills Review, Independent Challenges 1, 2, 4, Visual Workshop
Ex2002-3-2	Modify row and column settings	EXCEL C-10	Steps 1-6	Skills Review, Independent Challenges 1, 2
		EXCEL F-2	Steps 1-6	Skills Review
		EXCEL F-8	Steps 1-4	Skills Review
		EXCEL F-9	Table	Skills Review
Ex2002-3-3	Modify row and column formats	EXCEL C-6	Steps 6-7	Skills Review, Independent Challenges 2-4
		EXCEL C-7	Table	Skills Review
		EXCEL C-8	Steps 1-7	Skills Review, Independent Challenges 1-3
		EXCEL C-9	Clues to Use	Independent Challenge 3
Ex2002-3-4	Apply styles	EXCEL E-4	Step 4	Skills Review, Independent Challenge 2
Ex2002-3-5	Use automated tools to format worksheets	EXCEL C-7	Clues to Use	Independent Challenges 3, 4
Ex2002-3-6	Modify Page Setup options for worksheets	EXCEL C-16	Step 8	Independent Challenge 2
		EXCEL D-16	Step 4	Skills Review
		EXCEL E-16	Intro, Step 5 tip, Step 6	Skills Review, Independent Challenges 1, 3, 4, Independent Challenge 2
		EXCEL E-16	Tip Step 7	Independent Challenge 2
		EXCEL E-17	Clues to Use	Independent Challenge 2
		EXCEL F-5	Clues to Use	Skills Review, Independent Challenges 1-4, Visual Workshop
		EXCEL H-16	Step 2	Independent Challenge 2
		EXCEL H-17	Clues to Use	Independent Challenge 4
Ex2002-3-7	Preview and print worksheets and workbooks	EXCEL H-16	Step 2 Tip	Independent Challenge 2
		EXCEL H-17	Clues to Use	Skills Review, Independent Challenge 2

MOUS standardized coding number	Activity	Lesson page where skill is covered	Location in lesson where skill is covered	Practice
Ex2002-4	**Modifying Workbooks**			
Ex2002-4-1	Insert and delete worksheets	EXCEL F-4	Step 1	Skills Review, Independent Challenge 3
		EXCEL F-4	Step 3	Skills Review, Independent Challenge 2
Ex2002-4-2	Modify worksheet names and positions	EXCEL A-12 EXCEL A-12	Step 7 Step 3 Tip, 5-6	Skills Review Skills Review, Independent Challenge 3
Ex2002-4-3	Use 3-D references	EXCEL F-6	Step 3-5	Skills Review, Independent Challenges 1-3
Ex2002-5	**Creating and Revising Formulas**			
Ex2002-5-1	Create and revise formulas	EXCEL B-6	Steps 1-6	Skills Review, Independent Challenges 1, 2, 4, Visual Workshop
		EXCEL B-8	Steps 1-5, Clues to Use	Skills Review, Independent Challenges 1, 2, 4, Visual Workshop
		EXCEL B-10	Steps 4-6	Skills Review, Independent Challenge 2
		EXCEL B-14	All	Skills Review, Independent Challenges 1, 4
		EXCEL B-16	Steps 1-6	Skills Review, Independent Challenges 1, 4, Visual Workshop
		EXCEL B-18	Steps 4-7	Skills Review, Independent Challenges 1, 4, Visual Workshop
		EXCEL E-2	Steps 3-5	Skills Review, Independent Challenges 1,2
		EXCEL E-12	Steps 1-3	Skills Review
Ex2002-5-2	Use statistical, date and time, financial, and logical functions in formulas	EXCEL B-10 EXCEL B-11 EXCEL E-2 EXCEL E-8	Steps 1-4, 6 Clues to Use Steps 3-5 Steps 1-2	Independent Challenge 2 Skills Review Skills Review Skills Review, Independent Challenge 1
		EXCEL E-10 EXCEL E-12	Steps 1-4 Steps 1-8	Skills Review Skills Review, Independent Challenge 4
		EXCEL E-14	Steps 1-3	Skills Review, Independent Challenge 3, Visual Workshop
		EXCEL E-15	Clues to Use	Independent Challenge 4
Ex2002-6	**Creating and Modifying Graphics**			
Ex2002-6-1	Create, modify, position and print charts	EXCEL D-4	Steps 2-7	Skills Review, Independent Challenges 1-4
		EXCEL D-6	Steps 3-8	Skills Review, Visual Workshop
		EXCEL D-8	Steps 3-6	Skills Review, Independent Challenges 1-4
		EXCEL D-10	Steps 1-6	Skills Review, Independent Challenges 1-4
		EXCEL D-12	Steps 1-8	Skills Review, Independent Challenges 1, 3
		EXCEL D-14	Steps 1-8	Skills Review, Independent Challenges 2, 3, Visual Workshop
		EXCEL D-16	Steps 2-7	Skills Review, Independent Challenges 1-4, Visual Workshop
		EXCEL D-17	Clues to Use	

MOUS standardized coding number	Activity	Lesson page where skill is covered	Location in lesson where skill is covered	Practice
Ex2002-6-2	Create, modify and position graphics	EXCEL C-5 EXCEL D-14	Clues to Use Steps 1-8	Independent Challenge 3 Skills Review, Independent Challenges 2, 3, Visual Workshop
Ex2002-7	**Workgroup Collaboration**			
Ex2002-7-1	Convert worksheets into Web pages	EXCEL F-16	Steps 1-8	Skills Review, Independent Challenge 4, Visual Workshop
Ex2002-7-2	Create hyperlinks	EXCEL F-14	Steps 3-7	Skills Review, Independent Challenges 3, 4, Visual Workshop
		EXCEL F-14	Clues to Use	Skills Review, Independent Challenge 3
Ex2002-7-3	View and edit comments	EXCEL C-11 EXCEL F-17	Clues to Use Clues to Use	Skills Review Skills Review

Glossary

Excel 2002

3-D references A reference that uses values on other sheets or workbooks, effectively creating another dimension to a workbook.

Absolute reference A cell reference that contains a dollar sign before the column letter and/or row number to indicate the absolute, or fixed, contents of specific cells. For example, the formula $A$1+$B$1 calculates only the sum of these specific cells no matter where the formula is copied in the workbook.

Active cell The current location of the cell pointer.

Address See *Cell address*.

Alignment The placement of cell contents; for example, left, center, or right.

Area chart A line chart in which each area is given a solid color or pattern to emphasize the relationship between the pieces of charted information.

Arguments Information that a function needs to create an answer. In an expression, multiple arguments are separated by commas. All of the arguments are enclosed in parentheses; for example, =SUM(A1:B1).

Argument ToolTip A yellow box that appears as you build a function; shows function elements, which you can click to display online help for each one.

Arithmetic operator A symbol used in a formula (such as + or -, / or *) to perform mathematical operations.

Ask a Question box The list box at the right end of the menu bar in which you can type or select questions for the Help system.

Attribute The styling features such as bold, italics, and underlining that can be applied to cell contents.

AutoComplete A feature that automatically completes entries based on other entries in the same column.

AutoFill A feature that creates a series of text entries or numbers when a range is selected using the fill handle.

AutoFit A feature that automatically adjusts the width of a column to accommodate its widest entry when the boundary to the right of the column selector is double-clicked.

AutoFormat Preset schemes that can be applied to format a range instantly. Excel comes with 16 AutoFormats that include colors, fonts, and numeric formatting.

AutoSum A feature that automatically creates totals using the SUM function when you click the AutoSum button.

Background color The color applied to the background of a cell.

Bar chart A chart that shows information as a series of horizontal bars.

Border The edge of a cell, an area of a worksheet, or a selected object; you can change its color or line style.

Cancel button The X in the Formula bar; it removes information from the formula bar and restores the previous cell entry.

Cell The intersection of a column and row in a worksheet, datasheet, or table.

Cell address The location of a cell expressed by the column and row coordinates; the cell address of the cell in column A, row 1, is A1.

Cell pointer A highlighted rectangle around a cell that indicates the active cell.

Cell reference The address or name that identifies a cell's position in a worksheet; it consists of a letter that identifies the cell's column and a number that identifies its row; for example, cell B3. Cell references in worksheets can be used in formulas and are relative or absolute.

Chart A graphic representation of worksheet information. Types include 2-D and 3-D column, bar, pie, area, and line charts.

Chart sheet A separate sheet that contains only a chart linked to worksheet data.

Chart title The name assigned to a chart.

Chart Wizard A series of dialog boxes that helps you create or modify a chart.

Circular reference A formula that refers to its own cell location.

Clear A command on the Edit menu used to erase a cell's contents, formatting, or both.

Clipboard A temporary storage area for cut or copied items that are available for pasting. See *Office Clipboard*.

Clipboard task pane A task pane that shows the contents of the Office Clipboard; contains options for copying and pasting items.

Close A command that closes the file so you can no longer work with it, but keeps Excel open so that you can continue to work on other workbooks.

Column chart The default chart type in Excel, which displays information as a series of vertical columns.

Column heading The gray box containing the letter above the column.

Complex formula An equation that uses more than one type of arithmetic operator.

Conditional format A cell format that is based on the cell's value or the outcome of a formula.

Consolidate To combine values on multiple worksheets and show the result on another worksheet.

Control menu box A box in the upper-left corner of a window used to resize or close a window.

Copy A command that copies the selected cell's contents and places them on the Clipboard.

Cut A command that removes the cell contents from the selected area of a worksheet and places them on the Clipboard.

Database An organized collection of related information. In Excel, a database is called a list.

Data entry area The unlocked portion of a worksheet where users are able to enter and change data.

Data form In an Excel list (or database), a dialog box that displays one record at a time.

Excel 2002 — Glossary

Data Marker A graphical representation of a data point, such as a bar or column.

Data point Individual piece of data plotted in a chart.

Data series The selected range in a worksheet that Excel converts into a graphic and displays as a chart.

Delete A command that removes cell contents from a worksheet.

Dialog box A window that opens when a program needs more information to carry out a command.

Dummy column/row Blank column or row included at the end of a range that enables a formula to adjust when columns or rows are added or deleted.

Dynamic page breaks In a larger workbook, horizontal or vertical dashed lines that represent the place where pages print separately. They also adjust automatically when you insert or delete rows or columns, or change column widths or row heights.

Edit A change made to the contents of a cell or worksheet.

Electronic spreadsheet A computer program that performs calculations on data and organizes information into worksheets. A worksheet is divided into columns and rows, which form individual cells.

Enter button The check mark in the formula bar used to confirm an entry.

Exploding pie slice A slice of a pie chart that has been pulled away from the whole pie to add emphasis.

External reference indicator The exclamation point (!) used in a formula to indicate that a referenced cell is outside the active sheet.

Field In a list (an Excel database), a column that describes a characteristic about records, such as first name or city.

Field name A column label that describes a field.

Fill color The cell background color.

Fill Down A command that duplicates the contents of the selected cells in the range selected below the cell pointer.

Fill handle A small square in the lower-right corner of the active cell used to copy cell contents.

Fill Right A command that duplicates the contents of the selected cells in the range selected to the right of the cell pointer.

Find A command used to locate information the user specifies.

Find & Replace A command used to find one set of information and replace it with new information.

Floating toolbar A toolbar within its own window, not anchored along an edge of the worksheet.

Font The typeface or design of a set of characters.

Font size The size of characters, measured in units called points (pts).

Footer Information that prints at the bottom of each printed page; on the screen, a footer is visible only in Print Preview. To add a footer, use the Header and Footer command on the View menu.

Format The appearance of text and numbers, including color, font, attributes, borders, and shading. See also *Number format*.

Format Painter A feature used to copy the formatting applied to one set of text or in one cell to another.

Formatting toolbar A toolbar that contains buttons for frequently used formatting commands.

Formula A set of instructions used to perform numeric calculations (adding, multiplying, averaging, etc.).

Formula bar The area below the menu bar and above the Excel workspace where you enter and edit data in a worksheet cell. The formula bar becomes active when you start typing or editing cell data. It includes the Enter button and the Cancel button.

Formula prefix An arithmetic symbol, such as the equal sign (=), used to start a formula.

Freeze To keep columns or rows in place so they remain visible while other parts of the worksheet are viewed.

Function A special, predefined formula that provides a shortcut for a commonly used calculation; for example, AVERAGE.

Function Wizard A feature that provides assistance in entering the arguments for a selected function.

Gridlines Horizontal and/or vertical lines within a chart that make the chart easier to read.

Header Information that prints at the top of each worksheet in a workbook. To add a header, use the Header and Footer command on the View menu.

Help system A utility that gives you immediate access to definitions, steps, explanations, and useful tips.

Hide To make rows, columns, formulas, or sheets invisible to workbook users.

Hyperlink Text or an object in a document that, when clicked, opens another document, worksheet or Web page.

Hypertext Markup Language (HTML) The language used to describe the content and format of Web pages.

Input Information that produces desired results, or output, in a worksheet.

Insertion point The blinking vertical line that appears in the formula bar or in a cell during editing in Excel.

Intranet An internal computer network that is used by a group of people, such as employees in a company's office.

Keyword A representative word on which the Help system can search to find information on your area of interest.

Label Descriptive text or other information that identifies the rows and columns of a worksheet. Labels are not included in calculations.

Label prefix A character, such as the apostrophe, that identifies an entry as a label and controls the way it appears in the cell.

Landscape orientation A print setting that positions the worksheet on the page so the page is wider than it is tall.

Legend A key explaining how information is represented by colors or patterns in a chart.

Line chart A graph of data that is mapped by a series of lines. Line charts show changes in data or categories of data over time and can be used to document trends.

Glossary

Linking The dynamic referencing of data in other workbooks, so that when data in the other workbooks is changed, the references in the current workbook are automatically updated.

List The Excel term for a database, an organized collection of related information.

Lock To secure a row, column, or sheet so that data therein cannot be changed.

Logical test The first part of an IF function; if the logical test is true, then the second part of the function is applied, and if it is false, then the third part of the function is applied. In the function IF (Balance>1000, Balance*0.05,0), 5% of the balance is calculated if the balance exceeds $1,000.

Macro A set of instructions, or code, that performs tasks in the order you specify.

Menu bar The bar beneath the title bar that contains the names of menus, that when clicked, open menus from which you choose program commands.

Mixed reference A formula containing both a relative and absolute reference.

Mode indicator A box located at the lower-left corner of the status bar that informs you of a program's status. For example, when Excel is performing a task, the word "Wait" appears.

Module A program container attached to a workbook that holds a macro.

Mouse pointer A symbol that indicates the current location of the mouse on the desktop. The mouse pointer changes its shape to indicate what you can do next; for example, when you insert data, select a range, position a chart, change the size of a window or a column, or select a topic in Help.

Moving border The dashed line that appears around a cell or range that is copied to the Clipboard.

Name box The left-most area in the formula bar that shows the cell reference or name of the active cell. For example, A1 refers to cell A1 of the active worksheet. You can also display a list of names in a workbook using the Name list arrow.

Named range A range of cells given a meaningful name; it retains its name when moved and can be referenced in a formula.

New workbook task pane A task pane that lets you quickly open new or existing workbooks.

Number format A format applied to values to express numeric concepts, such as currency, date, and percentage.

Object A chart or graphic image that can be moved and resized and that contains handles when selected.

Office Assistant An animated character that appears to offer tips, answer questions, and provide access to a program's Help system.

Office Assistant tip A hint, indicated by the appearance of an onscreen light bulb, about the current action you are performing.

Office Clipboard A temporary storage area shared by all Office programs that can be used to cut, copy and paste multiple items within and between Office programs. The Office Clipboard can hold up to 24 items collected from any Office program. See also *Clipboard task pane*.

Open A command that retrieves a file from a disk and displays it on the screen.

Order of precedence The order in which Excel calculates parts of a formula: (1) exponents, (2) multiplication and division, and (3) addition and subtraction.

Output The end result of a worksheet.

Panes Sections into which you can divide a worksheet when you want to work on separate parts of the worksheet at the same time; one pane freezes, or remains in place, while you scroll in another pane until you see the desired information.

Paste A command that copies information on the Clipboard to a new location. Excel pastes the formula, rather than the result, unless the Paste Special command is used.

Paste Function A series of dialog boxes that helps you build functions; it lists and describes all Excel functions.

Paste Options Button A button that appears after an item is pasted; click its list arrow to keep source formatting, match destination cell formatting or keep the source cell's column widths.

Personal Macro Workbook A place to store commonly used macros that are available to all workbooks.

Pie chart A circular chart that represents data as slices of a pie. A pie chart is useful for showing the relationship of parts to a whole; pie slices can be extracted for emphasis. See also *Exploding pie slice*.

Plot area The area inside the horizontal and vertical chart axes.

Point A unit of measure used for fonts and row height. One inch equals 72 points, or a point is equal to $1/72$ of an inch.

Pointing method Specifying formula cell references by selecting the desired cell with the mouse instead of typing its cell reference; it eliminates typing errors. Also known as Pointing.

Portrait orientation A print setting that positions the worksheet on the page so the page is taller than it is wide.

Precedence Algebraic rules that Excel uses to determine the order of calculations in a formula with more than one operator.

Print Preview A command you can use to view a worksheet as it will look when printed. Also known as Previewing a worksheet.

Print title In a list that spans more than one page, the field names that print at the top of every printed page.

Program Task-oriented software (such as Excel) that enables you to perform a certain type of task, such as data calculation.

Program Code Program instructions used to create a macro.

Programs menu The Windows 95/98/ME/2000 Start menu that lists all available programs on your computer.

Publish Excel data Place a workbook or worksheet on a network or the Web.

Range A selected group of adjacent cells.

Range finder A feature that outlines an equation's arguments in blue and green.

Range format A format applied to a selected range in a worksheet.

Record In a list (an Excel database), data about an object or a person.

GLOSSARY 11

Excel 2002 — Glossary

Replace A command used to find one set of criteria and replace it with new information.

Relative cell reference A type of cell reference used to indicate a relative position in the worksheet. It allows you to copy and move formulas from one area to another of the same dimensions. Excel automatically changes the column and row numbers to reflect the new position. Also known as Relative reference.

Row height The vertical dimension of a cell.

Row heading The gray box containing the row number to the left of the row.

Run a macro Test or execute a macro.

Save To store a file permanently on a disk or to overwrite the copy of a file that is stored on a disk with the changes made to the file.

Save As Command used to save a file for the first time or to create a new file with a different filename, leaving the original file intact.

Selection handles Small boxes appearing along the corners and sides of charts and graphic images that are used for moving and resizing.

Series of labels Preprogrammed series, such as days of the week and months of the year. They are formed by typing the first word of the series, then dragging the fill handle to the desired cell.

Sheet A term used for a worksheet.

Sheet tab A description at the bottom of each worksheet that identifies it in a workbook. In an open workbook, move to a worksheet by clicking its sheet tab. Also known as Worksheet tab.

Sheet tab scrolling buttons Buttons that enable you to move among sheets within a workbook.

Sort keys Criteria on which a sort, or a reordering of data, is based.

Spelling check A command that attempts to match all text in a worksheet with the words in the dictionary.

Standard toolbar A toolbar that contains buttons for frequently used operating and editing commands.

Start To open a software program so you can use it.

Status bar The bar at the bottom of the Excel window that provides information about various keys, commands, and processes.

Style A combination of formatting characteristics.

SUM The most frequently used function, this adds columns or rows of cells.

Target The file that a hyperlink displays when you click it.

Task pane A window area to the right of the worksheet that provides worksheet options, such as creating a new workbook, conducting a search, inserting Clip Art, and using the Office Clipboard.

Template An Excel file saved with a special format that lets you open a new file based on an existing workbook's design and/or content.

Text annotations Labels added to a chart to draw attention to a particular area.

Text color The color applied to text in a cell or on a chart.

Tick marks Notations of a scale of measure on a chart axis.

Title bar The bar at the top of the program window that indicates the program name and the name of the current file.

Toggle button A button that turns a feature on and off.

Toolbar A bar that contains buttons that you can click to perform commands.

Toolbar Options button A button you click on a toolbar to view toolbar buttons not currently visible.

Truncate To shorten the display of cell information because a cell is too wide.

Values Numbers, formulas, or functions used in calculations.

Value axis Also known as the y-axis in a 2-dimensional chart, this area often contains numerical values that help you interpret the size of chart elements.

View A set of display and/or print settings that you can name and save for access at another time. You can save multiple views of a worksheet.

What-if analysis A decision-making feature in which data is changed and formulas based on it are automatically recalculated.

Wildcard Character A special symbol you use in defining search criteria in the data form or Replace dialog box. The most common types of wildcards are the question mark (?), which stands for any single character, and the asterisk (*), which represents any group of characters.

Window A rectangular area of a screen where you view and work on the open file.

Workbook A collection of related worksheets contained within a single file.

Worksheet An electronic spreadsheet containing 256 columns by 65,536 rows.

Worksheet menu bar The toolbar at the top of the Excel screen.

Worksheet tab See *Sheet tab*.

Workspace A group of workbooks that can be opened in one step.

World Wide Web (Web) A structure of documents, called pages, connected by hyperlinks over a large computer network called the Internet.

X-axis The horizontal axis in a chart; because it often shows data categories, such as months, it is also called the category axis.

X-axis label A label describing a chart's x-axis.

Y-axis The vertical axis in a chart; because it often shows numerical values in a 2 dimensional chart, it is also called the value axis.

Y-axis label A label describing the y-axis of a chart.

Zoom A feature that enables you to focus on a larger or smaller part of the worksheet in Print Preview.

Index

Special Characters

\> (greater than operator), EXCEL E-11
< (less than operator), EXCEL E-11
(hash mark), EXCEL C-8
$ (dollar sign), EXCEL C-2
% (percent sign), EXCEL B-7
' (apostrophe), EXCEL A-10
* (asterisk), EXCEL B-7, EXCEL H-8
\+ (plus sign), EXCEL B-7
– (minus sign), EXCEL B-7
/ (slash), EXCEL B-7
= (equal sign), EXCEL B-6
= (equal to operator), EXCEL E-11
? (question mark), EXCEL H-8
^ (caret), EXCEL B-7

A

absolute cell references, EXCEL B-14–15
   copying formulas, EXCEL B-18–19
active cells, EXCEL A-6
addition operator (+), EXCEL B-7
addresses, cells, inserting, EXCEL E-12
Ad View dialog box, EXCEL F-10, EXCEL F-11
alignment
   changing, EXCEL C-6, EXCEL C-7
   printing worksheets, EXCEL E-17
annotating charts, EXCEL D-14, EXCEL D-15
apostrophes ('), numbers not part of calculations, EXCEL A-10
area charts, EXCEL D-3
arithmetic operators, EXCEL B-6, EXCEL B-7
ascending order, EXCEL H-13
Ask a Question list arrow, EXCEL A-16, EXCEL A-17
asterisk (*)
   multiplication operator, EXCEL B-7
   wildcard, EXCEL H-8
attributes, changing, EXCEL C-6, EXCEL C-7
AutoCalculate feature, EXCEL E-6
AutoCorrect feature, EXCEL C-16
AutoFill, EXCEL B-16
AutoFilter, EXCEL H-5
AutoFit Selection command, EXCEL C-8
AutoFormat dialog box, EXCEL C-7
AutoFormat feature, EXCEL C-7
automating tasks. See macro(s)
AutoSum button, EXCEL B-10
AutoSum function, generating multiple totals, EXCEL E-6–7
AVERAGE function, EXCEL B-11, EXCEL E-13

B

backups, EXCEL H-12
bar charts, EXCEL D-3, EXCEL D-8, EXCEL D-9
Between option, conditional formatting, EXCEL C-15
Blank Workbook button, EXCEL A-9
Bold button, EXCEL C-7
borders, EXCEL C-12, EXCEL C-13
Bottom Border button, EXCEL C-13
buttons. See also specific buttons
   toolbars, EXCEL A-7

C

calculations
   AutoCalculate feature, EXCEL E-6
   future value, EXCEL E-15
   generating multiple totals, EXCEL E-6–7
   Paste Special command, EXCEL E-3
   payments, EXCEL E-14–15
   using dates, EXCEL E-8–9
capitalization, sorting, EXCEL H-14
caret (^), exponent operator, EXCEL B-7
case sensitivity, sorting, EXCEL H-14
category axis, EXCEL D-2, EXCEL D-3
cell(s), EXCEL A-6, EXCEL A-7
   active, EXCEL A-6
   addresses. See cell addresses
   columns. See column(s)
   contiguous, selecting, EXCEL C-2
   deleting, EXCEL B-19
   entries. See cell entries
   filling with sequential text/values, EXCEL B-17
   inserting, EXCEL B-19
   locking/unlocking, EXCEL F-8, EXCEL F-9
   names. See cell names
   ranges. See range(s)
   references. See cell references
cell addresses, EXCEL A-6
   inserting, EXCEL E-12
cell entries
   copying, EXCEL B-12, EXCEL B-13
   editing, EXCEL B-4–5
   indenting, EXCEL C-6
   moving, EXCEL B-12, EXCEL B-13
   rotating, EXCEL C-6
cell names
   deleting, EXCEL E-4
   listing, EXCEL E-5
cell pointer, EXCEL A-6, EXCEL A-7
cell references
   absolute, EXCEL B-14–15, EXCEL B-18–19
   circular, correcting, EXCEL E-11
   mixed, EXCEL B-15
   relative, EXCEL B-14–15, EXCEL B-16–17
   3-D references, EXCEL F-6–7
cell referencing, EXCEL B-6
chart(s), EXCEL A-2, EXCEL D-1–17
   annotating, EXCEL D-14, EXCEL D-15
   creating, EXCEL D-4–5
   drawing on, EXCEL D-14, EXCEL D-15
   editing, EXCEL D-8–9
   enhancing, EXCEL D-12–13
   formatting, EXCEL D-10–11
   moving, EXCEL D-6, EXCEL D-7
   Page Setup dialog box, EXCEL D-17
   planning and designing, EXCEL D-2–3
   previewing, EXCEL D-16, EXCEL D-17
   printing, EXCEL D-16, EXCEL D-17
   resizing, EXCEL D-6, EXCEL D-7
   text alignment, EXCEL D-13
   types, EXCEL D-3
Chart menu, EXCEL D-6
chart objects, EXCEL D-6
   identifying, EXCEL D-7
Chart Options dialog box, EXCEL D-10, EXCEL D-11
chart type buttons, EXCEL D-8
Chart Wizard, EXCEL D-4–5
circular references, correcting, EXCEL E-11
clearing formatting, EXCEL C-6
clip art, inserting, EXCEL C-5
Close command, File menu, EXCEL A-19
closing workbooks, EXCEL A-18, EXCEL A-19
Collapse dialog box, EXCEL E-12, EXCEL E-13
Collapse dialog box button, EXCEL B-10, EXCEL B-11
colors, EXCEL C-12, EXCEL C-13
column(s)
   adjusting widths, EXCEL C-8–9
   deleting, EXCEL C-10, EXCEL C-11
   freezing, EXCEL F-2, EXCEL F-3
   headings, EXCEL C-8, EXCEL C-9
   hiding/unhiding, EXCEL F-9
   inserting, EXCEL C-10, EXCEL C-11
   worksheet window, EXCEL A-6, EXCEL A-7
column charts, EXCEL D-3
combination charts, EXCEL D-3
comments
   adding and editing in worksheets, EXCEL C-11
   adding to macros, EXCEL G-9
comparison operators, EXCEL E-11
   searching using data forms, EXCEL H-8
complex formulas, EXCEL B-8–9
conditional formatting, EXCEL C-14–15
   deleting, EXCEL C-15
Conditional Formatting dialog box, EXCEL C-14, EXCEL C-15
conditional formulas, building with IF function, EXCEL E-10–11
copying
   cell entries, EXCEL B-12, EXCEL B-13
   formulas using absolute cell references, EXCEL B-18–19
   formulas using relative cell references, EXCEL B-16–17
   macros, EXCEL G-12
   worksheets, EXCEL A-13, EXCEL F-4
Copy pointer, EXCEL A-11
COUNTA function, EXCEL E-12, EXCEL E-13
COUNT function, EXCEL B-11, EXCEL E-12, EXCEL E-13
custom formats, numbers and dates, EXCEL E-9
Customize dialog box, EXCEL G-14, EXCEL G-15
customizing, toolbars, EXCEL G-16

INDEX 13

Index

custom menus, EXCEL G-14
custom sort order, EXCEL H-15
Custom Views dialog box, EXCEL F-10, EXCEL F-11

▶ D

data, finding in worksheets, EXCEL F-15
databases. *See also* lists
    lists versus, EXCEL H-3
data entry area, EXCEL F-8
data forms
    adding records to lists, EXCEL H-6–7
    editing records in lists, EXCEL H-10–11
    finding records, EXCEL H-8–9
data markers, EXCEL D-2, EXCEL D-3
data points, EXCEL D-2, EXCEL D-3
data series, EXCEL D-2, EXCEL D-3
date(s)
    calculations using, EXCEL E-8–9
    custom formats, EXCEL E-9
    formats, EXCEL C-2, EXCEL C-3
    inserting in worksheets, EXCEL E-8
decimal places, EXCEL C-2
Delete command, EXCEL C-10
Delete Conditional Formatting dialog box, EXCEL C-14
Delete dialog box, EXCEL H-10, EXCEL H-11
deleting. *See also* removing
    cell and range names, EXCEL E-4
    cells, EXCEL B-19
    columns, EXCEL C-10, EXCEL C-11
    conditional formatting, EXCEL C-15
    macros, EXCEL G-6
    records in lists, EXCEL H-10–11
    rows, EXCEL C-10, EXCEL C-11
    worksheets, EXCEL A-12
    worksheets in workbooks, EXCEL F-4, EXCEL F-5
descending order, EXCEL H-13
designing
    charts, EXCEL D-16, EXCEL D-17
    worksheets, EXCEL B-2–3
Diagonal resizing pointer, EXCEL D-7
discussion comments in worksheets, EXCEL F-17
displaying formula contents, EXCEL E-16, EXCEL E-17
division operator (/), EXCEL B-7
dollar signs ($), EXCEL C-2
drag-and-drop technique, copying cell entries, EXCEL B-12, EXCEL B-13
drawing on charts, EXCEL D-14, EXCEL D-15
Draw resizing pointer, EXCEL D-7
drop shadows, charts, EXCEL D-12, EXCEL D-13
dynamic page breaks, EXCEL F-12

▶ E

editing
    cell entries, EXCEL B-4–5
    charts, EXCEL D-8–9
    comments, EXCEL C-11
    formulas, EXCEL B-8
    macros, EXCEL G-8–9
electronic spreadsheets, EXCEL A-2–3. *See also* worksheets
    advantages, EXCEL A-2
    business uses, EXCEL A-3
e-mail, sending workbooks, EXCEL C-16

entering. *See also* inserting
    formulas, EXCEL B-6–7, EXCEL E-3
    values, EXCEL E-3
equal sign (=), formulas, EXCEL B-6
equal to operator (=), EXCEL E-11
Equal To option, EXCEL C-15
error correction
    spelling errors, EXCEL C-16–17
    typing errors, EXCEL A-10, EXCEL B-6, EXCEL B-8
Excel 2002
    exiting, EXCEL A-18, EXCEL A-19
    starting, EXCEL A-4–5
Exit command, File menu, EXCEL A-18, EXCEL A-19
exiting Excel, EXCEL A-18, EXCEL A-19
exploding pie slices, EXCEL D-15
exponent operator (^), EXCEL B-7

▶ F

fields in lists, EXCEL H-2
    multiple, sorting on, EXCEL H-14–15
    names, EXCEL H-4, EXCEL H-5
    single, sorting on, EXCEL H-12–13
file properties, workbooks, changing, EXCEL F-9
fill handle, EXCEL A-11, EXCEL B-16, EXCEL B-17
filtering lists using AutoFilter, EXCEL H-5
Find and Replace dialog box, EXCEL H-8, EXCEL H-9
finding
    clip art, EXCEL C-5
    records in lists, EXCEL H-8–9
    worksheet data and formats, EXCEL F-15
fonts, EXCEL C-4, EXCEL C-5
    sizes, EXCEL C-4, EXCEL C-5
footers, worksheets, EXCEL F-5
format(s)
    custom, numbers and dates, EXCEL E-9
    finding in worksheets, EXCEL F-15
Format Cells dialog box, EXCEL C-2, EXCEL C-3, EXCEL C-4, EXCEL C-5, EXCEL C-12, EXCEL C-13, EXCEL F-8, EXCEL F-9
Format Data Series dialog box, EXCEL D-10, EXCEL D-11
Format Painter button, EXCEL C-3
Format Tab Color dialog box, EXCEL A-12, EXCEL A-13
formatting
    charts, EXCEL D-10–11
    clearing, EXCEL C-6
    worksheets. *See* formatting worksheets
formatting shortcuts, EXCEL C-6
Formatting toolbar, EXCEL A-6, EXCEL A-7, EXCEL C-7
formatting worksheets, EXCEL C-1–17
    alignment, EXCEL C-6, EXCEL C-7
    attributes, EXCEL C-6, EXCEL C-7
    borders, EXCEL C-12, EXCEL C-13
    colors, EXCEL C-12, EXCEL C-13
    column widths, EXCEL C-8–9
    conditional formatting, EXCEL C-14–15
    deleting rows and columns, EXCEL C-10, EXCEL C-11
    fonts, EXCEL C-4–5
    inserting rows and columns, EXCEL C-10, EXCEL C-11
    patterns, EXCEL C-12, EXCEL C-13
    spell checking, EXCEL C-16–17
    values, EXCEL C-2–3

formula(s), EXCEL B-6–9, EXCEL E-1. *See also* calculations
    complex, EXCEL B-8–9
    conditional, building with IF function, EXCEL E-10–11
    copying, EXCEL B-16–17
    displaying and printing contents, EXCEL E-16–17
    editing, EXCEL B-8
    entering, EXCEL B-6–7, EXCEL E-3
    hiding/unhiding, EXCEL F-9
    names, EXCEL E-4–5
    order of precedence, EXCEL B-9
formula bar, EXCEL A-6, EXCEL A-7
formula prefixes, EXCEL B-6
freezing, columns and rows, EXCEL F-2
functions, EXCEL B-10–11, EXCEL E-1. *See also* calculations; specific functions
    modifying range, EXCEL B-10
    with several operators, EXCEL E-2
    statistical, EXCEL E-12–13
future value, calculating, EXCEL E-15
FV function, EXCEL E-15

▶ G

greater than operator (>), EXCEL E-11
gridlines, EXCEL D-10, EXCEL D-11

▶ H

hash mark (#), long values, EXCEL C-8
header(s), worksheets, EXCEL F-5
Header dialog box, EXCEL F-5
Help system, EXCEL A-16–17
    printing topics, EXCEL A-16, EXCEL A-17
Hide command, EXCEL C-8
hiding areas in worksheets, EXCEL F-8, EXCEL F-9
Horizontal resizing pointer, EXCEL D-7
hyperlinks
    navigating large worksheets using, EXCEL F-14
    removing, EXCEL F-14
    workbooks, EXCEL F-14–15
Hypertext Markup Language (HTML), EXCEL F-16

▶ I

I-beam pointer, EXCEL A-11
identifying chart objects, EXCEL D-7
IF function, building conditional formulas, EXCEL E-10–11
indenting cell entries, EXCEL C-6
Insert dialog box, EXCEL C-10, EXCEL C-11
Insert Function dialog box, EXCEL E-2, EXCEL E-3
Insert Hyperlink dialog box, EXCEL F-14, EXCEL F-15
inserting
    cell addresses, EXCEL E-12
    cells, EXCEL B-19
    clip art, EXCEL C-5
    columns, EXCEL C-10, EXCEL C-11
    hyperlinks in workbooks, EXCEL F-14, EXCEL F-15
    rows, EXCEL C-10, EXCEL C-11
    worksheets in workbooks, EXCEL F-4, EXCEL F-5
intranets, EXCEL F-16
Italic button, EXCEL C-7

▶ K

keywords
    Help system, EXCEL A-16
    searching for clip art, EXCEL C-5

Index

L

label(s), EXCEL A-10, EXCEL A-11
Label Ranges dialog box, EXCEL E-4
Left Border button, EXCEL C-13
legends, charts, EXCEL D-2, EXCEL D-3
less than operator (<), EXCEL E-11
line charts, EXCEL D-3
linking, workbooks. *See* workbook(s)
lists, EXCEL H-1–17
   adding records with data form, EXCEL H-6–7
   creating, EXCEL H-4–5
   databases versus, EXCEL H-3
   deleting records, EXCEL H-10–11
   fields, EXCEL H-2
   filtering using AutoFilter, EXCEL H-5
   finding records, EXCEL H-8–9
   planning, EXCEL H-2–3
   printing, EXCEL H-16–17
   sorting. *See* sorting lists
locking cells, EXCEL F-8, EXCEL F-9
logical tests, EXCEL E-10

M

macro(s), EXCEL G-1–17
   adding as menu items, EXCEL G-14–15
   adding comments, EXCEL G-9
   copying, EXCEL G-12
   deleting, EXCEL G-6
   editing, EXCEL G-8–9
   moving, EXCEL G-12
   naming, EXCEL G-2
   Personal Macro Workbook, EXCEL G-12–13
   planning, EXCEL G-2–3
   recording, EXCEL G-4–5
   running, EXCEL G-6–7
   security level, EXCEL G-6
   shortcut keys, EXCEL G-10–11
   stopping execution, EXCEL G-6
   toolbars for macros, EXCEL G-16–17
   viruses, EXCEL G-3
Macro dialog box, EXCEL G-6, EXCEL G-7
margins, printing worksheets, EXCEL E-17
mathematical operations, order of precedence, EXCEL B-9
MAX function, EXCEL B-11, EXCEL E-12, EXCEL E-13
MEDIAN function, EXCEL E-13
menu(s)
   adding macros as menu items, EXCEL G-14–15
   custom, EXCEL G-14
menu bar, EXCEL A-6, EXCEL A-7
MIN function, EXCEL B-11, EXCEL E-12, EXCEL E-13
minus sign (–), subtraction operator, EXCEL B-7
mixed cell references, EXCEL B-15
mode indicator, EXCEL B-4
modules, macros, EXCEL G-8, EXCEL G-9
Move or Copy dialog box, EXCEL A-13
Move pointer, EXCEL A-11
moving
   cell entries, EXCEL B-12, EXCEL B-13
   charts, EXCEL D-6, EXCEL D-7
   macros, EXCEL G-12
   worksheets, EXCEL A-12, EXCEL A-13

multiple panes, EXCEL F-3
multiple worksheets
   previewing and printing, EXCEL F-4
   printing, EXCEL H-16
multiplication operator (×), EXCEL B-7

N

name(s)
   cell ranges, EXCEL E-4
   cells. *See* cell names
   fields in lists, EXCEL H-4, EXCEL H-5
   formulas, EXCEL E-4–5
   macros, EXCEL G-2
   ranges, deleting, EXCEL E-4
   worksheets, EXCEL A-12, EXCEL A-13
name box, EXCEL A-6, EXCEL A-7
navigating worksheets, EXCEL A-11
   large worksheets, EXCEL F-14
New button, EXCEL A-8
New Toolbar dialog box, EXCEL G-16, EXCEL G-17
new workbook panes, EXCEL A-6
No Border button, EXCEL C-13
Normal pointer, EXCEL A-11
Not Between option, conditional formatting, EXCEL C-15
Not Equal To option, EXCEL C-15
number(s)
   custom formats, EXCEL E-9
   formatting in lists, EXCEL H-2, EXCEL H-4
   pages in worksheets, EXCEL F-12, EXCEL F-13

O

objects, EXCEL D-6
Office Assistant, EXCEL A-16, EXCEL A-17
   changing, EXCEL A-16
   opening, EXCEL A-16
Office Assistant Tips, EXCEL A-16, EXCEL A-17
Office Clipboard
   opening, EXCEL B-12
   using, EXCEL B-13
Open button, EXCEL A-8, EXCEL A-9
Open dialog box, EXCEL B-4
opening
   Clipboard, EXCEL B-12
   Office Assistant, EXCEL A-16
   workbooks, EXCEL A-8, EXCEL A-9
Options dialog box, EXCEL E-16, EXCEL E-17
order of precedence, formulas, EXCEL B-9

P

Page Break Preview, EXCEL F-13
page breaks in worksheets, EXCEL F-12, EXCEL F-13
page numbering in worksheets, EXCEL F-12, EXCEL F-13
Page Setup dialog box, EXCEL E-17, EXCEL H-16, EXCEL H-17
   charts, EXCEL D-17
panes, EXCEL F-2
   multiple, EXCEL F-3
Paste Options button, EXCEL B-12
Paste Special command, EXCEL E-3
patterns, EXCEL C-12, EXCEL C-13

payments, calculating using PMT function, EXCEL E-14–15
percent operator (%), EXCEL B-7
Personal Macro Workbook, EXCEL G-12–13
pie charts, EXCEL D-3
   exploding slices, EXCEL D-15
planning
   charts, EXCEL D-16, EXCEL D-17
   lists, EXCEL H-2–3
   macros, EXCEL G-2–3
   worksheets, EXCEL B-2–3
plot area, EXCEL D-2, EXCEL D-3
plus sign (+), addition operator, EXCEL B-7
PMT function, EXCEL E-14–15
pointers, EXCEL A-11
   changing, EXCEL D-14
   charts, EXCEL D-7
pound sign (#), long values, EXCEL C-8
previewing
   charts, EXCEL D-16, EXCEL D-17
   multiple worksheets, EXCEL F-4
   page breaks, EXCEL F-13
   worksheets, EXCEL A-14, EXCEL A-15
Print dialog box, EXCEL A-14, EXCEL A-15
printing
   charts, EXCEL D-16, EXCEL D-17
   formula contents, EXCEL E-16, EXCEL E-17
   Help system topics, EXCEL A-16, EXCEL A-17
   lists, EXCEL H-16–17
   multiple worksheets, EXCEL F-4
   worksheets, EXCEL A-14, EXCEL A-15
Print Preview
   charts, EXCEL D-16, EXCEL D-17
   documents, EXCEL A-14, EXCEL A-15
Print Preview window, EXCEL E-16, EXCEL E-17
print titles, EXCEL H-16
program code, EXCEL G-8, EXCEL G-9
program control menu box, EXCEL A-19
Programs menu, EXCEL A-4, EXCEL A-5
protecting areas in worksheets, EXCEL F-8, EXCEL F-9
publishing data on the Web, EXCEL F-16

Q

question mark (?), wildcard, EXCEL H-8

R

range(s)
   adding rows, EXCEL C-2
   multiple, printing at same time, EXCEL H-16
   names, EXCEL E-4
read-only status, EXCEL F-8, EXCEL F-9
recalculation, EXCEL A-2
recording macros, EXCEL G-4–5
record(s) in lists. See lists
Record Macro dialog box, EXCEL G-4, EXCEL G-5, EXCEL G-10, EXCEL G-11, EXCEL G-12, EXCEL G-13
recovering lost workbook files, EXCEL B-5
relative cell references, EXCEL B-14–15
   copying formulas, EXCEL B-16–17
removing. *See also* deleting
   hyperlinks, EXCEL F-14
replacing worksheet data and formats, EXCEL F-15

INDEX 15

Index

resizing charts, EXCEL D-6, EXCEL D-7
Right Border button, EXCEL C-13
rotating
    cell entries, EXCEL C-6
    3-D charts, EXCEL D-9
row(s)
    adding to ranges, EXCEL C-2
    deleting, EXCEL C-10, EXCEL C-11
    freezing, EXCEL F-2, EXCEL F-3
    hiding/unhiding, EXCEL F-9
    inserting, EXCEL C-10, EXCEL C-11
    specifying height, EXCEL C-9
    worksheet window, EXCEL A-6, EXCEL A-7
Row Height command, EXCEL C-9
running macros, EXCEL G-6–7

S

Save As dialog box, EXCEL A-8, EXCEL A-9, EXCEL F-16, EXCEL F-17
saving
    custom views of worksheets, EXCEL F-10–11
    workbooks, EXCEL A-8, EXCEL A-9
    worksheets. *See* saving worksheets
saving worksheets, EXCEL C-2
    saving as Web pages, EXCEL F-16–17
    saving custom views, EXCEL F-10–11
    saving for earlier versions of Excel, EXCEL F-16
scatter charts, EXCEL D-3
scrolling multiple tabs, EXCEL F-4
search criteria, wildcards, EXCEL H-8
searching. *See* finding
searching for clip art, EXCEL C-5
security level, macros, EXCEL G-6
selecting contiguous cells, EXCEL C-2
sending workbooks using e-mail, EXCEL C-16
sequential text/values, filling cells, EXCEL B-17
sharing information, EXCEL A-2
sheet tabs, EXCEL A-6, EXCEL A-7
Sheet tab scrolling buttons, EXCEL A-6, EXCEL A-7
shortcut(s), formatting, EXCEL C-6
shortcut keys, macros, EXCEL G-10–11
sizes
    fonts, EXCEL C-4, EXCEL C-5
    resizing charts, EXCEL D-6, EXCEL D-7
slash (/), division operator, EXCEL B-7
Sort dialog box, EXCEL H-14, EXCEL H-15
sorting lists
    case sensitivity, EXCEL H-14
    custom order, EXCEL H-15
    sorting on multiple fields, EXCEL H-14–15
    sorting on one field, EXCEL H-12–13
spell checking, EXCEL C-16–17
Spelling English dialog box, EXCEL C-16, EXCEL C-17
Standard toolbar, EXCEL A-6, EXCEL A-7
starting Excel 2002, EXCEL A-4–5
Start menu, EXCEL A-4, EXCEL A-5
statistical functions, EXCEL E-12–13

status bar, EXCEL A-6, EXCEL A-7
stopping execution of macros, EXCEL G-6
Stop Recording toolbar, EXCEL G-4
subtraction operator (-), EXCEL B-7
SUM function, EXCEL B-11

T

tabs, multiple, scrolling simultaneously, EXCEL F-4
targets, hyperlinks, EXCEL F-14, EXCEL F-15
task pane, EXCEL G-4
task pane list arrow, EXCEL A-6, EXCEL A-7
templates, EXCEL A-2
    opening workbooks, EXCEL A-9
text
    alignment in charts, EXCEL D-13
    sequential, filling cells, EXCEL B-17
text annotations, charts, EXCEL D-14, EXCEL D-15
Text Box button, EXCEL D-14
3-D charts, rotating, EXCEL D-9
3-D references, EXCEL F-6–7
tick marks, EXCEL D-2, EXCEL D-3
times, calculations using, EXCEL E-8
title bar, EXCEL A-6, EXCEL A-7
TODAY function, EXCEL E-8
toolbar(s), EXCEL A-6, EXCEL A-7
    buttons for macros, EXCEL G-16–17
    customizing, EXCEL G-16
Toolbar Options button, EXCEL A-7
truncation of labels, EXCEL A-10

U

Underline button, EXCEL C-7
Undo button, EXCEL B-4
undoing deletions, EXCEL H-11

V

value(s), EXCEL A-10, EXCEL A-11
    entering, EXCEL E-3
    formatting, EXCEL C-2–3
    sequential, filling cells, EXCEL B-17
value axis, EXCEL D-2, EXCEL D-3
views, custom, saving, EXCEL F-10–11
viruses, macros, EXCEL G-3
Visual Basic Editor
    editing macros, EXCEL G-8–9
    moving or copying macros, EXCEL G-12

W

Web, discussion comments in worksheets, EXCEL F-17
Web pages
    linking workbooks to, EXCEL F-14
    saving worksheets as, EXCEL F-16–17
what-if analysis, EXCEL A-2
Width command, EXCEL C-8
wildcards, search criteria, EXCEL H-8

workbook(s), EXCEL A-2–3, EXCEL A-6
    changing properties, EXCEL F-9
    closing, EXCEL A-18, EXCEL A-19
    creating, EXCEL A-8
    deleting worksheets, EXCEL F-4, EXCEL F-5
    inserting worksheets, EXCEL F-4, EXCEL F-5
    linking data between, EXCEL F-7
    linking to Web pages, EXCEL F-14
    linking using hyperlinks, EXCEL F-14–15
    opening, EXCEL A-8, EXCEL A-9
    protecting, EXCEL F-9
    recovering lost workbook files, EXCEL B-5
    saving, EXCEL A-8, EXCEL A-9
    sending using e-mail, EXCEL C-16
workbook control menu box, EXCEL A-19
worksheets, EXCEL A-2–3
    cells. *See* cell entries; column(s); row(s)
    copying, EXCEL A-13, EXCEL F-4
    creating new worksheets from existing worksheets, EXCEL A-2
    deleting, EXCEL A-12
    deleting from workbooks, EXCEL F-4, EXCEL F-5
    deleting records in lists using, EXCEL H-11
    discussion comments, EXCEL F-17
    footers, EXCEL F-5
    formatting. *See* formatting worksheets
    headers, EXCEL F-5
    hiding and protecting areas, EXCEL F-8–9
    hiding/unhiding, EXCEL F-9
    inserting in workbooks, EXCEL F-4, EXCEL F-5
    large, navigating, EXCEL F-14
    moving, EXCEL A-12, EXCEL A-13
    multiple. *See* multiple worksheets
    naming, EXCEL A-12, EXCEL A-13
    navigating, EXCEL A-11
    page breaks and page numbering, EXCEL F-12–13
    previewing, EXCEL A-14, EXCEL A-15
    printing, EXCEL A-14, EXCEL A-15
    printing parts, EXCEL H-16, EXCEL H-17
    protecting, EXCEL F-9
    saving. *See* saving worksheets
worksheet window, EXCEL A-6–7
workspaces, EXCEL F-11

X

x-axis, EXCEL D-2, EXCEL D-3
XY charts, EXCEL D-3

Y

y-axis, EXCEL D-2, EXCEL D-3

Z

zeros, EXCEL H-2, EXCEL H-4
Zoom button, Print Preview, EXCEL A-15